DATE DUE

DE 10 '93			
AG 18 '94			
DE 9 '94			
MY 19 '95 / AP 8 '97			
JU 22 '9			
MY 12 '98			
DE 15 98			
AP 5 00			
MR 15 03			
AP 8 03			
MY 27 '09			
MY 27 00			

THE CONSTITUTION AND RACE

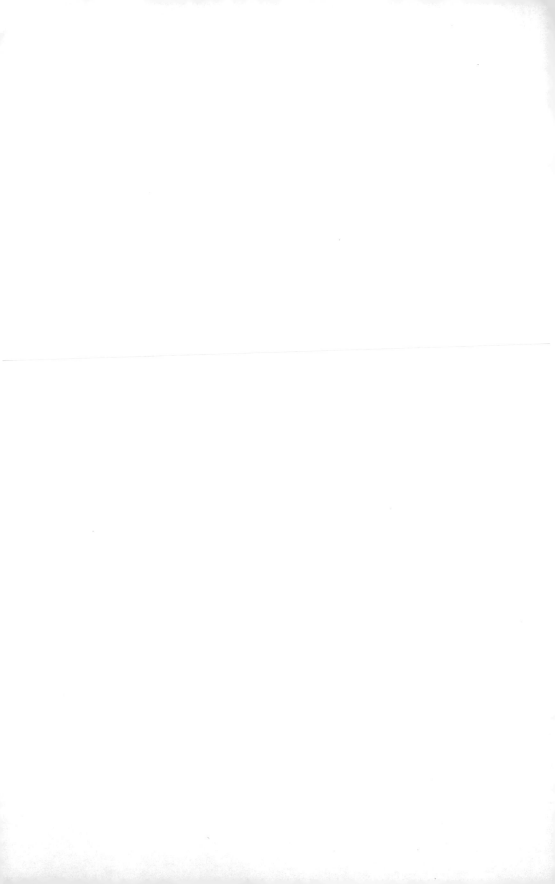

The Constitution and Race

DONALD E. LIVELY

New York
Westport, Connecticut
London

Library of Congress Cataloging-in-Publication Data

Lively, Donald E.
    The Constitution and race / Donald E. Lively.
        p.   cm.
    Includes bibliographical references and index.
    ISBN 0–275–93914–6 (alk. paper).—ISBN 0–275–94228–7 (pbk.)
    1. Race discrimination—Law and legislation—United States—
History.   2. Slavery—Law and legislation—United States—History.
3. Afro-Americans—Civil rights—History.   I.   Title.
KF4755.L57   1992
342.73′087—dc20
[347.30287]   91–30280

British Library Cataloguing in Publication Data is available.

Library of Congress Catalog Card Number: 91–30280
ISBN: 0–275–93914–6
        0–275–94228–7 (pbk.)

First published in 1992

Praeger Publishers, One Madison Avenue, New York, NY   10010
An imprint of Greenwood Publishing Group, Inc.

Printed in the United States of America

The paper used in this book complies with the
Permanent Paper Standard issued by the National
Information Standards Organization (Z39.48–1984).

10 9 8 7 6 5 4 3 2 1

To Donald and Dorothy Lively
for their values
and
Pamela and Rico Lively
for the opportunity to
share them

Contents

	Preface	ix
Introduction:	The Original Ordering of Constitutional Priorities	1
Chapter 1:	Constitutional Law and Slavery	11
Chapter 2:	Toward a More Perfect Union	39
Chapter 3:	Constitutional Amendment and Doctrinal Development	61
Chapter 4:	Separate But Equal	89
Chapter 5:	Desegregation and the Anti-Discrimination Principle	109
Chapter 6:	Color Blindness Revisited	137
Chapter 7:	Original Imperatives and Doctrinal Possibility	169
	Bibliography	187
	Index	191

Preface

Law is the means by which society governs itself. As the function of cultural priorities and ideals, law also affords insight into a society's nature and character. American constitutional law comprises the nation's charter document and two centuries of developmental jurisprudence. Because it iterates and amplifies principles that are basic and overarching, constitutional decision-making affords an especially apt reference point for gleaning societal truths and realities.

This book examines two centuries of accumulated constitutional jurisprudence pertaining to race. Accommodation of slavery in 1787 to facilitate the Union's actualization represented an original exercise in ordering priorities. The framers' interest in establishing a viable republic resulted in deferral rather than resolution of significant race-based issues. What was avoided then would be confronted later in the constitutional context of slavery, official segregation, and remediation.

Racial justice or injustice is a reflection of the values and ideals that define a society's moral character and inspire its laws. Over two centuries, race-dependent considerations of personhood, citizenship, liberty, and equality have presented the nation with significant moral and legal choices. Modern constitutional law case books—lacking attention to racially significant decisions influencing the Constitution's framing, making little if any reference to the Supreme Court's endorsement of slavery, and rushing through the separate but equal era, which has defined most of the Fourteenth Amendment's existence—suggest a discontinuity between past and present. Contemporary racial jurisprudence, which is quick to assert its distance and dissociate itself from embarrassing antecedents, reinforces an impression that reflects more illusion than reality.

Modern investment in constitutional color blindness, when race-conscious remediation is a paramount issue, denotes further how societal priorities are ordered and what dominant imperatives will countenance. Cultural norms and preferences similarly preordained the repudiation of color blindness a century ago when official segregation was the eminent question, and avoidance of the question two centuries ago when slavery and a viable union were competing interests. Much of the constitutional record pertaining to race, as modern jurisprudence acknowledges, is "sorry." Recognizing rather than disclaiming the ties between doctrinal past and present is essential not only for the purpose of affording meaningful context but also as a prerequisite for reckoning fully and finally with the Constitutional Convention's unfinished business.

ACKNOWLEDGMENTS

Several persons deserve special mention for their help in preparing this book. The original manuscript was facilitated by the processing efforts of Carmen Gonzalez, Fran Molnar, and Marie Liliane Wilks. Research assistance was provided by Patrick Casey, Sandra Czaykowsky, Joanne Guy, Lisa Lesperance, Neal Lechtner, Barbara McCalla, and Ellisa Taylor. Reverends Theodore Roddy, Charles Scott, and John White, of the African Methodist Episcopal Church, provided and facilitated access to information concerning racially significant events in Philadelphia during the year of the Constitutional Convention. Dr. Dennis Dickerson, A.M.E. Church historiographer, generously shared his insights into the framing process. Especially helpful were the comments of professors Henry Bourguignon and Stephen Plass, who reviewed an early manuscript. The author also is indebted to John Harney who as acquisitions editor has been a much appreciated source of encouragement, support, and patience.

Introduction

The Original Ordering of Constitutional Priorities

Philadelphia in 1787 was a city of two tales that disclosed significant truths with respect to the culture and the law it inspired. The time and place are well known as when and where the Constitutional Convention transpired. What eventually emerged from the deliberation and ratification processes was a blueprint of governmental power and an enumeration of basic rights and liberties. The resultant document also attended, albeit in rather furtive terms, to the institution of slavery. Although forthrightly charting federal powers and explicating fundamental guarantees previously reposing in the amorphous realm of natural law, the Constitution's architects avoided any overt mention of slavery. To secure the Deep South's support and thus ratification, however, the institution was accommodated in calculated if not direct terms.

Relevant passages in the nation's charter were striking for their failure either to use the term "slavery" or to identify the race that it victimized. The provision prohibiting congressional interference with the slave trade until 1808, for instance, was framed in terms of "[t]he Migration or Importation of such Persons as any of the States now existing shall think proper to admit."[1] Apportionment formulas for political representation and taxation in similarly cryptic fashion referred to "the whole Number of free Persons...and...three fifths of all other Persons."[2] Even the fugitive slave clause was crafted in facially race-neutral terms: "[n]o Person held to Service or Labour in one State, under the Laws thereof, escaping into another, shall, in Consequence of any Law or Regulation therein, be discharged from such Service or Labour, but shall be delivered up on Claim of the Party to whom such Service or Labour may be due."[3]

Such terminology may have reflected the tension between the ideals of liberty and equality enshrined in the Declaration of Independence and the pragmatic aims of forming a union and consequent accommodation of slavery. Although well established in five southern states, slavery already had been or was being abolished in the North and was regarded by many as a terminal institution.[4] In the same year that the framers met in Philadelphia, Congress prohibited slavery in the Northwest Territory.[5] Such results did not obscure the reality of racism and prejudice, which animated law and custom without regard to geography. Racial truths were disclosed less by lofty rhetoric than by contemporary deed. At Old St. George's Methodist Church, not far from where the republic's founders had assembled, black members were assigned segregated seating and advised they no longer could kneel in prayer with the rest of the congregation.[6] Threatened with expulsion, Richard Allen led a walk-out and subsequently founded what endures as the African Methodist Episcopal Church.[7]

Allen, who as a child was the slave of the future Chief Justice of the Pennsylvania Supreme Court,[8] became the nation's first ordained black minister.[9] Records do not reveal whether any of the framers were present at Old St. George's Methodist Church when Allen and others were singled out on the basis of their race. Nor, except for the sake of an effective historical anecdote, is their presence or absence critical to comprehending the cultural forces that inspired the Constitution. Moral sentiment against slavery at the time of the document's framing may have been developed enough that, absent any significant competing consideration, the institution would not have been tolerated, much less accommodated.[10]

Elimination of slavery, however, was not a strong enough priority that it would be allowed to jeopardize other aims. Rather, the institution's continuing existence and consequences were considered acceptable costs of effecting a union. Dominant attitudes not only accommodated slavery but also defined the existence of nominally free blacks who, North and South, were bound by a panoply of laws governing their employment opportunities, restricting their movement, and forbidding their presence. Terminological hedging in the nation's charter may disclose moral and legal tension, but the equivocation illuminates rather than obscures the reality that founding principles of liberty for practical purposes were selectively afforded.

Chief Justice Taney, in rendering the Supreme Court's opinion in *Scott v. Sandford* seven decades later, noted that when the Constitution was drafted, blacks "for more than a century [had been] regarded as beings of an inferior order, and altogether unfit to associate with the white race, either in social or political relations; and so far inferior, that they had no rights which the white man was bound to respect."[11] The *Scott* decision has been characterized as a "derelict[] of constitutional law"[12] and "the most frequently overturned decision in history."[13] Taney's depiction of racist ways and attitudes, however, was an accurate reflection of dominant conventions that endured long after the Constitution was ratified. Not until 1954 did the Court, in *Brown v. Board of Education*, meaningfully confront the consequences of official racism. Reality is that Taney's characterization is more rather than less apt with respect to most racially significant jurisprudence over the nation's history.

Ratification of the document proved to be a departure rather than a termination point for establishing the Constitution's meaning. Barely more than a decade later, the Supreme Court in *Marbury v. Madison* defined its own function in broad terms that included being the final authority on "what the law is."[14] Having defined the power of judicial review in expansive fashion, the Court was positioned to resolve questions that invariably would arise concerning open-ended constitutional terms and conditions. The Marshall Court over the next few decades fashioned a legacy of constitutional interpretation that facilitated a strong central government in the Federalist image. Given the economic tension and disorder among the several states, prompting reexamination of the Articles of Confederation and influencing the Constitution, early judicial attention to structural and material interests was expectable. Indeterminate and impressionable as the commerce, contracts and necessary and proper clauses may have been, their meanings were jurisprudentially amplified within the Court's first few decades.[15] The constitutional business of slavery, in contrast, was not directly reckoned with by the Court until the mid-Nineteenth Century.

Even as the republic was being chartered, slavery had proved itself to be potentially disruptive to a workable and durable political order. Although not the only obstacles to framing and ratifying the Constitution, the competing agendas of northern and southern states imperiled a new political system even more profoundly than the conflict over representation of large and small states. As James Madison observed, sectional divisions were not a function

of size, but...other circumstances; the most material of which resulted partly from climate, but principally from the effects of their having or not having slaves. These two causes concur in forming the great division of interests in the U[nited] States. It did not lie between the large [and] small states; it lay, between the Northern [and] Southern.[16]

Disagreement between North and South in 1787 was less suffused with the friction and acrimony that the slavery issue engendered in subsequent decades. Original stakes in the union's formation were considered significant enough, however, that concessions to slave interests were negotiated without significant resistance or misgiving. The Georgia and South Carolina delegations, representing interests most dependent on slave labor, warned that they would not join a union that separated them from their crucial economic resource. For many framers, including some southerners, slavery presented a moral issue and a practice that were difficult to square with the republic's founding principles of liberty and equality. Even if anti-slavery sentiment was broad, it was not profound enough to vie with the imperative of forming a republic. Historians have attributed the accommodation of slavery, despite significant hostility toward it, to

a small but vociferous proslavery group [which] fought tenaciously to protect and strengthen slavery. Whenever this group apprehended a danger to slavery, its members raised a protest, made a deal or threatened to start packing. Through bluster, compromise, and political blackmail over the question of union itself, they secured power and protection for slavery.[17]

Thus were obtained concessions on taxation, representation, the slave trade, and fugitive slaves.[18] Critics of the institution such as George Mason argued that "the general government should have power to prevent the increase of slavery,"[19] but eventually conceded that it would "involve us in great difficulties and infelicity to be now deprived" of slavery.[20] Thomas Dawes of Massachusetts observed that "[i]t would not do to abolish slavery,...[but] it...will die of a consumption."[21] The antislavery position in the framing process thus was reduced to precatory terms anticipating the institution's eventual and natural demise. Such contemplations, even if sincere rather than rationalized, may have been misplaced if premised upon the notion that slavery could not survive once cut off from its overseas source of replenishment. It has been noted that the South understood from its Revolutionary War experience that the institution could endure even when imports ceased, but pro-slavery delegates indulged northern assumptions to the contrary.[22] As Winthrop Jordan observed, in any event, "the Convention could not consider even the eventual termination of domestic slavery; propositions on this head would have sent half the delegates packing."[23]

The original ordering of constitutional priorities resulted in a charter that neither directly endorsed nor prohibited but nonetheless accommodated slavery. William Wiecek has identified at least ten charter provisions devoted entirely or partly to slavery.

1. Art. I, § 2, which apportioned representation in the House on the basis of population count, and considered slaves as three-fifths of a person.

2. Art. I, §§ 2 & 9, which required apportionment of direct taxes among the states pursuant to the same fractional formula.

3. Art. I, § 8, which vested Congress with power to suppress insurrections including those by slaves.

4. Art. I, § 9, which immunized the slave trade from congressional restriction until 1808.

5. Art. I, §§ 9 & 10, which exempted exports, including the output of slave labor, from federal and state taxation.

6. Art. IV, § 2, which precluded states from liberating fugitive slaves and required their return upon demand.

7. Art. IV, § 4, which obligated the federal government to protect states from domestic violence, including slave insurrections.

8. Art. V, which insulated constitutional provisions concerning the slave trade and direct taxes.[24]

Debate has persisted over the actual nature and extent of original attention to slavery. Provisions that some have identified as friendly to slavery, such as clauses empowering the federal government to quell violence or insurrection, have been explained by others as merely coincidental.[25] Arguments that allowance for the slave trade until 1808 denotes a pro-slavery constitution from the inception have elicited the counterpoint that a finite time limit effectively identified federal power to regulate and prohibit the institution over the long run.[26] Notwithstanding any uncertainty over the actual nature of original contemplations, the decision to delay proscription of the slave trade for twenty years allowed in James Madison's words "all the mischief that can be apprehended from the liberty to import slaves."[27] Despite eventual formal renunciation of such commerce, federal policy in practice consisted of lax enforcement and disinterest in British proposals for joint efforts at effective policing.[28] The exact shading of original expectations may be indeterminate but does not obscure significant and discernible realities. Accommodation of slavery, in greater or lesser terms, resulted from what were perceived as overarching societal interests. Concessions were made to a focused and fixed southern faction in the cause of establishing a union; what was considered as less significant was traded off for what was perceived as more important.

The norms of 1787 responsible for the calculated slighting of virtually an entire class of persons subsequently were deviated from, but the process of ordering priorities then has remained pertinent since. A century later, in *Plessy v. Ferguson*, the Supreme Court legitimized the dominant "customs, usages and traditions of the people" that supported official segregation and repudiated constitutional color blindness.[29] The passage of another century has found the Court, in *City of Richmond v.*

J. A. Croson Co., rejecting color-conscious remediation in part because such policies engender racial politics.[30] As in 1787, racial justice competes with concern for the viability of and perils to the political system.

The original compromise on slavery enabled the framers to bypass an otherwise inconvenient and confounding issue. Initial understanding reflected the sense that individual states possessed the power to permit or prohibit slavery and the federal government was to be neutral. A scheme dependent on mutual tolerance and noninterference was feasible to the extent North and South could sequester themselves from the effects of each other's preferences and interests. Territorial expansion and the problem of fugitive slaves, however, soon disclosed that mutual immunity was an impossibility.

The ultimate fate of slavery was an issue that the framers left to posterity. Territorial expansion from 1787 until the Civil War provided serial opportunities for revisiting the issue. During that period, the original premise of a disinterested federal government was transformed into a debate upon whether it had a constitutional duty to support or prohibit slavery. The decision in *Scott v. Sandford* represented an effort to end the debate in conclusive fashion, but it instead exacerbated sectional divisions. Despite the extensive criticism it elicited, the decision's inspiring racist ideology was not an immediate source of significant objection.

The institution of slavery ultimately was defeated by the Thirteenth Amendment. The ideology that supported it in 1787 and denied the humanity of all blacks in 1857, however, survived. Considerations of racial equality did not enter the mainstream of political debate until the Reconstruction period. Even then, black rights in a constitutional sense were introduced as a qualified notion. The Fourteenth Amendment, ratified in 1868, secured the Civil Rights Act of 1866 and established racial parity in contract and property rights and equality before the law. The Fifteenth Amendment, ratified in 1871, prohibited race-dependent impairment of the right to vote. Nevertheless, constitutional jurisprudence continued to accommodate preexisting attitudes and priorities. Racial segregation was characterized as a "[m]ere discrimination[]"[31] and tolerated to the extent separate could be regarded as equal.[32] Abrogation of voting rights was disregarded pursuant to Justice Holmes' sense that judicial intervention against racial prejudice would be "pointless."[33]

Notwithstanding the Fourteenth Amendment's repudiation of *Scott v. Sandford*, the Supreme Court did not meaningfully confront the racist ideology of the decision until the passage of another century. By declaring that racially separate education was "inherently unequal,"[34] the Court commenced the constitutionally mandated foreclosure of officially prescribed race-based distinctions. To the extent it postponed relief for a term, in hopes of overcoming resistance and eliciting cooperation, and required eradication of segregation with "all deliberate speed," the Court still factored in and at least accommodated the realities of racism. The strategy did not prevent widespread evasion, delay, and disregard of the new constitutional mandate. Within a couple of decades, moreover, equal protection demands were blunted, pursuant to a sense that the Court had "gone far enough in enforcing the Constitution's guarantee of equal justice."[35]

Constitutional jurisprudence concerning remediation of a two-century legacy of racism covers barely more than a decade. Within that time frame, however, the Court has moved from limited approval of minority preferences[36] to a general prohibition of race as a remedial factor.[37] Color-blindness, which was rejected when official segregation was the dominant racial issue a century ago, now operates when remediation is the prominent concern. The result is jurisprudence that acknowledges the nation's "sorry history of . . . racial discrimination"[38] but still attends to competing priorities. Pending analytical methodology that more effectively reckons with the interests of racial justice, within the purview of democratic consent, the business of 1787 will remain unfinished.

The original purpose of the Fourteenth Amendment has been the subject of extensive scholarly attention and debate. Some commentators have argued that it incorporated the Bill of Rights, fundamental liberties and guarantees derived from natural law, and equality in the broadest sense.[39] Others have expounded a more restrictive understanding of the amendment as the function of a narrow vision focused on basic opportunity for material self-development and equal standing before the law, rather than a broad spectrum of rights or comprehensive equality.[40] A thesis of this book, expressed in the final chapter, is that the minimalist view, glossed with indisputable anti-discrimination precepts that displaced official segregation, affords more potential than expansive concepts as a predicate for actuating the Fourteenth Amendment. Grander theories invariably engender resistance and dispute, which, among other things, render them academic. Some may interpret the Fourteenth Amendment in broader fashion, but all would agree that it at least covers what is described by the modified minimalist position. Such common ground, if fully mined, affords a promising basis of accounting for what is at least the amendment's core concern.

NOTES

1. U.S. Const. art. I, § 9, cl. 1.
2. *Id.* art. I, § 2, cl. 3.
3. *Id.* art. IV, § 2, cl. 3.
4. The pre-constitutional history of slavery, from the early colonial period forward, is accounted for comprehensively in A. Higginbotham, Jr., In the

Matter of Color (1978). The legal realities of slavery through the antebellum era are detailed in M. Tushnet, The American Law of Slavery (1981).

5. The nature and ambivalence of formative anti-slavery sentiment during and after the drafting process are detailed in D. Fehrenbacher, The Dred Scott Case 11–27 (1978); W. Wiecek, The Sources of Antislavery Constitutionalism in America, 1760–1848, at 62–105 (1977).

6. *See* R. Allen, The Life and Experience and Gospel Labors of the Rt. Rev. Richard Allen 6–7, 25 (1960).

7. *See id.* at 7, 25.

8. *See id.* at 5.

9. *See id.*

10. Delegates from as far south as North Carolina, including many of the convention's most notable figures, expressed their disapproval of or discomfort with slavery. Their objections were not collectively profound enough, however, to prevent compromise with the focused and insistent Deep South delegation. James Madison, in the course of the convention proceedings, observed that it would be "wrong to admit in the Constitution the idea that there could be property in men." 2 M. Farrand, The Records of the Federal Convention of 1787, 417 (1937). In the North Carolina ratification debates, future Supreme Court Justice James Iredell observed that the end of slavery would "be an event most pleasing to every generous mind, and every friend of human nature; but we often wish for things which are not attainable." II J. Elliot, The Debates in the Several State Conventions of the Adoption of the Federal Constitution, v. 4, at 100 (1941). Even so, objections to slavery often were equivocal and coupled with sympathy for the interests of slaveowners. *See id.* at 101 (Galloway).

11. Scott v. Sandford, 60 U.S. (19 How.) 393, 407 (1857).

12. Meese, *The Law of the Constitution*, 61 Tul. L. Rev. 979, 989 (1987). (quoting P. Kurland, Politics, the Constitution and the Warren Court 186 (1970)).

13. D. Bell, Race, Racism and American Law 21–22 (1973).

14. Marbury v. Madison, 5 U.S. (1 Cranch), 137, 177 (1803).

15. *See* Gibbons v. Ogden, 22 U.S. (9 Wheat.) 1 (1824) (commerce clause); Trustees of Dartmouth College v. Woodward, 17 U.S. (4 Wheat.) 518 (1819) (contracts clause); McCulloch v. Maryland, 17 U.S. (4 Wheat.) 316 (1819) (necessary and proper clause).

16. 1 M. Farrand, *supra* note 10, at 486.

17. P. Finkelman, An Imperfect Union 23 (1981).

18. *Id.*

19. II J. Elliott, *supra* note 10, v.5, at 458.

20. I J. Elliott, *supra* note 10, v.3, at 270.

21. *Id.*, v.2, at 41.

22. *See* P. Finkelman, *supra* note 17; W.E.B. Du Bois, The Suppression of the African Slave-Trade to the United States of America, 1638–1870 61–62 (1896).

23. W. Jordan, White over Black: American Attitudes Toward the Negro 323 (1968).

24. W. Wiecek, *supra* note 5, at 62–63.

25. The federal government used its authority to suppress insurrection to defeat the Whiskey Rebellion in 1794 and to respond to the South in 1861. Fehrenbacher, *Slavery, the Framers, and the Living Constitution*, in Slavery and Its

Consequences: The Constitution, Equality and Race (R. Goldwin & A. Kaufman eds. 1988).

26. *Id.* at 10–11.

27. 2 M. Farrand, *supra* note 10, at 415.

28. P. Finkelman, *supra* note 17, at 26.

29. Plessy v. Ferguson, 163 U.S. 537, 550 (1896).

30. City of Richmond v. J. A. Croson Co., 109 S. Ct. 706, 721 (1989).

31. The Civil Rights Cases, 109 U.S. 3, 25 (1883).

32. Plessy v. Ferguson, 163 U.S. at 550.

33. Giles v. Harris, 189 U.S. 475, 488 (1903).

34. Brown v. Board of Education, 347 U.S. 483, 495 (1954).

35. Milliken v. Bradley, 418 U.S. 717, 814 (1974) (Marshall, J., dissenting).

36. Regents of the University of California v. Bakke, 438 U.S. 265, 311–15 (1978) (Powell, J.).

37. City of Richmond v. J. A. Croson Co., 109 S. Ct. at 721. Race-conscious remedies are allowable to the extent they are narrowly tailored to fix a specific constitutional violation. *Id.* at 729–30. Race-dependent measures also have been upheld to the extent "they serve important governmental objectives within the power of Congress and are substantially related to achievement of those objectives." Metro Broadcasting, Inc. v. Federal Communications Commission, 110 S. Ct. 2997, 3008–09 (1990).

38. City of Richmond v. J.A. Croson Co., 109 S. Ct. at 724.

39. *E.g.*, J. Baer, Equality under the Constitution: Reclaiming the Fourteenth Amendment (1983); J. ten Broek, Equal under Law (1965).

40. *E.g.*, R. Berger, Government by Judiciary (1977).

Chapter 1

Constitutional Law and Slavery

The finessing of slavery at the republic's inception effectively accommodated the institution, albeit in terms that obscured the Constitution's connection to it. The calculated bypass, however, deferred rath r than avoided eventual reckoning. Despite Congress's explicit power to terminate the import of slaves beginning in 1808, the decision to allow or prohibit the institution itself was left to each state. Even before the ink had dried in Philadelphia, problematic questions pertaining to slavery had materialized. As the nation evolved over the next several decades, effective answers would be increasingly scarce. Original expectations that slavery would die of its own accord, or be satisfactorily reckoned with by the political process, were miscalculated or misplaced. Society instead became ever more deeply immersed in and confounded by the slavery issue.

In 1787, the Congress under the Articles of Confederation passed the Northwest Ordinance, which precluded "slavery . . . in the said territory, otherwise than in the punishment of crimes, whereof the party shall have been duly convicted."[1] Competing sentiment exists as to whether the enactment represented "a symbol of the [American] Revolution's liberalism" or was "part of a larger, and insidious bargain" constituting "the first and last antislavery achievement by the central government."[2] On its face, and despite inclusion of a fugitive slave clause, the Northwest Ordinance may seem consonant with a sense that slavery was a terminal institution. Some historians, noting that the ordinance was enacted by a southern dominated Congress one day after the three-fifths compromise on apportionment, suggest that the prohibition was an exercise in calculated cynicism. They propose that support for the territorial proscription was offered in exchange for constitutional concessions on slavery, to secure political debts that would translate into support of the South's agenda in Congress, and to establish a tacit understanding that slavery was permissible in the Southwest.[3]

Two years after the Northwest Ordinance was passed, the Southwest Territory, comprising the future states of Kentucky and Tennessee, was created in almost identical terms. The key difference in the new enactment was a provision to the effect that the federal government would not interfere with or prohibit slavery. A like restriction conditioned establishment of the Mississippi Territory. As the Nineteenth Century began to unfold, the Louisiana and Missouri territories elicited more extensive debate over slavery, and anti-slavery amendments to the respective enactments were defeated. Pertinent legislation eventually was structured without any explicit provisions for or against slavery. Congress, however, did prohibit slavery in Illinois, Indiana, and Michigan territories. By the early nineteenth century, slavery had become an increasingly complicating factor in the process of establishing new territories and expanding the union. Over the next few decades, what commenced as a thorny issue hardened into an intractable problem and national crisis.

An especially portentous confrontation between North and South on the issue of slavery occurred in 1819, as Congress considered proposals to grant Missouri statehood and to create an Arkansas territory. An initial House bill that would have banned slavery in Missouri, where it already was well established, provoked a profoundly negative southern response. Arkansas's territorial candidacy was advanced without restrictions on slavery, and southern representatives coalesced to block Maine's simultaneous application for admission to the union. With Maine's statehood held hostage by the South, the House eventually approved a Senate amendment that allowed Missouri to become a state without slavery restrictions and admitted Maine as a free state. The resultant Missouri Compromise provided that slavery would be forever forbidden in the remaining Louisiana Territory north of a line etched at 36° 30′ North. The Maine and Missouri controversy, although eventually settled, disclosed that the slavery debate was ratcheting in the direction of increasing sectional rancor. Despite persisting expressions that slavery was a dying institution and individual decisions by such luminaries as Jefferson, Madison, Taney, and others to liberate their slaves, the issue was enlarging rather than vanishing.

Early decades of territorial expansion indicate a general assumption that Congress possessed the power to determine slavery's permissibility in the territories and to condition statehood accordingly. That sense originally was disclosed by the South's endorsement of the Northwest Ordinance in anti-slavery terms. It persisted, despite sectional antagonisms manifested by the Missouri and Maine controversy. Evolving political thought, increasingly acrimonious debates over new territories and states, northern recognition of slavery's actual reach, and southern perceptions of vulnerability, however, eventually destabilized initial assumptions. Further challenging the basic premise of federal neutrality and the models of compromise and accommodation was the emergence of radical abolitionism.

During the 1830s, abolitionism burst into American thinking with new arguments about what the Constitution required or prohibited. The South's intolerant response to the promulgation of abolitionist views evidenced not only the region's heightened sense of imperilment but also its evolving sense that the issue was no longer debatable. Southern prohibition of anti-slavery literature would have presented in later times a First Amendment crisis.[4] Asserting that Congress had no power over slavery, southern representatives maintained also that abolitionists had no freedom to petition for anti-slavery legislation.[5] Southern political assumptions, previously consonant with the exercise of federal power on questions of slavery, began to challenge the legitimacy of such authority. Debates concerning slavery in the District of Columbia and Texas further evidenced the hardening of pro-slavery sentiment. Although Congress possessed authority "[t]o exercise exclusive Legislation in all Cases whatsoever" in the District of Columbia,[6] southern influence assured the vitality of slavery there.

As perceived threats to slavery had magnified and the stakes accordingly had increased, southern strategists searched for more secure doctrinal footing. A key reference was the Constitution itself, which, although originally avoiding outright endorsement or repudiation of slavery, was increasingly the object of revisionist interpretive notions. Abolitionist thinking would divide over whether the Constitution was an anti-slavery document that should be so animated or a pro-slavery charter that should be structurally overhauled. The South, meanwhile, turned toward doctrinal formulations that would not just accommodate but support slavery. In championing slavery in the District of Columbia, southern legislators asserted that the federal government was an agent of the several states with the affirmative obligation of supporting their various institutions, including slavery. Presaging a significant premise in *Scott v. Sandford*, they also argued that slaves were property protected by the Fifth Amendment.[7]

The issue of Texas annexation, which Congress faced in the 1840s, disclosed further how constitutional thought was coursing beyond premises of a neutral federal role to competition over whether the document required an affirmative position for or against slavery. The Wilmot Proviso, which would have prohibited slavery in all territory acquired from Mexico, ultimately failed but not without sharpening sectional divisions. The proviso was significant, even if not enacted, insofar as it contemplated a deviation from the lines drawn and the sectional balance struck by the Missouri Compromise. Its mere proposal suggested a movement in the North and South away from accommodation and toward confrontation.

Such events were the backdrop against which consensus was fragmenting. Pro-slavery sentiment, as noted previously, progressed toward an assertive interpretation of the Constitution as prohibiting interference with the institution. Anti-slavery thinking, which never merged into a unified front, presented a variety of sometimes conflicting positions. The perspective of William Lloyd Garrison was that the Constitution endorsed slavery. For him, the deficiency could be accounted for only by dissolving the union. Competing with Garrison's analysis was the notion that the federal government had no power over slavery in the states and must dissociate itself from any support for the institution.[8] Other theorists, described as "constitutional utopians," considered the due process and privileges and immunities clauses, notwithstanding their operation against federal power, as potential reference points for an anti-slavery charter or at least a theory of review favoring liberation.[9]

Multiplying perspectives of what the Constitution did or did not require were consistent with the expanding contours of debate beyond the original question of whether Congress had the authority to ban slavery in territories. Congress's territorial powers, if analyzed without the distorting frictions of the time, may not have presented such difficult questions or have been so susceptible to competing interpretation. The exercise of such power during and after the Constitution's drafting, with southern participation and support, suggests that the federal interest and role were apt and initially uncontroversial. This impression is reinforced by review of congressional power in circumstances unrelated to slavery. In *American Insurance Co. v. Canter*, the Supreme Court had determined that "[i]n legislating for the territories, Congress exercises the combined powers of the general, and of a state government."[10] Despite recognition of broad federal power over the territories, reflected by jurisprudence and by actual practice, arguments for slavery sought to redefine congressional authority. The debate thus reflected movement beyond original considerations of state determination and federal neutrality and toward an eventual constitutional showdown.

Attention to the Constitution's meaning for slavery was renewed and revised as a function not merely of the nation's expansion but of other realities and perceptions as well. Like territorial governance, the question of fugitive slaves originally presented no significant controversy. The fugitive slave clause of the Constitution was not a subject of significant attention or debate when framed. Soon after ratification, Congress enacted a fugitive slave law which also was notable for its immediate uncontroversiality. As the nation's attention became more focused on slavery in subsequent decades, however, the fugitive slave clause would move from the margins to the center of debate. Even if the actual number of slave renditions was relatively few, fugitive slave legislation, more discernibly than territorial compromise, manifested congressional aiding and abetting of the institution. The fugitive slave controversy effectively heightened northern awareness of the reality that slavery implicated the entire nation rather than just a region. Even if a slave was apprehended and returned, his or her economic value was diminished by the act of running away and the consequently disclosed risk of future escape. The fugitive slave issue nonetheless acquired significant political meaning. For the South, it represented a test of the federal government's willingness to accommodate and later support slavery. For the North, it clarified how entangled the entire society was in the institution.

Fugitive slave legislation, more visibly than its constitutional predicate, directly implicated the federal government in the cause of slavery. The Constitution's fugitive slave clause provided that

[n]o person held to Service or Labour in one State, under the Laws thereof, escaping into another, shall, in Consequence of any Law or Regulation therein, be discharged from such Service or Labour, but shall be delivered up on Claim of the Party to whom such Service or Labour may be due.[11]

The provision was housed in Article IV, which concerns interstate relations, rather than in Article I, which delineates the powers of Congress. Because it also did not have an explicit implementation provision, like the Full Faith and Credit clause in the same article, a credible argument existed that it provided no authority for a congressional enactment.[12] Although the clause eventually elicited intense constitutional controversy, its original purpose is uncertain. The provision was drafted and adopted without debate or formal vote as the convention was winding down. Not surprisingly, given its vagueness and relative inattention afforded it, the fugitive slave clause was a source of diverging interpretations ranging from the sense that it established a right of recovery anywhere in the nation to the perception that it simply precluded another state's emancipation of runaway slaves.[13] The observation has been made that, during the framing process, no one "could foresee a federally regulated Fugitive Slave Law with marshals and special commissioners."[14] Soon after ratification, however, Congress enacted legislation that enshrined the clause as a predicate for affirmative federal support of slavery.

Congress initially accounted for the fugitive slave problem by passing the Fugitive Slave Act of 1793. The act (1) imposed on a state the duty to return fugitives upon official demand, and (2) enabled a slave owner to cross state lines, apprehend the alleged fugitive, and, upon proof of ownership to a judicial officer, reclaim and remove the person.[15] Although the act itself provided no incidents of due process, such as the right to a hearing, several states enacted laws prohibiting the kidnapping of blacks or at least providing opportunities to contest the claims of slave owners or their agents.[16]

Fugitive slave legislation represented an early paradox in the federal system. Slavery had been constitutionally accommodated pursuant to the premise of federal neutrality and individual state determination. Imposition of universal obligations to account for fugitive slaves constituted an early exercise in the expansion of federal power. The constitutional predicate for the policy, as previously noted, was dubious but originally uncontroverted. Reaction to and debate over the fugitive slave clause and federal legislation, therefore, was effective in illuminating sectional incompatibility and enhancing mutual disaffection.

The fugitive slave controversy also revealed some significant truths with respect to the North. The variance between the status of slaves in the South and nominally free blacks in the North was reducible essentially to a difference between full and partial disability. As Chief Justice Taney accurately noted in *Scott v. Sandford*, presumptions of racial inferiority were pervasive and unqualified by geography.[17] Reality was that Taney's racist premises were reflected as much by northern customs and attitudes as by southern priorities. Freedom for blacks was more common in the North than in the South, where it became an increasingly rare phenomenon. Blacks in the South were denied virtually any incident of citizenship and most basic constitutional protections. By their mere presence, or as a consequence of violating the law, they risked reverting into slavery.

Even if the danger of enslavement in the North was limited to possibilities created by fugitive slave legislation, legal burdens and social exclusion there nonetheless were profound. Most free blacks were not allowed to vote, and at least two states, Indiana and Illinois, enacted laws prohibiting their immigration. Congress excluded blacks from military service and certain federal jobs. In Washington, D.C., where slavery flourished until the middle of the nineteenth century, blacks were denied voting rights and prohibited from engaging in various types of businesses.

Particularly indicative of northern racial attitudes were official policies of segregation. The Massachusetts Supreme Court, for instance, articulated the principle of separate but equal nearly half a century before the U.S. Supreme Court subscribed to it in *Plessy v. Ferguson*. In *Roberts v. City of Boston*, the state supreme court upheld a racial segregation requirement at variance with state law, which generally provided for student placement at the nearest school. Assignment of a black student to a school across town was upheld on grounds she was afforded an equal education.[18] Not until 1954, when the Court in *Brown v. Board of Education* declared separate to be "inherently unequal,"[19] would the racially separatist doctrine introduced in *Roberts* and reiterated in *Plessy* be defeated. Even then, transportation burdens, which did not impress the *Roberts* court when carriage was less efficient, would be reintroduced as a premise for limiting desegregation remedies.

Despite their common linkage to racial animus, inconsistent state policies toward blacks, even apart from slavery, engendered constitutionally awkward circumstances. Before the Constitution was amended after the Civil War to secure liberty and equality notwithstanding race, as discussed in the next chapter, questions concerning possible citizenship and rights of free blacks directed attention to the constitutional possibilities. Early attention focused on the provision that "[t]he Citizens of each State shall be entitled to all Privileges and Immunities of Citizens in the several States."[20] The privileges and immunities clause essentially provided that a state could not differentiate between its citizens and those of other states with respect to the rights and protections it afforded. Although not prompted by any preconception or contemplation of black citizenship, Article IV, Section 2 would have had profound implications if glossed in such terms. Southern states in particular would have been required to afford black citizens of other states equality of legal status. The issue was not directly addressed but at least was implicated in a lower court decision in 1823 and an attorney general's opinion in 1824. Both rulings determined that a South Carolina law, prohibiting entry of black sailors into the state's ports, was precluded by exclusive federal power over interstate and foreign commerce and foreign relations.[21] Confrontation of the question in terms of citizenship or freedom, however, was avoided.

Several years later, following adoption of similar restrictions by other southern states, another attorney general's opinion depicted race-dependent exclusions as a legitimate exercise of state power under the Tenth Amendment.[22] It also did not attend specifically to the status or rights of free blacks. That issue was directly confronted in yet another attorney general's opinion authored by Roger Taney in 1832. Consistent with his opinion in *Scott v. Sandford* a quarter of a century later, Taney's affirmance of state power disclosed an official sense of a class properly reduced to slavery. He thus observed that

[t]he African race in the United States even when free, are everywhere a degraded class, and exercise no political influence. The privileges they are allowed to enjoy, are accorded to them as a matter of kindness and benevolence rather

than of right. They are the only class of persons who can be held as mere property, as slaves. . . . They were never regarded as a constituent portion of the sovereignty of any state. . . . They were not looked upon as citizens by the contracting parties who formed the Constitution. They were evidently not supposed to be included by the term *citizens*. And were not intended to be embraced in any of the provisions of that Constitution but those which point to them in terms not to be mistaken.[23]

Although not officially published, Taney's opinion succinctly previewed the sentiments he would express in upholding slavery twenty-five years later.

The exclusion of black sailors from southern ports surfaced as a congressional issue during the early 1840s. A House report asserted that such state action was contrary to the supremacy clause and the privileges and immunities clause.[24] The report, although suggesting the potential of the privileges and immunities clause, had no impact on policy. Congress enacted no legislation that would have enforced or effectuated the terms of Article IV, Section 2 in a racially significant way. Such inaction was consistent with dominant northern sentiment, which, even if opposed to slavery and supportive of broad federal power in the field of commerce, assumed the legitimacy of race-dependent burdens and distinctions.

Northern blacks, existing in a twilight zone between slavery and full citizenship, presented a special challenge to the legal system. With racial questions having been largely avoided since the republic's origination, it is not surprising that standards for possible citizenship or standing to sue were underdeveloped or nonexistent. The status of blacks, however, was not without possibilities for contemporaneous analogy. Corporations were entities whose identity also did not fit into any preexisting legal categories.

In 1809, the Supreme Court had found that a corporation was an "artificial, invisible body, existing only in contemplation of law" and thus was without the standing of citizenship.[25] By 1844, the Court had determined that a corporation qualified as a citizen for purposes of suing and being sued.[26] Although corporations eventually would be regarded as citizens for general purposes, their split or uncertain legal personality was akin to the contemporary status of free black persons in the North. Just as corporations had fewer rights and privileges than did actual persons, the list of guarantees and liberties for blacks was shorter than that for whites. The similarities eventually would prove academic, however, when the Court in 1857 denied any notion of black citizenship and reduced the affected class to a status beneath even fictional persons.

Although it never directly or meaningfully addressed the possibility of black citizenship during the first half of the nineteenth century, the

Supreme Court rendered several racially significant decisions. In *The Josefa Segunda*, for instance, the Court upheld a federal law which prohibited importation of slaves and took effect when the constitutional moratorium on such enactments expired.[27] The opinion of the Court referred to the slave trade as an "inhuman traffic, for the abolition of which the United States have rendered an early and honorable anxiety."[28] Such a characterization may have reflected a jurisprudential sense of the slave trade as "contrary to the laws of nature."[29] The Court, however, declined opportunities to explore the possibilities of personal liberty under law and limited its focus to relatively narrow or technical considerations.[30] Despite invitations to restrict slavery further, the Court's decisions prior to the 1840s evinced no interest in broadly reviewing the institution or its incidents.

Constitutional jurisprudence at least until the *Scott* decision was calculated largely to avoid disrupting the premises of federal neutrality and state determination. Cases concerning the moratorium clause and the commerce power thus were relatively simple and uncontroversial compared to the issues that surfaced in an increasingly venomous and divisive political context. As noted previously, the fugitive slave problem was congressionally tended to by legislation that accommodated the interests of the South. Consistent with that slant, the Court invariably decided fugitive slave issues in terms favorable to slavery. Choice of law questions presented when freedom was claimed in the North were resolved in favor of southern law. Such rulings, although determining relatively technical legal issues, had profound decisional consequences. Because liberty could not be effected by the state of refuge, it was an exclusive function of the slave jurisdiction. So long as slavery endured, therefore, legal freedom could be secured only in rare and discretionary instances of manumission.

Fugitive slave jurisprudence reflected an ordering of priorities akin to what influenced the Constitution itself. The original emphasis on the imperatives of establishing a union was reiterated in terms of maintaining intramural cooperation and thus the union's continuing viability. Despite its formalistic appeal, such reasoning necessitated denial of practical realities. In *Commonwealth v. Aves*, the Supreme Judicial Court of Massachusetts thus related how it was

well known that when this Constitution was formed, some of the States permitted slavery and the slave-trade, and considered them highly essential to their interest, and that some other States had abolished slavery within their own limits, and from the principles deduced and policy evolved by them, might be presumed to desire to extend such abolition further. It was therefore manifestly the interest and the object of one party to this compact to enlarge, extend and secure, as far as possible, the rights and powers of the owners of slaves, within their own limits, as well as in other States, and of the other party to limit and restrain them. Under these circumstances the clause in question was agreed on and introduced into the constitution; . . . was intended to secure future peace and harmony . . . [and should be interpreted] to afford effectual security to the owners of slaves. The States have a plenary power to make all laws necessary for the regulation of slavery and the rights of the slave owners, while the slaves remain within their territorial limits; and it is only when they escape, without the consent of their owners, into other States, that they require the aid of other States, to enable them to regain their dominion over the fugitives.[31]

The *Aves* decision diminished a free state's legal interest in slaves, whether sojourning or seeking refuge, and indicated a constitutional duty to accommodate slavery. It thus acknowledged but soft-pedaled the reality of how federal law drew the entire nation into the service of slavery.

The implications of fugitive slave arrangements could not be permanently avoided or downplayed, however, given a system in which sectional competition over slavery in general was enlarging and deepening. Many northern states, responding to Congress's failure to afford basic legal process or to deter disregard of even pro forma legal procedure, enacted personal liberty laws. Legislation in some instances provided for writs of habeas corpus or like devices and prohibited the kidnapping of blacks. During the 1820s, Pennsylvania authorized detention of alleged fugitives only by judicial officers, required more extensive proof of ownership, and criminalized private seizure of a black person. The legislation endeavored to balance the state's obligation under the 1793 act with due process concerns, especially for free blacks who otherwise were vulnerable to mistaken identification or exploitation. It also resulted in comprehensive judicial review of the fugitive slave law. The consequent decision, in *Prigg v. Pennsylvania*, has been described as "rival[ing] *Dred Scott v. Sandford* in historical importance."[32]

The circumstances of the *Prigg* decision illuminated precisely the concerns that prompted enactment of the Pennsylvania law. At issue was the status of a Maryland slave couple's daughter, never herself previously claimed as a slave, and her children. The woman had married a free man and moved to Pennsylvania where some of her children were born. After she had resided in Pennsylvania for five years, descendants of her parents' owner sought to have her and the children returned to Maryland. Although the offsprings' agent Edward Prigg obtained a warrant for arrest, the Pennsylvania court refused to provide a certificate for removal. Prigg nonetheless took the woman and her children in violation of the state law. Maryland initially refused to extradite Prigg, but the Pennsylvania legislature enacted a law providing him with special procedural consideration and safeguards so that the constitutionality of the state law could be assessed. Prigg was convicted and, within a year, had appealed to the U.S. Supreme Court.[33]

The *Prigg* decision was authored by Justice Story who had been a long-time critic of slavery. Story nonetheless rendered a decision that invalidated the Pennsylvania law on the grounds it conflicted with the Fugitive Slave Act of 1793 and the Constitution. In sum, he determined that the federal law was constitutional, a state law at odds with the statute was impermissible, and slave owners could recapture fugitive slaves on their own initiative and by their own devices.

Determination that the federal law of 1793 was constitutional, although perhaps unsettling to Story's moral precepts, was consistent with a jurisprudential style characterized by a nationalist ideology and a commitment to judicial restraint.[34] He discerned that congressional power to enact the Fugitive Slave Act of 1793 was reasonably inferred from the fugitive slave clause of the Constitution.[35] Simple as the premise was, the Court's analysis was not airtight. Because the fugitive slave clause is set forth in Article IV, as noted previously, a credible argument existed that it spoke to relations among the states instead of providing a basis for congressional action. The Court itself avoided meaningful inquiry into whether the act was at odds with specific constitutional guarantees. The federal law denied even the rudimentary incidents of due process to free blacks who might be wrongly or mistakenly apprehended. As a consequence, Congress and the Court permitted a deprivation of fundamental liberty that they almost certainly would have repaired if white persons had been similarly slighted. The enactment and Story's response to it suggest that Taney's subsequent blurring of legal distinctions between free blacks and slaves was neither aberrational nor unique.

A critical aspect of the Court's decision was the determination that fugitive slaves were within the federal government's exclusive jurisdiction.[36] This finding was consistent with jurisprudence that, in the time between *Marbury v. Madison* and *Scott v. Sandford*, had invalidated no federal statute. The grounding of the Fugitive Slave Act in Article IV at least offered an eminent point for distinguishing *Prigg* from otherwise expansive readings of national power. The Court, however, bypassed any such analysis.

The *Prigg* decision warned against state legislation that would "interfere with or . . . obstruct the just rights of the owner to reclaim his slave."[37] Favorable as the ruling was to the immediate interests of slavery, it nonetheless communicated a mixed message to the South. Although resolving the fugitive slave question in terms favorable to southern interests, the decision introduced the unsettling prospect that slavery itself was a federal rather than a state concern. Chief Justice Taney sensed the possibility that if the federal government could provide for slavery, it also could operate against it. He thus wrote separately to make the point that states were not only prohibited from interfering with a slave owner's rights but also obligated to protect them.[38]

The Court's decision, if examined solely within the context of its four corners, would seem to have an undeniably pro-slavery cast. Endorsement of a virtually unqualified right to recapture a slave, pursuant to a slave owner's own methodology, effectively extended the law of southern states into the North. Despite constitutional and statutory intimations of at least minimal procedural protection,[39] the only limitation on recapturing a slave or kidnapping a free black was that it be effected "without any breach of the peace, or illegal violence."[40] Demands of the South, at least for fugitive slave purposes, thus became requirements of the nation.

The *Prigg* ruling, however, enhanced rather than terminated the controversy. By illustrating how inextricably the whole nation was bound up in slavery, it compounded anti-slavery sentiment and destabilized rather than secured the institution. For radical abolitionists, the *Prigg* ruling further validated their view of the Constitution as a pro-slavery document. The manifest implication of the entire nation in slavery defeated imagery of a wall between northern and southern custom and enhanced the conviction that the Constitution should be resisted even at the cost of disunion. In his abolitionist publication *The Liberator*, William Lloyd Garrison observed that allowing a slave owner to claim his property in any state "establish[ed] the constitutionality of slavery in every State in the Union."[41]

Despite the criticism it engendered, the decision soon became a source for undermining the interests it supposedly had secured. Story had determined that Congress could authorize state courts to enforce the law but could not, without abridging state powers, require them to do so.[42] He further ventured that "it might well be deemed an unconstitutional exercise of power of interpretation, to insist that the states are bound to carry into effect the duties of the national government, nowhere delegated or instructed to them by the Constitution."[43] Story also noted that state judges, although not obligated to enforce federal law, nonetheless could do so "unless prohibited by state legislation."[44] Such observations restated common understandings of the imperatives and incidents of federalism. Offered in the context of a profoundly divisive ideological conflict, however, effect proved disproportionate to purpose. As Chief Justice Taney accurately forecast, these statements, although not part of the Court's holding and thus not binding, became a departure point for neutralizing the otherwise pro-slavery cast of the *Prigg* decision. Noting the scarcity of federal judges in many states, he warned that "if the state authorities are absolved from all obligation to protect this right, and may stand by and see it violated without an effort to defend it, the act of Congress of 1793 scarcely deserves the name of a remedy."[45]

Taney's worst fears promptly were confirmed, as many northern legislatures and courts, respectively, enacted laws and rendered decisions
transforming a principle favorable to slavery into one antagonistic to the
institution. Several states prohibited their judges from enforcing the
federal law. Even without legislation, courts cited to *Prigg* itself for purposes of disclaiming authority to hear fugitive slave actions. Five years
after the decision, Pennsylvania enacted a law precluding jurisdiction in
all fugitive slave cases. Instead of settling an account in favor of slavery,
therefore, the ruling actually advanced the anti-slavery cause. Having
been sensitized to their nexus with the institution they condemned,
northern states responded in terms and deeds calculated to sever their
linkage. Ambivalence that could accommodate slavery thus became increasingly susceptible to displacement by cognition of the institution's
real and broad demands.

By enhancing northern awareness of slavery's national significance,
the *Prigg* decision quickened and deepened societal antagonisms. Prior
to *Prigg*, the law had accommodated slavery while largely avoiding the
imagery of real involvement with the institution. Evidencing how effectively that illusion was pierced, northern participation in rendering fugitive slaves actually diminished after *Prigg*. Despite pervasive racism in
the North, conversion of an essentially pro-slavery decision into an anti-
slavery principle disclosed an enhanced sense of how slavery infected
the entire nation and consequent effort to minimize its reach.

So extensively and effectively was *Prigg* repudiated and offset in the
following decade that Congress enacted a new fugitive slave law. Central
to the legislation was neutralization of the dicta that had become the
basis for northern resistance to rather than cooperation in recaption and
rendition. To compensate for state reluctance to effectuate the law, a
federal bureau was established and vested with enforcement power. For-
tification of the fugitive slave law was part of a broad congressional effort
to resolve several thorny problems associated with the general question
of slavery. Not only did the resultant Compromise of 1850 codify new
fugitive slave legislation. It also provided for California's admission to
the union as a free state, organized the Utah and New Mexico territories
as slave jurisdictions, and prohibited the slave trade in the District of
Columbia. Architects and supporters of the compromise envisioned it
as a final resolution of the slavery issue. The legislative premises, however, were grounded in the problem-solving model of the past when the
South perceived less peril to slavery and the North was less conscious
of its connection to the institution. Given the significantly altered op-
erational circumstances, it is not surprising that the Compromise of 1850
proved to be a temporary rather than a permanent melioration.

Just how unsettled pertinent norms and practices had become was
evinced shortly after the Compromise of 1850 was enacted. Southern

opposition to the creation of Nebraska as a free territory challenged the long-established dividing line etched by the Missouri Compromise. Instead of maintaining a geographical bright line, Congress considered more complex premises for determining how territories were to be established and states admitted to the union. Competing for acceptance were Democratic Party concepts of popular sovereignty and competing notions of free soil.[46] Experience in Kansas and Nebraska was defined by the Democratic principle of allowing a territory's populace to determine its institutions. The result was unbridled turmoil, chicanery, and violence. The Democratic consensus itself would soon subdivide into competing northern and southern positions respectively staked to readings of the Constitution as neutral but accommodating slavery and actually supporting and protecting it.

Having wrestled with slavery for more than half a century, and having crafted policy yielding ever-diminishing returns, Congress appeared increasingly incapable of formulating a durable solution. Hardened differences between northern and southern legislators of different parties, compounded by the split between northern and southern Democrats, augured unfavorably for a consensus on federal policy. In its representative capacity, Congress was a microcosm of the profound sectional antagonism and mutual distrust that had come to define the nation. Increasing attention to constitutional imperatives, although a competitive exercise among slavery's supporters and detractors, pointed toward the judiciary as a possible forum for resolving the issue. What the framers had avoided and Congress could not successfully compromise thus eventually was reckoned with by means of litigation.

Constitutional jurisprudence by the midpoint of the century already had established a favorable disposition toward the South at least in terms of accommodating slavery. Dominated by southern jurists, the Court in the 1850s enhanced that tradition. Decisions preceding *Scott v. Sandford* revealed an enthusiasm for the southern position that at times was excessive. In *Strader v. Graham*, the Court dismissed a case on procedural grounds but proceeded to decide substantive questions anyway.[47] The action originated in Kentucky, where a slaveowner sued a party who helped his slaves escape to Canada. The defense was premised on the argument that upon setting foot in Ohio the slaves were free. The Kentucky court rejected the proposition, and the Supreme Court dismissed the case for lack of jurisdiction.[48] Normative principle of review precluded the Court from resolving issues unnecessary for disposition of a case. Despite that basic premise, the Court gratuitously observed that the law of a slave state applied in determining the issue of freedom.[49] Although the principle was not essential to the action's resolution, the Court in 1852 asserted the primacy of the slave state's interest.

A decade after *Prigg*, the Court revisited fugitive slave questions. In

Moore v. Illinois, it upheld a state law punishing individuals who aided fugitive slaves.[50] The decision was an extension of *Prigg* insofar as the Court earlier had suggested that state police power could be used to promote and aid but not interfere with the interest of slave owners.[51] Unlike *Prigg*, the ruling was an unequivocal reminder of the North's unwanted obligations to the South. Northern understanding of slavery as a national rather than a regional phenomenon accordingly was further enhanced.

By 1850, the debate between North and South was notable for how it had been redefined. With respect to slavery, original thinking had contemplated a neutral federal role and individual state determination. Over the course of several decades, that premise was unsettled by fugitive slave experience and territorial expansion. Congress effectively extended the reach of slavery nationwide in 1793 when it enacted legislation protecting slaveowner interests in runaways. Despite jurisprudential efforts to effectuate the act and legislative attempts to enhance it, southern attitudes increasingly and accurately assumed that the North wished to distance itself from and minimize the operation of slavery. The refusal of free states to turn over fugitive slaves, contrary to the Supreme Court's delineation of duty, represented an exercise in detachment. Refusal to respect the claims and interests of slave owners, which the South had secured through the legislative and judicial processes, revealed that a final and comprehensive decision on the institution itself could not be avoided forever.

Intense competition between North and South already was manifesting itself in efforts to define policy in the remaining territories. The admission of California as a free state denoted the South's failure to extend the Missouri Compromise line to the Pacific. Southern legislators responded by defeating a bill for the Nebraska Territory, which was introduced on the premise that slavery was prohibited north of the latitude of compromise. The Kansas-Nebraska Act, passed the following year, divided what originally was one territory into two and provided that eventual admission of each as a free or a slave state would depend on what their respective constitutions resolved. Implicit in the act was the possibility that the proposition of slavery might be resolved according to the concept of popular sovereignty. Subsequent political events and violence in Kansas over the content of the state's constitution indicated the high stakes involved for North and South.[52]

Dispute over the status of Kansas and Nebraska revealed compounding fractures in the body politic and a further diminished congressional capacity. The Republican party emerged from the Kansas-Nebraska episode as a national force and primary exponent of free soil principles. The Democratic party split into northern and southern wings, divided by subtle but significant distinctions over the meaning of popular sovereignty. At issue was not the general question of territorial or state status but when and by whom the decision would be made. For southern Democrats, popular sovereignty enabled the people of a territory to permit or prohibit slavery when framing the constitution for statehood. Northern Democrats maintained that territorial legislatures could determine whether slavery should be permitted or prohibited. Both shared the view that the Constitution's territory clause did not vest the federal government with power to provide for or against slavery. The northern position, expounded most notably by Senator Stephen A. Douglas of Illinois, differed from the southern view in that territories were regarded as incipient states with full sovereignty. Such a perspective was inimical to southerners, concerned that if Congress could delegate power to prohibit slavery in the territories, it could pass judgment on the institution in general. The Douglas formula, which has been referred to as territorial rather than popular sovereignty,[53] represented an effort to bridge the widening gap between North and South. Its failure demonstrated the profundity and insurmountability of sectional differences.

The Kansas-Nebraska controversy and contemporary political developments disclosed how vexing and convoluted the slavery problem had become for representative governance. The Kansas-Nebraska Act advanced a notion of popular sovereignty that, although subject to varying interpretations, added a new wrinkle to the traditional federal policy of neutrality. Self-determination in the new jurisdictions was made "subject only to the Constitution."[54] Given the manifest division over constitutional meaning and requirements, such direction was at least imprecise. It also was superfluous because judicial review is appropriate for any legislative action alleged to be unconstitutional. Even if unintended, passage of the act symbolized a timely invitation for judicial attention to an otherwise intractable problem. The Court, although having rendered several decisions concerning slavery, had yet to confront the territorial question. Judicial review thus loomed as an option for an effectively stalemated legislative process and the nation's interest in a final constitutional resolution of a seemingly interminable problem.

In 1857, the Supreme Court attempted to resolve the slavery controversy as a function of constitutional imperative. Its effort, however, exacerbated rather than muted sectional differences. The case of *Scott v. Sandford* resulted when the slave of a military doctor, who had lived on extended assignments in Illinois and the Minnesota Territory, claimed his liberty as a consequence of lengthy residence in free jurisdictions. The case could have been decided without reaching the general issue of slavery or its constitutionality. A judgment against Scott could have been premised on choice of law principles requiring disposition pursuant to Missouri rather than Illinois law. The Court also might have followed the precedent of *Strader*; it could have determined that the parties were not citizens of different states and thus federal jurisdiction did not exist. Instead, Chief Justice Taney attended comprehensively to questions of black citizenship, congressional and territorial power, and the rights of slave owners. The result was a decision that enhanced the controversy and diminished the Court's prestige.[55]

The *Scott* decision comprised nine separate opinions, including six concurrences and two dissents. Chief Justice Taney's rendering was presented as the opinion of the Court, and because its status was not contested by the other justices, it may be considered authoritative. Immediately evident in Taney's opinion was an inclination to avoid a narrowly premised decision and instead to reckon with slavery in sweeping terms.

Scott's complaint in the Missouri trial court had elicited a plea in abatement which, under common law pleading, challenged the time, place, or manner in which an action was brought. The pleading asserted that the defendant had assaulted and falsely imprisoned the plaintiff, his wife, and two children. Sandford's plea in abatement challenged the court's jurisdiction on the grounds the plaintiff, as a black man, was not a citizen and thus could not sue. The trial court, although not determining citizenship in broad terms, found that at least for purposes of suing in federal court Scott qualified as a citizen under the Constitution's diversity clause.[56] The Supreme Court rejected Scott's argument that the defendant waived the jurisdictional issue by eventually pleading to the substantive merits of the case.[57] As Chief Justice Taney properly noted, jurisdiction if contested at the trial court level remains a proper issue upon appeal.[58]

Analysis of whether any black person qualified as a citizen, although not essential to a decision that could have rested on choice of law or diversity principles or that could have been narrowed to whether slaves were citizens, constituted nearly half of Taney's opinion. For the chief justice,

[t]he question is simply this: can a negro, whose ancestors were imported into this country and sold as slaves, become a member of the political community formed and brought into existence by the Constitution of the United States, and as such become entitled to all the rights, and privileges, and immunities, guaranteed by that instrument to the citizen.[59]

To sue in federal court as a citizen of the United States, Taney determined that a person would have to possess full citizenship under the Constitution. Because blacks were considered "a subordinate and inferior class of beings" at the time the document was framed, he concluded that any "rights or privileges" accruing to them were a function not of the Constitution but of governmental discretion.[60] The constitutional status of blacks, or more precisely the lack thereof, thus was fixed by a sense that the entire race originally was regarded as a slave class.

By focusing on national citizenship, Taney did not disturb the power of any state to confer rights and privileges on black persons. Refusal to acknowledge that they were "citizen[s] in the sense in which that word is used in the Constitution of the United States," however, not only disabled blacks from suing in federal court but also limited any rights "to the State which gave them."[61] The privileges and immunities clause, which required states to accord a "perfect equality to its citizens and those of other states as to rights of persons and rights of property," was construed to protect only the incidents of national rather than state citizenship.[62] It thus was not pertinent to black persons, whether emancipated or not, who had been afforded no national citizenship and were state citizens only to the extent so provided.

Taney noted that persons recognized by the states as citizens when the Constitution was adopted also were citizens of the nation.[63] To offset the reality that some blacks were recognized as state citizens and thus qualified as national citizens, the chief justice offered his understanding of the society's founding values and attitudes. Taney related that for more than a century before the Declaration of Independence and the Constitution were framed, black persons had

been regarded as beings of an inferior order, and altogether unfit to associate with the white race, either in social or political relations; and so far inferior, that they had no rights which the white man was bound to respect and that the negro might justly and lawfully be reduced to slavery for his benefit.[64]

The conclusion that black persons "had no rights which the white man was bound to respect" represented a perversion of the historical record. Reality was that blacks in several states at the time of the republic's founding possessed rights to sue in court, to contract, and to acquire, own, and sell property.[65] Although anti-miscegenation laws were common and discrimination pervasive, the notion that blacks were entirely bereft of rights represented an exaggeration.

The chief justice also suggested that neither the Declaration of Independence nor the Constitution contemplated black citizenship. Taney dismissed facial indications in the Declaration that its self-evident truths comprehended all of humanity by referring to contemporaneous political exclusions of and attitudes toward blacks. In spite of the document's unqualified terms, he opined that it was "too clear for dispute, that the enslaved African race were not intended to be included" within its purview.[66] To fortify his premise, Taney found the slave trade and fugitive slave clauses to be evidence that blacks were not "a portion of the people or citizens of the Government then formed."[67] Glossed over were the

Constitution's own distinctions referenced toward slavery rather than color.

Resolving the question of general black citizenship was not essential to the disposition of the *Scott* case. As noted previously, the question was reducible to whether a slave could sue in federal court. Insofar as the Court had determined that corporations were state citizens for purposes of diversity, if not under all circumstances, a legitimate precedent existed for at least allowing a right to sue.[68] By converting a dispositive jurisdictional issue into a question of whether all blacks were entitled to national citizenship and its incidental rights and protections, Tancy deviated from the principle that courts should avoid unnecessary issues.

Having determined that blacks were not citizens, Taney then depicted them for constitutional purposes as property. Referring to provisions for ending the slave trade and accounting for fugitive slaves, the chief justice concluded that the Constitution identified a property right entitled to federal protection.[69] Acknowledging only an authority "coupled with the duty of guarding and protecting the [slave] owner in his rights," Taney found Congress powerless to compromise the property rights of slave owners.[70] The depiction of slaves as property was crucial for purposes of identifying an interest that a citizen could not be deprived of "without due process of law."[71] It translated the Constitution, which by its original terms had evaded and at best accommodated slavery, into a prohibition of federal interference with and an endorsement of the institution.

Although having pursued the citizenship question further than necessary, the Court had reached a logical termination point for its decision. Determined to resolve the slavery question in conclusive and comprehensive terms, however, Taney proceeded to confront the dominant and divisive political question of the time. He thus concluded that Congress had no power to prohibit slavery in territories and that the Missouri Compromise itself was unconstitutional. Over the course of the nineteenth century, the Supreme Court consistently had interpreted federal powers expansively, and the *Scott* decision represented the first time since *Marbury v. Madison*[72] that it had struck down a federal law. The result reflected a narrow reading of the territory clause, which, by its terms, authorized Congress "to dispose of and make all needful Rules and Regulations respecting the territory...belonging to the United States...."[73] Taney maintained that this provision related only to land claimed by the United States in 1789[74] and was not a basis for exercising power over subsequently acquired territories.[75]

The interpretation was problematic for several reasons. It rationalized congressional action, contemporaneous with the Constitution's framing, providing for governance of the Northwest Territory in terms that prohibited slavery. Taney's view conflicted, however, with the established principle that, under the necessary and proper clause,[76] Congress may enact laws reasonably related to an enumerated power, provided they do not conflict with a specific constitutional prohibition.[77] His reading also departed from precedent to the effect that a territory was "governed by virtue of that clause in the Constitution which empowers Congress 'to dispose of and make all needful rules and regulations, respecting the Territory, or other Property belonging to the United States.' "[78] Finally, the chief justice's analysis was contrary to the actual exercise of congressional power for seven decades.

Taney nevertheless introduced the notion that persons in federal territories and existing states were on a constitutional par. He maintained that

an act of Congress which deprives a citizen of the United States of his liberty or property, merely because he came himself or brought his property into a particular Territory of the United States, and who had committed no offense against the laws, could hardly be dignified with the name of due process of law.[79]

Contrary to the argument he had made successfully a quarter of a century earlier, in *Barron v. Mayor and City Council of Baltimore*,[80] Taney then identified the Fifth Amendment as a specific check on Congress's territorial power.[81] He thereby planted in constitutional jurisprudence the seeds of substantive due process. By the end of the century, as discussed in Chapter 4, the premise would become a significant source of unenumerated but nonetheless fundamental rights and liberties.

Given his earlier disposition against substantive due process notions, Taney may have seemed an unlikely exponent of such an activist principle. Identification of a fundamental, albeit constitutionally unspecified right, however, was a useful premise in foreclosing federal territorial governance. Consistent with the views of southern Democrats, Taney further concluded that if Congress could not set the terms of territorial rule, it "could not authorize a Territorial Government to exercise them ...[or] confer [any] power on any local government, established by its authority, to violate the provisions of the Constitution."[82]

As the chief justice related it, delimitation of congressional power was the function not of constitutional implication or radiation but rather of "a right of property in a slave [that] is distinctly and expressly affirmed in the Constitution."[83] Even if such a guarantee was not manifest pursuant to an objective reading of the document, Taney found it expressed by the slave trade clause, allowing "a right to traffic in it ... for twenty years."[84] From the fugitive slave clause, he also deduced an affirmative federal duty to protect the institution at least to the extent of accounting for runaway slaves.[85] The conclusion that a right of slavery was "expressly affirmed" at minimum turned any notion of literalism on its ear. Identification of a property right in slavery also was at variance with the original sense of a neutral federal role and state determination. The slave trade clause itself was a dubious source of a durable right insofar as the provision connoted eventual prohibitive power. To the extent slavery was under comprehensive review, the fugitive slave clause was a logical candidate for reevaluation rather than reiteration and extension. The reasonable possibility that the clause defined imperatives of inter-state cooperation, instead of furnishing a basis for federal action, none-theless received no attention.

Having identified multiple predicates for its holding, the Court con-cluded that "[u]pon these considerations it is the opinion of the court that the act of Congress which prohibited a citizen from holding and owning property of this kind in the territory of the United States north of the line therein mentioned, is not warranted by the Constitution, and is therefore void."[86] The immediate consequence of the decision was that "neither Dred Scott nor his family were made free by virtue of their transit to free territory even if their owner had intended to be a per-manent resident."[87] Its broader significance was a translation of the Con-stitution into terms not only recognizing the right of slavery but also denying the personhood of an entire race.

The Court thus resolved the issue of slavery by clothing its ideology in constitutional fabric of its own weave. Because its underlying philos-ophy and consequent doctrine remained in dispute, the decision fueled rather than dampened the controversy. It accordingly has been observed that "[a]s a bid to settle political issues, the Dred Scott venture was a ghastly failure. Instead of pacifying, it created worse turbulence. It forced politicians and the public into more intense and agonizing reap-praisals of constitution and priorities."[88] Rather than ameliorating sec-tional frictions, the Court hardened the split between northern and southern Democrats, Democrats and Republicans, and North and South. Its judgment and opinion facilitated the southern agenda and predict-ably prompted northern outrage. Criticism except in radical abolitionist circles, however, was selective and qualified. The Court was condemned primarily for its invalidation of the Missouri Compromise.[89] Objection to the constitutional reduction of blacks was muted and disclosed that, despite their differences on the general question of slavery and federal power, the North and the South shared significant common ground with respect to racial ideology.

Notwithstanding the northern outcry in response to the *Scott* decision, racism and racial phobias were widespread phenomena. Although the Court's endorsement of slavery became a dominant issue for congres-sional elections in 1858 and the presidential election in 1860, political marketing responded to racial reality. While advocating free soil and criticizing the *Scott* decision, Republicans avoided identification with the plight of slaves or blacks. Even if opposed to fugitive slave legislation and territorial expansion of slavery, they still acknowledged a constitutional obligation to abide by fugitive laws and accommodate the institution at least where established. Concern with the civil circumstances of black persons was considered so risky that even opponents of slavery were moved to emphasize their racial disdain. Lincoln thus emphasized a "natural disgust in the minds of nearly all white people to the idea of an indiscriminate amalgamation of the white and black races."[90] His pronouncement differed from Taney's insofar as it suggested a subclass rather than non-class of persons. Critical focus and caution were revealing not only with respect to the candidates but also the society toward which their message was pitched.

Even if selective, objections to the *Scott* decision were trenchant. The Court had deviated from the traditional premise that slavery was allowable pursuant only to positive state law and not when specifically prohibited. Although some critics anticipated the possibility that the decision eventually would be overruled, Lincoln presented a significant challenge to the principle of judicial review. Essentially he argued that the Court's judgment, although controlling with respect to the actual parties, did not bind government or become general law until it became "fully settled."[91] Barring indisputable coextension of legal principle and public belief, Lincoln asserted that Congress should not consider itself bound by the decision.[92]

The possibility of northern defiance manifested itself when a Wisconsin court freed two persons, convicted in federal court for facilitating the escape of runaway slaves in violation of federal law, pursuant to a writ of habeas corpus.[93] The state court effectively assumed the responsibility of filling "the procedural gap Congress left in the Fugitive Slave Law when it omitted jury trials for alleged runaways and prohibited testimony by them."[94] In *Ableman v. Booth*, the Supreme Court upheld the national law and emphasized the imperatives of federal court immunity from state challenge.[95] The decision, authored by Chief Justice Taney, ironically urged respect for the conditions of a national union which the *Scott* ruling helped imperil.

The 1860 presidential election devolved into a three-way campaign among southern Democrats, northern Democrats, and Republicans. Southern Democrats maintained that the *Scott* decision had settled the territorial issue conclusively and established affirmative constitutional support for slavery. Northern Democrats asserted that the territorial question remained open but could be resolved by a future ruling. Republicans continued to challenge the decision's legitimacy and maintained that Congress still could exclude slavery from new territories. Even after Lincoln was elected, Congress made a final effort to mediate sectional differences and forestall the union's unraveling. A Senate committee proposed several constitutional amendments designed to resolve the slavery issue permanently. The amendments among other things allowed and required protection of property including slaves in territories south of the Missouri Compromise line, prohibited abolition of or interference with slavery in states where it existed and made unamendable all constitutional provisions directly pertinent to the institution.[96] The proposal was defeated as Republicans held fast to principles of slavery's containment.

The *Scott* ruling itself was nullified for practical purposes by the Lincoln administration's calculated neglect of it. Failure of the political (legislative and executive) and judicial branches to resolve the issues of societal division led inevitably to civil war. The conflict commenced over the scope of congressional power but terminated with the abolition of slavery, repudiation of *Scott*, and a commitment to secure black citizenship. In the years immediately following civil war, the Thirteenth Amendment prohibited slavery, the Fourteenth Amendment established black citizenship and at least limited equality, and the Fifteenth Amendment prohibited racial discrimination in voting rights.

Despite its constitutional renouncement, the *Scott* decision remained a fair reflection of geographically unqualified values and attitudes. The opinion and judgment were rendered at a time when racism was rampant in the North, racial disadvantage was effectuated and maintained nationwide, and racial phobias were accentuated by the concern that emancipated slaves would migrate North and compete in a largely if not exclusively white job market.[97] Although mainstream abolitionism promoted liberation, it did not contemplate racial equality in a comprehensive legal or normative sense. Even when eventually ordering emancipation, Lincoln continued to disclaim notions of racial parity, observing that

[t]here is an unwillingness on the part of our people, harsh as it may be, for you freed colored people to remain with us.... [Even] when you cease to be slaves, you are far removed from being placed on an equality with the white man.... I cannot alter it if I could. It is a fact.[98]

When read against such a moral and ideological backdrop, Taney's opinion offers more than an idiosyncratic reflection of southern values. The sense of a racial group as "beings of an inferior order, ... altogether unfit to associate with the white race"[99] comports not only with the imperatives of slavery but also with the priorities of general society which by law had pervasively and overtly expressed its racism. Notwithstanding context, the *Scott* opinion's infamy has been seen as radiating from "its smug assumption of racial superiority; ... its shameful equation of citizenship with whiteness; ... its sweeping exclusion of black people from belonging to America; ... its bland acceptance of their relegation to an inferior caste."[100]

To the extent the *Scott* decision was an extension of dominant values, it does not fit retrospective characterization as a "derelict[] of constitutional law."[101] Modern understanding of it as an aberration may reflect functional if not real exorcism from the nation's jurisprudence. A sense that the decision is relatively insignificant for modern purposes may be intimated by its virtual disappearance from most contemporary constitutional law case books.[102] Dismissal of *Scott* as irrelevant, however, is misconceived.

Original accommodation of slavery, even if merely anticipating deferral of a final decision, at least assumed the risk that the institution would ultimately be endorsed rather than disavowed. Although the Thirteenth and Fourteenth Amendments eventually repudiated *Scott*, its spirit endured in subsequent jurisprudence. By the late nineteenth century, the Supreme Court had ratified the separate but equal doctrine in a ruling criticized at the time for being "quite as pernicious as ... the *Dred Scott Case*."[103] Parallels also can be argued with respect to curtailment of the desegregation mandate and foreclosure of affirmative action in the latter half of the twentieth century. The influences and considerations that defined antebellum law and culture did not vanish with the abolition of slavery. Subsequent history has disclosed that although the *Scott* decision was formally disowned within a decade, its ordering of racial priorities and underlying spirit would prove more durable.

NOTES

1. Ordinance of 1787: The Northwest Territorial Government, art. VI.

2. P. Finkelman, An Imperfect Union 83 (1981) (*quoting* S. Lynd, Class Conflict, Slavery, and the United States Constitution 186 (1967)); U. Phillips, American Negro Slavery 128 (1918).

3. *See* S. Lynd, *supra* note 2, at 185–213.

4. *See* W. Wiecek, The Sources of Antislavery Constitutionalism in America, 1760–1848, at 172–82 (1977). Not until the next century would the First Amendment be applied to the states through the Fourteenth Amendment. *See* Near v. Minnesota, 283 U.S. 697, 707 (1931); Gitlow v. New York, 268 U.S. 652 (1925).

5. *See* W. Wiecek, supra note 4, at 183–89.

6. U.S. Const. art. I, § 8, cl. 17.

7. D. Fehrenbacher, The Dred Scott Case 122 (1978).

8. *See id.* at 236–48.

9. *See* R. Cover, Justice Accused 154–56 (1975). Some analysts regard the utopian vision as apprehending a constitution that was affirmatively anti-slavery. *See* J. ten Broek, Antislavery Origins of the Fourteenth Amendment (1951); Graham, *The Early Antislavery Backgrounds of the Fourteenth Amendment*, 1950 Wis. L.Rev. 610 (1950). The perception has elicited criticism to the effect that the

utopians merely looked to principles of superseding natural law. *See* R. Cover at 156.

10. American Insurance Co. v. Canter, 26 U.S. (1 Pet.) 511, 546 (1828).

11. U.S. Const. art. IV, § 2, cl. 3.

12. *See* D. Fehrenbacher, *supra* note 7, at 25; R. Cover *supra* note 9, at 163.

13. *See* P. Finkelman, *supra* note 2, at 27.

14. *Id.*

15. 1 Stat. 302 (1793).

16. *See* D. Fehrenbacher, *supra* note 7, at 61–64.

17. 163 U.S. 537 (1896), discussed in Chapter 4.

18. Roberts v. City of Boston, 59 Mass. (5 Cush.) 198 (1850).

19. Brown v. Board of Education, 347 U.S. 383, 393 (1954).

20. U.S. Const. art. IV, § 2, cl. 1.

21. *See* D. Fehrenbacher, *supra* note 7, at 69; W. Wiecek, *supra* note 4, at 137–38.

22. *See* D. Fehrenbacher, *supra* note 7, at 70.

23. The Taney opinion is excerpted in Mr. Justice 43–45 (A. Dunham & P. Kurland eds. 1964).

24. W. Wiecek, *supra* note 4, at 138.

25. Bank of the United States v. DeVeaux, 9 U.S. (5 Cranch) 61, 73 (1809) (emphasis in original).

26. Louisville, Cincinnati & Charleston Railroad Co. v. Letson, 43 U.S. (2 How.) 497, 559 (1844).

27. The Josefa Segunda, 18 U.S. (5 Wheat.) 338, 356–57 (1820).

28. *Id.* at 357.

29. The Antelope, 23 U.S. (10 Wheat.) 66, 120 (1825).

30. *See supra* notes 27–29 and accompanying text. *See also* Queen v. Hepburn, 11 U.S. (7 Cranch) 290 (1813); Scott v. Negro Ben, 10 U.S. (6 Cranch) 3 (1810).

31. Commonwealth v. Aves, 35 Mass. (18 Pick.) 191, 220–21 (1836).

32. D. Fehrenbacher, *supra* note 7, at 43.

33. Background of the case is detailed in Finkelman, *Prigg v. Pennsylvania and Northern State Courts*, in The Law of American Slavery 160 (K. Hall ed. 1987).

34. Story regarded the Court's function as nondisruptive and viewed the Constitution as "practical [in] nature . . . designed for common use and fitted for common understanding." J. Story, Commentaries on the Constitution of the United States 345 (1905).

35. Prigg v. Pennsylvania, 41 U.S. (16 Pet.) 539, 613 (1842).

36. *Id.* at 616–17.

37. *Id.* at 625.

38. *Id.* at 627–28 (Taney, C. J., concurring).

39. Fugitive slave provisions, for instance, spoke in terms of "be[ing] delivered up on Claim of the Party. . . . " U.S. Const. art. IV, § 2, cl. 3; 1 Stat. 302.

40. Prigg v. Pennsylvania, 41 U.S. (16 Pet.) at 613.

41. Liberator, Mar. 11, 1842, *quoted in* Finkelman, *supra* note 33, at 172.

42. Prigg v. Pennsylvania, 41 U.S. (16 Pet.) at 614.

43. *Id.* at 625.

44. *Id.* at 615–16.

45. *Id.* at 628–29 (Taney, C. J., concurring).

46. *See* D. Fehrenbacher, *supra* note 7, at 172–87.

47. Strader v. Graham, 51 U.S. (10 How.) 82 (1850).

48. *Id.* at 97.

49. *Id.* at 93–94.

50. Moore v. Illinois, 55 U.S. (14 How.) 13, 17 (1853).

51. Prigg v. Pennsylvania, 41 U.S. (16 Pet.) at 625.

52. An account of the violent and convoluted efforts to define Kansas as a slave or a free state is provided by D. Fehrenbacher, *supra* note 7, at 193–201.

53. *See id.* at 196.

54. *Id.* at 184.

55. A. Mason, The Supreme Court from Taft to Warren 37–38 (1958).

56. *See* Scott v. Sandford, 60 U.S. (19 How.) 393, 400 (1857); U.S. Const., art. III, § 2, cl. 1.

57. Scott v. Sandford, 60 U.S. (19 How.) at 402–03.

58. *Id.*

59. *Id.* at 403.

60. *Id.* at 404–05.

61. *Id.* at 405.

62. *Id.* at 406–07.

63. *Id.* at 406.

64. *Id.* at 407.

65. *See* D. Fehrenbacher, *supra* note 7, at 349–50.

66. Scott v. Sandford, 60 U.S. (19 How.) at 410.

67. *Id.* at 411.

68. *See* Louisville, Cincinnati & Charleston Railroad v. Letson, 43 U.S. (2 How.) at 559.

69. Scott v. Sandford, 60 U.S. (19 How.) at 451–52.

70. *See id.* at 452.

71. *Id.*

72. 5 U.S. (1 Cranch) 137 (1803).

73. U.S. Const. art. IV, § 3, cl. 2.

74. Scott v. Sandford, 60 U.S. (19 How.) at 432.

75. *Id.* at 442.

76. U.S. Const. art. I, § 8, cl. 18.

77. McCulloch v. Maryland, 17 U.S. (4 Wheat.) 316, 421 (1819).

78. American Insurance Co. v. Canter, 26 U.S. (1 Pet.) at 542 (quoting U.S. Const. art. IV, § 3 [2]).

79. Scott v. Sandford, 60 U.S. (19 How.) at 450.

80. As attorney general of Maryland, Taney had argued against adding substantive meaning to the Fifth Amendment's due process clause. *See* Barron v. Mayor and City Council of Baltimore, 32 U.S. (7 Pet.) 243 (1833).

81. *See* Scott v. Sandford, 60 U.S. (19 How.) at 450.

82. *Id.* at 451.

83. *Id.*

84. *Id.*

85. *Id.* at 451–52.

86. *Id.* at 452.

87. *Id.*

88. H. Hyman, A More Perfect Union 22 (1973).

89. See *id.*

90. D. Fehrenbacher, *supra* note 7, at 436.

91. *Id.* at 442.

92. *Id.* at 442–43.

93. *See* H. Hyman, *supra* note 88, at 25.

94. *Id.*

95. Ableman v. Booth, 62 U.S. (21 How.) 506 (1859).

96. *See* D. Fehrenbacher, *supra* note 7, at 546.

97. *See* R. Berger, Government by Judiciary 12 (1977).

98. C. Woodward, The Burden of Southern History 81 (1960).

99. Scott v. Sandford, 60 U.S. (19 How.) at 407.

100. K. Karst, Belonging to America 44 (1989).

101. Meese, *The Law of the Constitution*, 61 Tul. L.Rev. 979, 989 (1987) (*quoting* P. Kurland, Politics, the Constitution, and the Warren Court 186 (1870).

102. *See* Lively & Plass, *Equal Protection: The Jurisprudence of Denial and Evasion*, 40 Am. U.L. Rev. 1307 (1991).

103. Plessy v. Ferguson, 163 U.S. 537, 559 (1896) (Harlan, J., dissenting).

Chapter 2

Toward a More Perfect Union

Civil war and its aftermath presented the opportunity to redefine the union and tend especially to the deficiencies that had compromised its viability. Armed conflict was calculated to determine whether the republic as created would endure or divide. Northern objectives originally consisted of saving the union but by war's end had broadened to include the elimination of slavery. Actual abolition required not only disregard of the *Scott* decision but also formal proscription of slavery. Insofar as blacks as a class generally had been denied recognition as persons, much less citizens, laws also proved necessary to define the incidents of their new status.

In the years immediately following the Civil War, the Constitution was amended so as to repudiate *Scott*, prohibit slavery, and establish the citizenship and basic liberties and equality of black persons. Such change was exceptional for a society that, barely a decade before, largely was unresponsive to criticism of Taney's racist ideology. Evidencing how profoundly political direction and opportunity had been redefined was the fact that, in early 1861, Congress with Republican support had approved a constitutional amendment "in the direction of a perpetual commitment to the sanctity of slave property in *states* where it then existed."[1] The amendment quickly became "a casualty of the war it was designed to prevent."[2] Constitutional change, albeit with significant qualification, was a logical extension of societal experience and developments during the war years.

Even before the post-war amendments, the *Scott* decision was undermined by legislative and executive action. Congress in 1862 repealed the Fugitive Slave Act and eliminated slavery in the District of Columbia. It also enacted confiscation laws, which were to operate against disloyal southerners. Insofar as they contemplated deprivation of slaves, the statutes actually perpetuated the premise of persons as property. The irony, however, did not persist long. Effective the first day of 1863, the Emancipation Proclamation liberated slaves in any state still engaged in rebellion. Given the realities of secession, the proclamation's significance largely was symbolic. Presidential and congressional action evidenced, however, that federal power no longer would be exercised to facilitate or accommodate slavery. The emancipation order itself was premised on the president's authority as commander-in-chief and did not pertain to slave states that were either loyal or occupied. Its basis thus was almost as narrow as its reach was limited.

The war experience influenced public opinion, so as to make attention to the status of blacks a politically feasible rather than risky proposition. Attitudes still were characterized by a sense of white superiority and phobias concerning racial mixing. The participation and performance of blacks in combat contributed to a sense that it was illogical to deny their personhood and citizenship. Given the basis and scope of the Emancipation Proclamation, it was evident that freedom would have to be fastened to a more secure predicate. With the war having been fought eventually to defeat slavery, it became both sensible and possible to account politically for the consequences of victory and the incidents of incipient citizenship.

Early notions of reconstruction included a sense that rebel states not only would have to renounce secession but repudiate slavery.[3] As noted before, emancipation's limited basis and ambit as a function of presidential war power militated toward identification of an indisputable and durable predicate to eliminate slavery. Turning initially to the Constitution as it existed, the Republicans in 1864 maintained that slavery was inconsonant with Article IV, Section 4's provision that "[t]he United States shall guarantee to every State in this Union a Republican Form of Government...."[4] The construction reflected a novel reading of the article that was never argued in *Scott* and was unlikely to have been contemplated by the framers. Such interpretive creativity nonetheless demonstrated the reality of moral development, which for the first time was supporting political efforts to reckon with racial injustice. The Republican party, which in 1860 had avoided the slave issue as a race issue, by 1864 was defining a Constitution that not only repudiated slavery but also afforded civil equality.[5]

The possibility of reconstructing the nation without altering the Constitution soon proved unrealistic. Congress in 1864 enacted Reconstruction legislation that, among other things, prohibited slavery, guaranteed the freedom of all persons within the states, and extended "the laws for the trial and punishment of white persons...to all persons."[6] Lincoln pocket-vetoed the law for reasons that included doubt over whether Congress could emancipate merely by legislation.[7]

Defeat of the Reconstruction proposal delayed formal effectuation of black freedom. Lincoln's concern that congressional authority was inadequate to emancipate left liberty dependent, for the time being, on the even narrower authority of executive decree. The vulnerability of presidentially declared emancipation to constitutional challenge was noted by legislative critics. As they observed, "the right of a slave to freedom is an open question before the State courts [and]...[w]hat the Supreme Court would say, who can tell?"[8] Such commentary reflected not only distrust of the high court, whose reputation still was diminished by the *Scott* decision,[9] but also a growing sense that existing authority was deficient for the task at hand. Rather than stretch the Constitution in a way that evoked uncertainty and doubt, logic favored changing it to account directly for new reality.

Reconstruction eventually was defined after the war and without Lincoln's participation. The question of slavery, however, was resolved in conclusive constitutional fashion early in his second term. Shortly before Lincoln's assassination, Congress framed and the president endorsed the Thirteenth Amendment. The amendment as ratified reads as follows:

Section 1. Neither slavery nor involuntary servitude, except as a punishment for crime whereof the party shall have been duly convicted, shall exist within the United States, or any place subject to their jurisdiction.
Section 2. Congress shall have power to enforce this article by appropriate legislation.[10]

The Thirteenth Amendment unequivocally extinguished the institution of slavery in the United States. It also introduced more possibilities and concerns than it resolved. Until the amendment's ratification, provision and protection of civil rights and liberties were a function of state responsibility. The Thirteenth Amendment made freedom a national interest and vested Congress with power to enforce it against the states. Federal policies that might define that national interest, as well as state actions that might offend it, remain subjects of constitutional debate. For Lincoln, the amendment effectively incorporated the essence of the Declaration of Independence into the Constitution.[11] Viewed from his perspective, the Thirteenth Amendment not only foreclosed slavery but also established civil rights as an incident of freedom. The notion that such rights flowed from the constitutionally secured status of freedom was not an illogical inference. It was not a premise, however, that would inspire the meaning of the Thirteenth Amendment then or later.

Even if civil guarantees were not manifestly incidental to the Thirteenth Amendment, Section 2 provided a credible basis for Congress to identify and secure basic rights attendant to freedom. Prior to the Civil War, concepts of citizenship and personal allegiance were associated with the states. The war, defined and pursued in terms of saving the union and the consequent emergence of the Thirteenth Amendment, helped engender a transcendent sense of citizenship and loyalty. The experience accelerated evolution of a national identity and established a departure point for fastening the rights and freedoms of federal citizenship.[12] Explication and vitalization of those interests were hastened by post-war developments in the South. Despite the North's battlefield triumph and the constitutional eradication of slavery, it was soon evident that the South was committed to undermining and evading the new political and social order.

Although the Thirteenth Amendment eliminated slavery, it did not uproot the ideology on which it had been premised. Notwithstanding the expectations of Lincoln and many of the Thirteenth Amendment's architects, civil rights and equality were not to flow naturally from the provision's ratification. Much like the desegregation mandate a century later, which would be responded to with widespread evasion and resistance,[13] abolition was circumvented and frustrated by methodologies that sought to establish slavery's functional equivalence.

Racially calibrated law and established custom effectively reduced blacks in the post-war South to a status not meaningfully distinguishable from slavery. The Black Codes in particular imposed special legal disabilities that mocked concepts of civil freedom and equality. State constitutions were rewritten in terms that prohibited slavery but effectively denied any meaning to liberation.

The Black Codes, adopted immediately after the Civil War, represented a slave society's effort to change as little as possible, if at all. Although itemizing the legal rights of blacks, the codes were notable primarily as devices for maintaining the traditional social status of and distance between whites and blacks. Their introduction communicated a swift and powerful message that civil rights would not be self-actuating as a result of the Thirteenth Amendment's ratification. Although southern laws had been revised to acknowledge contractual, property, marital, and litigative rights and liberty to travel, such guarantees effectively were vitiated by provisions that

defined racial status, forbade blacks from pursuing certain occupations or professions (e.g., skilled artisans, merchants, physicians, preaching without a license); forbade owning firearms or weapons; controlled the movement of blacks by systems of passes, required proof of residence; prohibited the congregation of groups of blacks; restricted blacks from residing in certain areas; . . . specified an etiquette of deference to whites; ... forbade racial intermarriage and provided the death penalty for blacks raping white women, while omitting special provisions for whites raping black women ... [and] excluded blacks from jury duty, public office, and voting. Some Codes required racial segregation in public transportation. Most Codes authorized whipping and the pillory as punishment for freedmen's offenses.[14]

The codes accounted for the interests of a free labor system vitiated by slavery's prohibition. Laws concerning vagrancy and paupers, regulations for apprenticeship, and punishment for impoverished criminal offenders effectively redirected emancipated blacks into a master-servant relationship. In sum, the codes preserved slavery in fact after it had been abolished in theory. Their introduction and operation disclosed that efforts to secure racial justice, instead of culminating in the Thirteenth Amendment, had barely commenced. The codes also were evidence that the conflict between federal and regional interests had reverted from the battlefield to the political process where it would be pursued throughout the next century and beyond.

In 1865, the Joint Committee on Reconstruction was established and charged with formulating and coordinating reconstruction policy. The committee, created by the Thirty-Ninth Congress, consisted of six senators and nine representatives. Also established, several months earlier, was the Bureau of Freedmen, Refugees, and Abandoned Land. Functioning within the War Department, the Freedmen's Bureau was vested with "control of all subjects relating to refugees and freedmen in the rebel states."[15] Its responsibilities included providing legal protection for recently freed blacks and for white unionists who were subject to retributive harassment and disability.

The bureau's experience and performance previewed the difficult task confronting the reconstruction committee. As a consequence of presidential policy, inadequate funding, and indefeasible racial prejudice and custom, the Freedmen's Bureau failed to realize its potential. Plans for land redistribution were frustrated when President Johnson ceased confiscation proceedings and granted pardons to many former Confederates. Funding of the bureau was dependent largely on private donations. Efforts to effectuate new legal relationships between blacks and whites were confounded by inadequately trained or insensitive personnel and southern intransigence. To the extent bureau agents actually attempted to ensure the rights of newly freed blacks, southern officials and courts used the Black Codes to resist, evade, and confound their efforts.

The reconstruction committee assumed its responsibilities in 1865, therefore, with a clear sense that civil rights and equality would not be self-fulfilling incidents of freedom. As Reconstruction commenced, it also was evident that, despite improvements in the legal condition of northern blacks, prejudice and discrimination still were pervasive. Actual policy was to be a function not only of what was necessary to effectuate meaningful freedom in the South but also of what was politically acceptable in the North. At minimum, the war had demonstrated that federal power was not the only source of official peril to civil rights and liberties. As originally focused, constitutional attention to official imperilment of rights and liberties was directed toward the national government. Prior to the Civil War, the Court had resisted efforts to translate the Fifth Amendment into a check on state power.[16] Post-war use of state authority to deny basic freedoms, however, prompted a reexamination and eventuated a profound restructuring of the constitutional system.

The Thirteenth Amendment, as noted previously, made freedom a national policy and empowered Congress to enforce it. What the amendment accomplished by its own terms beyond eradication of slavery became an immediate subject of debate. President Johnson, consistent more with the Democratic position than the drift of his own party, expounded the minimalist position. He maintained that the amendment only abolished the institution of slavery and did not alter the preexisting relationship between nation and states.[17] Congressional action and subsequent constitutional retooling, however, soon dated the notion that federal and state powers and the union itself were not being substantially redefined. The South's response to the Thirteenth Amendment, characterized by the harassment of unionists, impedance of black freedom, and negation of the Freedmen's Bureau, convinced Congress that the elimination of slavery was not enough to guarantee in every state the incidents of a republican form of government.

The plight of southern blacks, a consideration freshly removed from the political closet, had become by 1866 a prime focus for further constitutional and statutory attention. Action was prompted by recognition that the war's objectives and achievements, as eventually defined and attained, were in danger of being compromised if not altogether vitiated by southern recalcitrance. Despite the racial phobias and ideologies that persisted in and pervaded the North, the South's response to the Thirteenth Amendment thus made possible a national accounting for civil rights.

Federal attention to civil rights was inspired by post-war realities but was nonetheless constrained by two significant factors. Concepts of black liberty and equality were limited by societal moral development, which was still rooted in white supremacy. Racial considerations aside, disagreement existed with respect to the nature and extent of civil rights. The very concept of such guarantees defied consensus insofar as civil freedoms had descended from innately amorphous natural rights. Defining civil rights thus was to be a competitive process influenced by the perimeters of racial tolerance and agreement on what the essential incidents of citizenship were. Radical Republicans, for instance, asserted that civil rights at minimum were defined by the Declaration of Independence and the Bill of Rights. Although most of the Bill of Rights has been incorporated jurisprudentially into the Fourteenth Amendment, the radicals' position of comprehensive effectuation was a minority position then and now.

Even if civil rights could not be readily and neatly itemized, it generally was agreed that they represented the privileges and immunities appurtenant to status as a free person. Such rights traditionally had been defined by the state, as noted previously, and had been perceived largely in economic terms. Incipient federal interest in securing them, although introducing a new basis, evinced no consensus for altering their linkage to material considerations. At minimum, civil rights as then conceived included the rights to contract, own and transfer property, sue and be sued, travel, and enjoy personal security.

Southern interference with those incidents, considered crucial to full and equal participation in civil society, prompted a reformulation of basic law, which recontoured the relationship between federal and state government. Political power was redefined and redistributed, as Congress further repudiated the *Scott* decision and negated another antebellum ruling that had regarded constitutionally furnished guarantees as a check only on the federal government.[18] Statutory and constitutional reckoning was a function of the freshly demonstrated abusive potentiality and actuality of state power. Congress responded to the circumstances with legislation calculated to advance Thirteenth Amendment aims and to fortify the Constitution itself and thereby better secure the civil rights of all citizens.

Accounting for the incidents of freedom required policy that, unlike the prohibition of slavery, was affirmative in nature. The Civil Rights Act of 1866, as an extension of the Thirteenth Amendment and a preface to the Fourteenth Amendment, represented a seminal effort to secure what neither the war nor the Thirteenth Amendment itself had attained. Like its constitutional predicate, the civil rights bill was rooted in the relatively new concept of national citizenship and concomitant federal obligation to protect its incidents. Neither the 1866 act nor the Fourteenth Amendment catalogued civil rights. The lack of itemization, as previously mentioned, is consistent with the imprecise nature and extent of civil rights. It also has been suggested "that the framers found it natural to adopt the mode of generality already used elsewhere in the Constitution to express limitations on the states and on the national government."[19] Although failure to specify these rights presents problems in understanding their actual scope and coverage, perceptual difficulties would not be avoided entirely even in the event of particularization. Disagreement over the ambit of contractual rights, indisputably secured in 1866, manifests itself even in modern times.[20]

Prior to 1866, the closest approximation to a comprehensive judicial definition of civil rights was related by a federal court in *Corfield v. Coryell*.[21] The decision, authored by Justice Washington as circuit justice, alluded to those rights "which are, in their nature, fundamental; which belong, of right, to the citizens of all free governments; and which have, at all times, been enjoyed by the citizens of the several states which compose this Union."[22] Included among the fundamental privileges of citizenship were

Protection by the government; the enjoyment of life and liberty, with the right to acquire and possess property of every kind, and to pursue and obtain happiness and safety; ... [t]he right of a citizen of one state to pass through, or to reside in any other state, for purposes of trade, agriculture, professional pursuits, or otherwise; to claim the benefit of the writ of habeas corpus; to institute and maintain actions of any kind in the courts of the state; to take, hold and dispose of property, either real or personal; and an exemption from higher taxes than are paid by other citizens of the state; ... [and] the elective franchise, as regulated and established by the law or constitution of the state in which it is to be exercised.[23]

The *Corfield* decision arose out of circumstances that, in comparison to those inspiring the Civil Rights Act of 1866 and the Fourteenth Amendment, seemed relatively trifling. At issue were the rights of another state's citizens to harvest oysters in the waters of New Jersey.[24] From that context emerged principles of equal respect for citizens of all states.[25]

While precedent established that a state must be even-handed toward the citizens of other states, to the extent it afforded any rights to its own citizens, the 1866 act and the Fourteenth Amendment sought to secure incidents of national citizenship as a matter of constitutional imperative rather than comity—the principle of respect for the law of other jurisdictions. Instead of merely forbidding discrimination against citizens of another state, the Thirty-Ninth Congress prohibited discrimination by states against their own citizens. It did so by means of legislation that sketched basic rights in general terms, akin to the articulations of *Corfield*, and prohibited qualification of these rights on the basis of race.

The civil rights enactment thus provided that

there shall be no discrimination in civil rights or immunities ... on account of race ... but the inhabitants of every race ... shall have the same rights to make and enforce contracts, to sue, be parties, and give evidence, to inherit, purchase, lease, sell, hold and convey real and personal property, and to full and equal benefit of all laws and proceedings for the security of persons and property, and shall be subject to like punishment.[26]

The enumeration, described by one legislator as "the fundamental rights of citizenship,"[27] was consonant with *Corfield*'s characterization of the basic incidents of citizenship. What was revolutionary about the civil rights bill was the regard of fundamental freedom as a federal interest.

Civil rights legislation in its seminal form responded to the introduction and operation of the Black Codes. Given Congress's use of language broader than necessary to invalidate the codes, and aims characterized as otherwise "too inconsiderable," the Civil Rights Act of 1866 has been styled as a "statute of permanent and universal applicability" calibrated toward establishing "a federal principle of racial equality in the enjoyment of state-created rights."[28]

The newly established federal interest, however, reflected neither a congressional nor a public mandate for an expansive definition of civil rights. Despite Justice Washington's inclusion of suffrage as a civil right a few decades earlier in *Corfield*, his perception was not consensually subscribed to even after the war. The congressional record itself is suffused with commentary disclaiming any intention to secure voting rights, depicting the franchise as a political right, and distinguishing suffrage from civil rights.[29] Nor was an integrated education system or other modern accoutrements of the Fourteenth Amendment, such as the rights of privacy and personal autonomy, on the mind of Congress in 1866. Public education, which eventually would be regarded as so crucial to citizenship that desegregation would be judicially mandated,[30] was a marginal and underdeveloped institution and not a primary object of legislative attention. The general sense at the time, consistent with established custom, was that racial separation in schools and other contexts presented no constitutional affront. Contemporaneous with the adoption of the Civil Rights Act of 1866 and the Fourteenth Amendment, in fact, Congress provided for segregated education in the District of Columbia.

Consistent with a congressional aim that was qualified rather than comprehensive, the House chair of the Joint Committee on Reconstruction repudiated the notion

that in all things, civil, social, political, all citizens, without distinction of race or color, shall be equal [...] By no means can [civil rights and immunities] be so construed. ... Nor do they mean that all citizens shall sit on juries, or that their children shall attend the same schools. ... I understand civil rights to be simply the absolute rights of individuals, such as "The right to personal security, the right of personal liberty, and the right to acquire and enjoy property." [Nor should anyone] be subjected to obligations, duties, pains and penalties from which other citizens are exempted. . . . This is the spirit and scope of the bill and does not go one step beyond.[31]

Understanding the basic and limited aims of the Civil Rights Act of 1866 is essential for appreciating the contemplated ambit of the Fourteenth Amendment as ratified in 1868. Like its legislative precursor, the Fourteenth Amendment was the function of a qualified civil rights agenda. It reflected, however, further experience with the post-war South and a mounting apprehension that hard-won achievements might be at risk when Reconstruction was finished and the South regained its political influence. The possibility that a reemergent South might dominate the federal government and repudiate the aims of war and reconstruction was a real concern. Given a response to the Thirteenth Amendment, resulting in the vitiation of black freedom, it was not hard to imagine how the South actually might function in the new political structure. With congressional representation no longer bound by the "three-fifths of a person" formula applied to slaves, the South might deny blacks the right to vote and still expand its representative basis. Concern with the prospect of a renascent but effectively unreconstructed South was accentuated by a sense among some legislators, compounded by President Johnson's unsuccessful veto of the civil rights bill, that the enactment might be vulnerable to constitutional challenge.[32] Constitutionalization of the 1866 act by means of the Fourteenth Amendment thus removed any doubt about the existence and basis of federally secured civil rights.

The Fourteenth Amendment as originally conceived represented an effort to enshrine the incidents of citizenship "beyond normal politics . . . [and] fix [them] in the serene sky, in the eternal firmament of the Constitution, where no storm of passion can shake . . . and no cloud can obscure."[33] It did so in the following terms:

Section 1. All persons born or naturalized in the United States and subject to the jurisdiction thereof, are citizens of the United States and of the State wherein they reside. No State shall make or enforce any law which shall abridge the privileges or immunities of citizens of the United States; nor shall any State deprive any person of life, liberty, or property, without due process of law; nor deny to any person within its jurisdiction the equal protection of the laws.

Section 2. Representatives shall be apportioned among the several States according to their respective numbers, counting the whole number of persons in each State, excluding Indians not taxed. But when the right to vote at any election for the choice of electors for President and Vice President of the United States, Representatives in Congress, the Executive and Judicial officers of a State, or the members of the Legislature thereof, is denied to any of the male inhabitants of such State, being twenty-one years of age, and citizens of the United States, or in any way abridged, except for participation in rebellion, or other crime, the basis of representation therein shall be reduced in the proportion which the number of such male citizens shall bear to the whole number of male citizens twenty-one years of age in such State.

Section 3. No person shall be a Senator or Representative in Congress, or elector of President and Vice President, or hold any office, civil or military, under the United States, or under any State, who, having previously taken an oath, as a member of Congress, or as an officer of the United States, or as a member of any State legislature, or as an executive or judicial officer of any State, to support the Constitution of the United States, shall have engaged in insurrection or rebellion against the same, or given aid or comfort to the enemies thereof. But Congress may by a vote of two-thirds of each House, remove such disability.

Section 4. The validity of the public debt of the United States, authorized by law, including debts incurred for payment of pensions and bounties for services in suppressing insurrection or rebellion, shall not be questioned. But neither the United States nor any State shall assume or pay any debt or obligation incurred in aid of insurrection or rebellion against the United States, or any claim for the loss or emancipation of any slave; but all such debts, obligations and claims shall be held illegal and void.

Section 5. The Congress shall have power to enforce, by appropriate legislation, the provisions of this article.[34]

Discerning the original understanding of the Fourteenth Amendment is complicated by more than a century of jurisprudence that has extended its meaning far beyond its relatively simple beginnings. The amendment was designed to secure civil rights against future tampering by a post-Reconstruction Congress. Support for the Fourteenth Amendment, as with most enactments, represented a mixture of justifications and motives. Some of its champions urged a broad meaning that would have transcended the Civil Rights Act of 1866. During the framing process itself, they advocated the Fourteenth Amendment as a means for implementing broad concepts of rights and equality reposing in the Declaration of Independence and the Bill of Rights.[35] Such expansive incorporation, however, was not subscribed to by a congressional majority still cautious with the novelty of national citizenship and protective of traditional state powers and functions. Even supporters of a broadly encompassing guarantee eventually acknowledged that "(v)irtually every speaker in the debates on the Fourteenth Amendments—Republicans and Democrats alike—said or agreed that [it] was designed to embody or incorporate the Civil Rights Act."[36] As originally conceived, therefore, Section 1 of the Amendment provided the necessary framework for the rights incidental to citizenship.

The significance of Section 1's structure has proved a durable subject of debate. Some scholars maintain that each clause had a well-defined and particularized function. From Raoul Berger's perspective, for instance, the privileges and immunities clause accounted for the substantive rights secured by the Civil Rights Act of 1866; the equal protection clause prohibited legislative discrimination with respect to those rights; and the due process clause ensured recourse to an impartial judiciary.[37] Competing with that formalistic understanding of Section 1 is the sense that "[t]here was no serious effort to differentiate the function of the various clauses . . . [and] the section in its entirety was taken to guarantee equality in the enjoyment of the rights of citizenship."[38] Consistent with the latter premise is the notion that whatever was or might be accomplished pursuant to a particular clause is achievable by extrapolation from Section 1's conferral of national citizenship.[39]

What the Fourteenth Amendment did not clearly account for, at least originally, were rights that many considered political rather than civil in nature. Although theoretically useful to the Republican party's vitality, black suffrage was not well established in the North and was strongly resisted by most whites. A constitutional demand on the South, which would have required northern states to extend rights they were not prepared to offer themselves, did not translate into a politically viable option. As a Kentucky senator observed, "Negro suffrage is political arsenic. If it is not, why do not the free States open wide their throats and gulp down the graceful and invigorating drought."[40]

Even if black suffrage was not immediately feasible, the linkage between voting and the meaningful operation of civil rights was not entirely unappreciated. A prominent architect of Reconstruction policy characterized the franchise as "the Great Guarantee; and the only sufficient Guarantee."[41] Ratification, however, required endorsement by three-fourths of the states and thus concession to political reality. As members of the Reconstruction committee concluded, "it was our opinion that [such support] . . . could not be induced to grant the right of suffrage, even in any degree or under any restriction, to the colored race."[42] Reiterating the basic point, the Senate chair identified not "the slightest probability that [black suffrage] will be adopted by the States . . . [or] would commend itself to anybody."[43]

The framers of the Fourteenth Amendment thus confronted a dilemma in accounting satisfactorily for citizenship and its incidents. Black freedom and equality were to be secured in a society still rooted in tenets of white superiority and still resistant to the notion of fully sharing political and economic power and opportunity. The more precise and immediate challenge was to preclude the emergence of a fortified white southern bloc in Congress without offending northern constituents generally opposed to black suffrage. Section 2 of the Fourteenth Amendment thus provided an incentive but did not require southern states to extend the franchise to blacks. Its key provision reduced the basis of representation if the right to vote was denied or abridged. Even if an indirect or convoluted methodology, the section was clear in its purpose "to deprive the lately rebellious states of the unfair advantage of a large representation in this House, based on their colored population, so long as that people shall be denied political rights."[44]

The Fourteenth Amendment effectively left determination of voting rights to the individual states. Even the forthcoming introduction of a constitutional proscription proved inadequate, for nearly a century, in defeating racially motivated deprivations of voting rights in the South. As subsequent events demonstrated, southern states were bent on maintaining an exclusively white political process without regard to constitutional risk. Such intransigence, as discussed later, eventually would help engender the Fifteenth Amendment.

Meanwhile, experience with the South was demonstrating that respect even for the limited range of rights and liberties contemplated by the Fourteenth Amendment would not be easily established. The Black Codes were effective not only as an instrumentality of oppression but in radiating the South's determination to define the contours of civil rights and liberties pursuant to the criteria it saw fit. Despite introduction of the Thirteenth Amendment, most southern blacks remained the functional equivalent of slaves.[45] It was toward the Black Codes in particular that the equal protection clause responded as a guarantor of "equality of protection in those enumerated civil rights which the States may deem proper to confer upon any race."[46] As another emanation of the Civil Rights Act of 1866, it required "each State [to] provide for equality before the law, equal protection to life, liberty, and property, equal right to sue and be sued."[47]

Modern equal protection analysis, which concerns itself with suspect classifications—those based on race, gender, alienage, and parental marital status—and impairment of fundamental rights, represents a substantial jump from the original sense that "[w]hatever law protects the white man shall afford *equal protection* to the black man."[48] Consistent with the Fourteenth Amendment's initial concern with a discrete set of rights and liberties, equal protection as initially calibrated did not comprehend perfect equality. Advocates of a broader guarantee, like proponents of sweeping rights and freedoms, were compelled to defer their aims to the reality of a society not yet prepared for such a cultural overhaul.[49] Although itself not a source of rights, the equal protection guarantee prohibits race-dependent denial or qualification of any state-created rights or immunities.[50]

From the Fourteenth Amendment's due process clause, over the course of its existence, has emerged a panoply of fundamental rights and liberties. Although such guarantees are not specified by the amendment or otherwise enumerated in the Constitution, the Supreme Court in less than a century cultivated the due process clause in substantive terms that accounted for economic liberty, privacy rights, and personal

autonomy. Such jurisprudence has been the source of extensive controversy and criticism of the Court's function. Investment in substantive
due process coupled with cramped readings of the commerce power
eventually prompted a serious political challenge to the judiciary when,
in response to persistent invalidation of New Deal legislation, President
Roosevelt introduced a plan for packing the Court and redefining its
ideology.[51] Even in disclaiming jurisprudentially glossed economic rights
doctrine, the Court has continued to identify unenumerated interests as
fundamental.[52]

Such developments diverge from strict notions of due process as "only
applicable to the process and proceedings of the courts or justice; they
can never be referred to an act of the legislature."[53] The characterization,
related by Alexander Hamilton, pertained to the meaning of due process
afforded by the Fifth Amendment. Raoul Berger maintained that the
absence of extensive attention to due process or evidence of a profoundly
different meaning, in debates concerning the Fourteenth Amendment,
indicates that due process was not reinvented or substantially redefined.[54]
His understanding is not universally shared. Thomas Cooley, within a
decade of the Fourteenth Amendment's ratification, observed that nothing "necessarily implies that due process of law must be judicial process."[55] Justice Field contemporaneously advanced the sense "that the
Amendment and related legislation reflected Congress' intent to place
a dynamic, broad body of common rights, including economic interests,
under national judicial protection."[56] Specifics of the due process clause
itself are further diminished in significance if substantive protection is
inferred from Section 1's creation of national citizenship.[57] What the
Fourteenth Amendment at least changed, if not the meaning of due
process, was its scope and beneficiaries. As one legislator put it, "[t]he
Constitution already declares generally that no person shall be deprived
of life, liberty, or property without due process of law ... ; [the Fourteenth Amendment] declares particularly that no State shall do it."[58] The
due process clause, even if merely enabling all citizens to enforce civil
rights and equality by means of access to a fair and impartial judicial
system,[59] further denoted a redistribution of federal and state interests.

Included in the Fourteenth Amendment are sections that, at least for
modern purposes, are vestigial. Section 2, as noted previously, reduced
the political strength of states that denied or limited the franchise.[60]
Section 3 precluded officials who had supported rebellion from holding
federal or state office.[61] Section 4 reaffirmed the validity of the nation's
war debt and disclaimed liability for Confederate borrowings or claims
for the loss of slaves.[62] Each of those provisions has been rendered
obsolete by altered political realities and the passage of time. Of more
enduring significance is Section 5, which conferred on Congress "power
to enforce ... the provision of this article."[63]

The assignment of enforcement power to Congress rather than the judiciary may have reflected abiding distrust of an institution that had validated slavery a mere decade before.[64] One of the legacies of the *Scott* decision was the Supreme Court's self-inflicted loss of credibility and prestige. The Court's reputation had been diminished by the perception that it was "the citadel of Slaveocracy."[65] Section 5 imposed "upon Congress the responsibility of seeing to it, for the future, that all the sections of the amendment are carried out in good faith, and that no State infringes the rights of person and property."[66] The assignment of enforcement power was further evidence of how profoundly the relationship between federal and state government had been recontoured. Section 1 provided a benchmark against which state action could be measured. Section 5 suggested that the federal legislature might enact laws on matters previously reserved to the states. Although not charged with plenary authority for purposes of establishing a body of comprehensive municipal law, Congress at least might supersede state enactments implicating Section 1. A central meaning of the Fourteenth Amendment, therefore, was that civil rights were a national interest that might be effectuated by national policy.

Even in redistributing power between federal and state government, the Fourteenth Amendment generally and Section 5 specifically were influenced by traditional considerations of federalism. Although fashioning and endorsing the Fourteenth Amendment, many Republicans second-guessed whether "the nation...could, or should police every Southern hamlet."[67] The amendment was recognized as a cutting edge with the potential for paring traditional state powers and concerns. The law of contracts, for instance, reflected a generally local interest qualified by a newly and constitutionally established federal policy of non-discrimination. The new mix of federal and state concerns not only challenged traditional political perceptions and thought but, as discussed in the next chapter, also resulted in tension with evolving principles of laissez-faire economics.

As the 1860s drew to a close, southern resistance to new statutory and constitutional demands hardened rather than abated. Persisting intransigence doused northern hopes, even if unrealistic, for a cooperative, harmonious, and efficient Reconstruction. Feeding the South's intractability were the words and deeds of President Johnson in opposition to forceful Reconstruction policies. Congressional attention and energy during the post-war period thus were spread between two adversaries— the chief executive and the remnants of the Confederacy. Mixed signals radiated from congressional passage and presidential veto of civil rights legislation and from contrary legislative and executive rhetoric. Not surprisingly, the South tuned in to the message of its liking.

Despite the political risks attached to the cause of black suffrage, which

previously had limited and foreclosed its championing, unvarying southern attitudes and diminishing patience with Reconstruction resulted in
serious attention to the subject. For advocates of comprehensive liberty
and equality, the right to vote was the missing constitutional link for
meaningful citizenship. They assumed that no state would tamper with
civil rights if it faced accountability at the ballot box. Black suffrage, for
those who may have resisted or avoided it before, presented an opportunity to end the post-war era and its seemingly intractable problems. For
a nation becoming increasingly weary of Reconstruction, extending the
franchise offered a final solution that would clear race from the political
agenda and enable society to move beyond Reconstruction.

The Fifteenth Amendment thus was proposed by Congress in 1869
and ratified in 1870. More like the Thirteenth than the Fourteenth
Amendment in its length and detail, the Fifteenth Amendment provides
that

Section 1. The right of citizens of the United States to vote shall not be denied
or abridged by the United States or by any State on account of race, color, or
previous condition of servitude.
Section 2. The Congress shall have power to enforce this article by appropriate
legislation.[68]

Pursuant to its enforcement power, Congress promptly enacted implementing legislation. The Enforcement Act of 1870 made public or
private interference with the right to vote a criminal offense.[69] The
voting process itself was subjected to oversight, as legislation passed the
following year provided for federal supervision of registration and certification of election results.[70] Contemporaneous with its effort to secure
voting rights pursuant to the Fifteenth Amendment, Congress also
sought to reckon with racially motivated violence and intimidation that
jeopardized civil rights in the South. Fourteenth Amendment enforcement power was the basis for the Ku Klux Klan Act adopted in 1871.[71]
That legislation directed itself not only to deprivation of civil rights under
color of state law but also to private action denying equal protection.

Debate over the Ku Klux Klan Act reignited the controversy as to
whether the Thirteenth Amendment could support legislation that was
not directly and proximately concerned with eradicating slavery. In spite
of arguments that Section 2 of the amendment enabled Congress to
enforce by positive enactment the prohibition provision of Section 1,[72]
doubt persisted with respect to whether it afforded an adequate legislative departure point. Similar concern prompted reenactment of the
Civil Rights Act of 1866 pursuant to the Fourteenth Amendment. Such
action, coupled with passage of the Ku Klux Klan Act and voting rights
legislation, represented the post-war apex in federal accounting for civil

rights. The outburst of initiative, however, would prove to be only a preface to subsequent court decisions delimiting the Fourteenth Amendment's potential as a source of racial justice and transforming it into a platform for new rights and liberties of a general nature.

The Reconstruction amendments and implementing legislation nonetheless had effected profound change in the blueprint of governmental power and personal freedom. Reality was that "as the years passed and fervor for racial equality waned, enforcement of [voting rights] laws became spotty and ineffective, and most of their provisions were repealed in 1894."[73] Pursuant to the Fourteenth Amendment, Congress in 1875 passed further civil rights legislation prohibiting discrimination in public accommodations.[74] Concern with the reach of federal power into the private sector and impatience with still intractable problems of race soon prompted a trimming of Congress's enforcement power. Depicting the racial classifications proscribed by the Civil Rights Act of 1875 as "[m]ere discriminations"[75] and a function of private rather than official action, the Court in the *Civil Rights Cases* invalidated the law.[76] Within a decade of Reconstruction, therefore, doctrine repudiated the special constitutional or legislative attention to the interest of the nation's new citizens.[77]

Jurisprudential cramping of congressional power disclosed an immediate irony that remained significant in the framing of modern civil rights legislation. By reenacting the Civil Rights Act of 1866 pursuant to the Fourteenth Amendment, Congress had sought to clarify and fortify the law's constitutional premises. Although the enactment may have been secured against challenges to legislative authority, redirection traded away the potential utility of an amendment not subject to a state action requirement. Given the temper of society as it coursed through and past Reconstruction, legislation directed toward private discrimination and premised on the Thirteenth Amendment probably would have been invalidated anyway. Congress in recent times has been allowed to account for "the badges and incidents of slavery"[78] in a broader sense, but early Thirteenth Amendment analysis favored a restrictive reading of those terms. As the Court noted in 1883, "[m]ere discriminations" that denied certain privileges afforded white citizens or limited access to public accommodations, reflected settled custom rather than badges of slavery.[79] Although the Court eventually comprehended that discrimination in public venues merited congressional attention,[80] initial restrictions on legislative authority survived as constitutional impediments to modern reckoning with discrimination. The Civil Rights Act of 1964, which prohibits discrimination not only in public accommodations but in education, employment and other contexts, thus was predicated alternatively on the Fourteenth Amendment and the commerce power.

Collectively, the reconstruction amendments established a national interest in the incidents of national citizenship and enabled Congress to secure them against racially discriminatory action by the states. The amendments have been described as "equating the rights of United States citizenship to the natural rights of free men.... In short, the legal theory of national civil rights enforcement authority under the Thirteenth and Fourteenth Amendments posited a virtually unlimited national authority over civil rights."[81] Despite such grand descriptions, the process of charting respective perimeters of federal and state interests and powers has been central especially to the Fourteenth Amendment's evolution and meaning. The amendment may not have established a consensus for eliminating all racial prejudice and discrimination. Broad support existed, however, for the limited aim of ensuring that racism did not deny basic opportunities for material development and equal standing before the law.

Although voting rights were tended to by the Fifteenth Amendment, initial reluctance to constitutionalize the franchise reinforces the sense that the Fourteenth Amendment originally was intended to account for a narrow band of rights and equality. Reality is that the framers, as agents of the society they represented, did not enact a broad anti-discrimination principle. Nor did they intend to eradicate racial distinctions that did not implicate basic interests of life, liberty, person, and property. Subsequent jurisprudence has construed expansively the provision's racially nonspecific text. Principles evolving from the amendment's core concern, however, have been mostly circumspect or circumscribed. Within a few years of its ratification, the provision was subject to review that permanently would distort its original concern and meaning. The Fourteenth Amendment's legacy, at least until the middle of the twentieth century, would prove notable primarily for doctrines that responded to interests unrelated to race or solidified race-dependent impairment of citizenship and its incidents.

NOTES

1. H. Hyman, A More Perfect Union 46 (1973) (emphasis in original). Pertinent terms of the provision were that "no amendment shall be made to the Constitution which will authorize or give to Congress the power to abolish or interfere, within any state, with the domestic institutions thereof, including that of persons held to labor or service by the laws of said state." Cong. Globe, 36th Cong. 2d Sess. 1284–85 (1861). President Lincoln's position was that the measure comported with what constitutional law already implied and thus he would not object to its explication and irrevocability. See H. Hyman, *supra*, at 47.

2. See H. Hyman, *supra* note 1, at 47.

3. See H. Hyman & W. Wiecek, Equal Justice Under the Law 269 (1982).

4. U.S. Const. art. IV, § 4.

5. See H. Hyman & W. Wiecek, *supra* note 3.

6. *Id.* at 272–73.

7. *See id.* at 274.

8. *Id.* at 275.

9. A. Mason, The Supreme Court from Taft to Warren 38 (1958).

10. U.S. Const. amend. XIII.

11. *See* H. Hyman & W. Wiecek, *supra* note 3, at 278.

12. *See* R. Kaczorowski, The Politics of Judicial Interpretation: The Federal Courts, Department of Justice and Civil Rights, 1866–1876 108 (1985).

13. *See* Chapter 5.

14. H. Hyman & W. Wiecek, *supra* note 3, at 319. The experience of the Freedmen's Bureau is examined in R. Koczorowski, *supra* note 12, at 27–48.

15. H. Hyman & W. Wiecek, *supra* note 3, at 315.

16. *See* Barron v. Mayor and City Council of Baltimore, 32 U.S. (7 Pet.) 243, 250–51 (1833).

17. H. Hyman & W. Wiecek, *supra* note 3, at 389.

18. Barron v. Mayor and City Council of Baltimore, 32 U.S. (7 Pet.) at 250–51.

19. K. Karst, Belonging to America 55 (1989). It also has been noted that, given the need to accommodate competing purposes as in any multi-sided political debate, "one time-honored way to achieve compromise . . . is to enact broad language that is capable of bearing more than one meaning." *Id.* at 55–56. *See* Sandalow, *Constitutional Interpretation*, 79 Mich. L.Rev. 1033, 1046 (1981).

20. The Court determined that 42 U.S.C. § 1981, a direct statutory descendant of the 1866 act, prohibits discrimination in the making of contracts but does not concern itself with post-information harassment. *See* Patterson v. McLean Credit Union, 109 S. Ct. 2363, 2373 (1989). The distinction was criticized as an unjustified exercise by the Court in "snatch[ing] away with one hand [what] it gives with the other." *Id.* at 2379 (Brennan, J. dissenting).

21. 6 F. Cas. 546 (C.C.D. Pa. 1823). Evolution of the concept and meaning of citizenship in American society, from the early colonial period to the Civil War's immediate aftermath, is examined in J. Kettner, The Development of American Citizenship, 1608–1870 (1978).

22. Corfield v. Coryell, 6 F. Cas. at 551.

23. *Id.* at 551–52.

24. *Id.* at 547.

25. Disagreement is discernible before and after *Corfield* with respect to whether privileges and immunities were a function of state determination or fundamental incidents deriving from national citizenship. *See* J. Kettner, *supra* note 21, at 258–61.

26. Cong. Globe, 39th Cong., 1st Sess. 474 (1866).

27. *Id.* at 1151 (Rep. Thayer).

28. C. Fairman, VI History of the Supreme Court of the United States, Reconstruction and Reunion, pt. 1, at 1228 (1971). R. Berger, Government by Judiciary 26 (1977). For an account of how civil rights evolved from concepts of national citizenship, including initial concerns for whites and blacks in the South, *see* H. Hyman, *supra* note 1, at 414–32.

29. *See, e.g.*, Cong. Globe, *supra* note 26, at 599 (Rep. Trumbull); *id.* at 606 (Sen. Saulsbury); *id.* at 632 (Rep. Moulton); *id.* at 704 (Sen. Fessender); *id.* at

744 (Sen. Sherman); *id.* at 1124 (Rep. Cook); *id.* at 1151 (Rep. Thayer); *id.* at 1159 (Rep. Windom); *id.* at 3034–35 (Sen. Henderson).

30. *See* Chapter 5.

31. Cong. Globe, *supra* note 26, at 1117 (Rep. Wilson).

32. K. Karst, *supra* note 19, at 51; R. Berger, *supra* note 28, at 23 n.12.

33. Cong. Globe, *supra* note 26, at 2462 (Rep. Garfield).

34. U.S. Const. amend. XIV.

35. *See* W. Nelson, The Fourteenth Amendment: From Political Principle to Judicial Doctrine 71–77, 117–19 (1988).

36. H. Graham, Everyman's Constitution 291 n.73 (1968).

37. *See* R. Berger, *supra* note 28, at 18.

38. *See* K. Karst, *supra* note 19, at 18.

39. *See* C. Black, Jr., Structure and Relationship in Constitutional Law 51–66 (1969).

40. Cong. Globe, *supra* note 26, at 246 (Sen. Davis).

41. *Id.* at 685 (Sen. Sumner).

42. *Id.* at 2766 (Sen. Howard).

43. *Id.* at 704 (Sen. Fessenden).

44. *Id.* at 141 (Rep. Blaine).

45. *See* C. Fairman, VII History of the Supreme Court of the United States, Reconstruction and Reunion, pt. 1, at 134 (1987); R. Berger, *supra* note 28, at 169.

46. Cong. Globe, *supra* note 26, at 1293 (Rep. Shellabarger). *See* C. Fairman, *supra* note 45, at 134 (equal protection reckoned with the "gross injustice and hardship" of the Black Codes).

47. *Id.* at 1622 (Rep. Moulton).

48. *Id.* at 2459 (Rep. Stevens) (emphasis in original).

49. Even champions of comprehensive equality conceded that prerequisite societal remolding was unrealistic, and thus "we shall be obliged to be content with patching up the worst portions of the ancient edifice." *Id.* at 3148 (Rep. Stevens).

50. As noted in Chapters 5 and 6 the equal protection clause eventually became the basis for challenging official racial discrimination.

51. For a discussion of the operation and criticism of substantive due process and the political friction it caused earlier in this century, *see* L. Tribe, American Constitutional Law (567–58 2d ed. 1988).

52. *See, e.g.,* Zablocki v. Redhail, 434 U.S. 374 (1978) (right to marry); Moore v. City of East Cleveland, 431 U.S. 494 (1977) (sanctity of family); Roe v. Wade, 410 U.S. 113 (1973) (liberty to elect abortion); Griswold v. Connecticut, 381 U.S. 479 (1965) (right of privacy).

53. R. Berger, *supra* note 28, at 196 n.11 (*quoting* Alexander Hamilton).

54. *See id.* at 193–200.

55. Weimar v. Bunbury, 36 Mich. 203 (1874), in H. Hyman, *supra* note 1, at 169.

56. H. Hyman, *supra* note 1, at 536 (*quoting* Slaughter-House Cases, 83 U.S. (16 Wall.) 36 (1873) (Field, J., dissenting)). Support for an expansive reading of due process also exists in J. ten Broek, The Antislavery Origins of the Fourteenth Amendment 222–23 (1951).

57. *See supra* note 39 and accompanying text.

58. Cong. Globe, *supra* note 26, at 256 (Rep. Baker).

59. *See id.* at 1117–18 (Rep. Wilson).

60. U.S. Const. amend. XIV, § 2.

61. *Id.* § 3.

62. *Id.* § 4.

63. *Id.* § 5.

64. *See* R. Berger, *supra* note 28, at 222–23.

65. A. Mason, *supra* note 9, at 16.

66. Cong. Globe, *supra* note 26, at 2766 (Sen. Howard).

67. H. Hyman & W. Wiecek, *supra* note 1, at 404.

68. U.S. Const. amend. XV.

69. 16 Stat. 170 (1870).

70. 16 Stat. 433 (1871).

71. 17 Stat. 13, now codified as 42 U.S.C. §§ 1983, 1985(3).

72. Cong. Globe 42d Cong., 1st Sess. 85 (1871) (Rep. Stevens). *See* H. Hyman & W. Wiecek, *supra* note 3, at 470–71.

73. South Carolina v. Katzenbach, 383 U.S. 301, 310 (1966).

74. Civil Rights Act of 1875, 18 Stat. 335 (1875).

75. Civil Rights Cases, 109 U.S. 3, 25 (1883).

76. *Id.* at 20.

77. *Id.* at 25.

78. Jones v. Alfred H. Mayer Co., 392 U.S. 409, 439–41 (1968).

79. Civil Rights Cases, 109 U.S. at 25.

80. The Civil Rights Act of 1964, 42 U.S.C. §§ 2000a to 2000a–6, insofar as it prohibits discrimination in public accommodations, was upheld as a proper exercise of Congress's commerce power. Katzenbach v. McClung, 379 U.S. 294 (1964); Heart of Atlanta Motel v. United States, 379 U.S. 241 (1964).

81. R. Kaczorowski, *supra* note 12, at 1.

Chapter 3

Constitutional Amendment and Doctrinal Development

The Reconstruction amendments resolved some fundamental issues that had been bypassed or deferred when the Constitution originally was drafted. The Thirteenth, Fourteenth, and Fifteenth Amendments, individually and collectively, demanded profound political and social change. Eventual meaning would be defined by jurisprudential glossing, with the Fourteenth Amendment eventually becoming an especially prolific source of constitutional jurisprudence and eminent departure point for congressional action. The provision with the most immediate and obvious impact, however, was the Thirteenth Amendment which permanently foreclosed slavery.

Early readings of the Reconstruction amendments reflect an abiding discomfort with and even resistance to enhancement of the federal government's interest and power. Although quick in acknowledging the amendments' primary concern with the nation's new citizens, the Supreme Court soon fashioned doctrine that limited their utility with respect to core interests but increased their potential for facilitating other aims. Early jurisprudence thus reflected the nation's drifting interest from racial affairs to other priorities such as economic growth and development. Early case law and practical constitutional meaning thus developed as a function of superseding considerations and racial fatigue.

The scope of the Thirteenth Amendment had been a source of controversy and uncertainty almost since its ratification. As noted in the preceding chapter, many framers considered it a dubious predicate for establishing or securing civil rights. To alleviate precisely that doubt,

Congress had reenacted the Civil Rights Act of 1866 pursuant to the Fourteenth Amendment. Whether the Thirteenth Amendment prohibited more than personal bondage or could be a basis for civil rights legislation ultimately was to be resolved by the Supreme Court. Congress's final significant Reconstruction enactment, the Civil Rights Act of 1875, was based on the Thirteenth and Fourteenth Amendments. The act prohibited discrimination in public accommodations, much like the Civil Rights Act of 1964. In 1883, however, the Court in the *Civil Rights Cases* determined that such discrimination did not constitute a badge of slavery or servitude.[1] The Thirteenth Amendment[2] was found inadequate as a basis for the 1875 act, and Congress's enforcement powers were accordingly trimmed.

For several decades, the Thirteenth Amendment was considered pertinent only to the extent a nexus was discerned between a challenged practice and the institution of slavery itself.[3] Not until the middle of the twentieth century, after having vitalized the Fourteenth Amendment with anti-discrimination principles, did the Court finally revisit the question of whether the Thirteenth Amendment affords a sufficient basis for civil rights legislation. Specifically at issue, in *Jones v. Alfred H. Mayer Co.*, was whether Congress could ban private racial discrimination in the sale of real estate on the grounds it constituted a badge or incident of slavery.[4] The statute under review, 42 U.S.C. § 1982, descended directly from the Civil Rights Act of 1866. Contrary to its restrictive approach and displacement of legislation nearly a century earlier, the Court afforded Congress broad latitude in determining what constituted "badges and incidents of slavery" and enacting legislation rationally related to eliminating them.[5]

In *Griffin v. Breckenridge*, the Court emphasized that unlike the other Reconstruction amendments the Thirteenth Amendment did not impose a state action requirement.[6] Victims of a racially motivated attack on a public road in Mississippi during the height of the civil rights movement thus were allowed to sue under federal law.[7] The pertinent statute, 42 U.S.C. § 1985(3), afforded relief from private racially inspired efforts to interfere with equal protection or privileges and immunities and was construed specifically to secure the right of interstate travel.[8] Although previous interpretations of the law had required state action,[9] the Court found no such qualification to the extent the enactment was rooted in the Thirteenth Amendment.[10]

The aims of the Civil Rights Act of 1866 were further invigorated and ties to the Thirteenth Amendment renewed when the Court, in *Runyon v. McCrary*, upheld a provision prohibiting racial discrimination in making and enforcing private contracts.[11] It thus found that a private school could not deny black students the right to contract for an education.[12] Pursuant to 42 U.S.C. § 1981, the Court determined that the "right 'to make and enforce contracts' is violated if a private offeror refuses to extend to a Negro, solely because he is a Negro, the same opportunity to enter into contracts as he extends to white offerees."[13]

The validity and scope of the law were revisited more than a decade later in *Patterson v. McLean Credit Union*.[14] The consequent decision reaffirmed that Section 1981 prohibited racial discrimination in the making and enforcement of contracts.[15] Although the law was found applicable to employment contracts, the Court qualified its reach in finding that the provision did not extend to post-formation racial harassment by an employer.[16]

Despite enhanced congressional latitude for legislation pursuant to the Thirteenth Amendment, litigation has been less extensive and doctrine more circumscribed than under the Fourteenth Amendment. The narrower perimeters may reflect the Thirteenth Amendment's more obviously discrete focus, the early curtailment of its operation, and the absence of an inherent limiting principle equivalent to a state action requirement. Recent Supreme Court decisions demonstrate a continuing disinclination to animate the amendment forcefully.

In *City of Memphis v. Greene*, the Court was unmoved by arguments that erection of a street barrier, routing black traffic around a white neighborhood, constituted a "restraint on the liberty of black citizens that is in any sense comparable to the odious practice the Thirteenth Amendment was designed to eradicate."[17] Despite the city's long and not too distant history of formal segregation and the evident racial impact, the Court was satisfied that racially neutral safety considerations justified the traffic diversion measure.[18]

The Court also has indicated that legislation enacted pursuant to the Thirteenth Amendment is subject to significant limiting principles. In *General Building Contractors Association, Inc. v. Pennsylvania*, the Court determined that a Section 1981 offense did not exist without proof of discriminatory intent.[19] Given the identical origins of Sections 1981 and 1982, it would follow that the discriminatory motive requirement would apply to both. Such a standard is consistent with criteria that define modern equal protection review. As discussed in Chapter 6, however, discerning motive is a vexing exercise to the extent intent may be hidden, mixed, or impossible to identify. It thus represents a qualifying standard of major proportion.

The Thirteenth Amendment was introduced in response to an institution that characterized and defined a discrete region. By contrast, the Fifteenth Amendment operated against general inclinations and methodologies for excluding blacks from voting. In 1869, when the Fifteenth Amendment was introduced, only twenty states gave blacks the right to vote. Half of those were southern states obligated to provide such rights in exchange for readmission to the union. Proposals for extending the franchise to blacks consistently had been defeated in northern states, where opposition remained so intense that Republicans in 1868 advocated black suffrage as a function of federal law in the South but state determination in the North. Supporters fought hard for the amendment, and its ratification was narrowly secured. Significant support for the amendment was prompted by the sense that, with voting rights assured, the nation could dispatch the problem of race. The Fifteenth Amendment thus confronted a culture that had extended the franchise as a function of convenience rather than enthusiasm.

Within a year of the amendment's ratification, Congress enacted enforcement legislation. The Force Acts criminalized public or private impairment of the right to vote and provided for federal supervision of registration processes and certification of election results.[20] Although reflecting genuine enforcement commitment, the laws were soon victimized by southern resistance, the nation's shifting attention and priorities, and the eventual repeal of statutory conspiracy provisions in 1894.

Judicial review of Fifteenth Amendment claims, until the middle of the twentieth century, was largely unproductive. The Supreme Court refused, for instance, to read the provision as prohibiting private interference with voting rights.[21] The distinction between private and public action seemed largely immaterial. In *Giles v. Harris*, the Court concluded that it would be "pointless" to intervene, even if a state refused to register black voters.[22] Confronted in 1903 with a constitutional mandate and state disrespect for it, the Court declined to order what it sensed would be ignored.[23] The Court thus reckoned with manifest racism by accommodating it and advising, in Justice Holmes' words, that "relief from a great political wrong, if done, as alleged by the people of a State and the State itself, must be given by them or by the legislature and the political department of the government of the United States."[24]

For the better part of the twentieth century, the Court remained mostly unresponsive to racially inspired interference with voting rights. Consistent with its endorsement of official segregation, the Court allowed the operation of devices calculated to exclude blacks from meaningful civil and political participation. Methods of disfranchisement—such as poll taxes, literacy and general knowledge tests, property requirements, and character qualifications—effectively served their racially exclusionary purpose and were generally upheld by the Court.[25] Impediments, unless overtly race-dependent, withstood constitutional challenge even into the desegregation era. In *Guinn v. United States*, the Court invalidated a literacy test that applied by law only to persons qualified to vote in 1867 and thus manifestly excluded blacks.[26] The existence of state action and overt purpose also were critical to decisions, based on the Fourteenth Amendment, invalidating Texas laws that resulted in exclusion of blacks from primary elections. The Court struck down enactments establishing all-white primaries[27] and enabling political parties to exclude blacks.[28] By the middle of the century, the Court had emphasized the linkage of party-run primaries to general elections and found racially based exclusions and restrictions offensive also to the Fifteenth Amendment.[29]

Pursuant to the enforcement powers which the reconstruction amendments afforded, Congress in the decade after *Brown v. Board of Education* renewed its attention to civil rights legislation. Notwithstanding Justice Holmes' observation that "relief from a great political wrong" must come from the legislature, Congress was a generally unproductive source with respect to civil rights. Such inaction and inattention reflected the grip of southern legislators who, under the seniority system, dominated key leadership and committee positions in Congress. As the legislative branch finally began to respond to the law's new direction charted by *Brown*, new enactments secured civil and voting rights. Pursuant to its commerce power and authority to enforce the Fourteenth Amendment, Congress passed the Civil Rights Act of 1964, which prohibits discrimination in public accommodations and facilities, public schools and employment.[30] The act also expedited certain voting rights cases and prohibited various methods that denied the franchise. The 1964 act was preceded by the Civil Rights Act of 1957,[31] authorizing the Justice Department to seek injunctions against racially inspired interference with voting rights, and by the Civil Rights Act of 1960,[32] providing federal access to local voting records and empowering courts to register voters where they had been systematically disfranchised.

Congress eventually adopted the Voting Rights Act of 1965, which established a clear national interest in and provided for federal monitoring of state and local elections.[33] Among other things, the act empowers the Attorney General to review all changes of election qualifications and procedures in states governed by the law. The statute covered jurisdictions (1) where prior to November 1, 1964, a test or device to determine voting rights had been used, and (2) where less than half of the potential voters were registered on the aforementioned date or actually voted in the 1964 presidential election.

The Court in *South Carolina v. Katzenbach* upheld the 1965 act.[34] In so doing, it construed congressional enforcement power broadly and refused to limit legislative reach to violations of the amendment itself. Drawing on necessary and proper clause standards of review, it determined that if Congress's objective is "legitimate . . . [and] within the scope of the constitution, . . . all means which are appropriate, which are plainly adapted to that end, which are not prohibited, but consist with the letter and spirit of the constitution, are constitutional."[35] Pursuant to its most recent extension in 1982, the Voting Rights Act continues to operate in states that historically denied or impaired the franchise on racial grounds.

Thirteenth and Fifteenth Amendment jurisprudence, although spanning more than a century, has been less copious than Fourteenth Amendment case law. Until fairly recently, it also has been bound by standards that limited the amendments' independent significance or cramped congressional enforcement power. The Fourteenth Amendment, in contrast, has been a source of extensive judicial attention and creativity. From the Court's original sense that the amendment was concerned essentially with securing civil rights and equality for the nation's new citizens, to subsequent premises that countenanced "[m]ere discriminations" and official segregation, and then to modern anti-discrimination and color-blind principles, doctrine concerning race has been plentiful, complex, and often convoluted. The Fourteenth Amendment also has proved multidimensional insofar as it has evolved as a source of fundamental rights unenumerated by the Constitution, unrelated to race, and beyond the original vision of the framers. The balance of this chapter will focus on seminal reading and development of the Fourteenth Amendment. Subsequent chapters will cover official segregation, the desegregation mandate and anti-discrimination principles, and race-conscious remediation.

Just as the antebellum Supreme Court had to reckon with the unfinished business of the original framing process, the Court during the latter decades of the nineteenth century had to account for loose ends in the Fourteenth Amendment's creation. Seminal review reflected many of the same tensions and conflicts over redistribution of government power that had been evident during the amendment's drafting stage. Competing against vindication of the new national interest was abiding reverence for the states and for the traditions of federalism. Eventually, the national interest represented by the Fourteenth Amendment was acknowledged and with respect to non-racial concerns actually magnified by the Court. Although its immediate response was to trim some significant documental threads, the Court soon began fashioning a constitutional design created in large part from fabric it supplied and stitched.

Predictive of the Fourteenth Amendment's future elasticity and malleability, the Court's initial interpretive exercise did not pertain to the provision's race-dependent concern. The *Slaughter-House Cases* arose from challenges to a Louisiana law prohibiting all but one slaughterhouse in New Orleans.[36] Even if the litigation seemed to distance principle from race, contemporary reality emphasized the association. The day before the Court rendered its judgment was memorable for the Colfax Massacre in Grant Parish, Louisiana, where a dispute over political power culminated in a white-led attack upon a black-defended courthouse. What followed was what the media described as a "Horrible Massacre" in which multitudes of blacks were shot or burned to death and some whites were killed.[37]

Although obligated to rent space to any butcher who applied, the state-created monopoly at issue in the *Slaughter-House Cases* elicited claims that it interfered with the right to pursue a trade and thus compromised the Fourteenth Amendment. A lower court decision, authored by Justice Bradley sitting as a circuit judge, responded favorably to arguments for a broadly defined set of rights. Bradley described the privileges and immunities clause as comprehending personal freedom "to adopt and follow such lawful industrial pursuit" and affording protection "in the possession and enjoyment of [one's] property."[38] Although conceding that these rights were subject to reasonable regulation pursuant to state police powers, he found the monopoly at odds with the Fourteenth Amendment.[39]

Bradley's expansive interpretation failed to carry a majority of the Supreme Court. In a 5–4 decision authored by Justice Miller, the Court maintained that the Fourteenth Amendment was concerned with establishing "the freedom of the slave race, the security of and firm establishment of that freedom, and the protection of the newly-made free man and citizen from the oppressions of those who had formerly exercised unlimited dominion over him."[40] Despite acknowledging the amendment's concern, the Court construed it in a way that significantly blunted its potential to protect the rights of blacks. The majority opinion reflected an exercise in resistance to expanded federal power. Its characterizations of state and national citizenship were, respectively, generous and parsimonious.

In reading the Fourteenth Amendment, the Court focused initially on the first sentence of Section 1 which "opens with a definition of citizenship—not only citizenship of the United States, but citizenship of the States."[41] Recognizing that the provision introduced the new concept of national citizenship, which further invalidated the *Scott* decision, the Court determined that the primary and indisputable purpose of the clause was "to establish the citizenship of the negro."[42] From the phrase "citizens of the United States and of the State wherein they reside," the Court discerned a concept of citizenship that was bifurcated rather than integrated or intertwined. It found "quite clear, then, that there is a citizenship of the United States and a citizenship of a State, which are distinct from each other and which depend upon different characteristics or circumstances in the individual."[43]

The distinction between national and state citizenship preordained effective and enduring devitalization of the privileges and immunities clause. In further dissecting the provision, the Court determined that the clause "speaks only of the privileges and immunities of citizens of the United States, and does not speak of those of citizens of the several States."[44] Such a reading proved fatal to the plaintiffs' claim, which assumed that the two types of citizenship were the same and the interests secured also were identical.[45] Focusing specifically on language that "[n]o State shall make or enforce any law which shall abridge the privileges or immunities of the citizens of the United States," the Court found it

a little remarkable, if this clause was intended as a protection to the citizen of a State against the legislative power of his own State, that the words "citizen of the State" should be left out when it is so carefully used, and used in contradistinction to "citizens of the United States" in the very sentence which precedes it. It is too clear for argument that the change in phraseology was adopted understandingly and with a purpose.[46]

The assertion, that the significance of separately referenced citizenships was "too clear for argument," was challenged by the Court's own division. Especially for being only a few years removed from the extensive and well-covered debates over the Fourteenth Amendment, review seemed to reflect a dubious inquiry into the amendment's meaning. Given the manifest intention of the framers to transfer at least the guarantees of the Civil Rights Act of 1866 to the privileges and immunities clause, the exercise suggested more an evasion of than a search for actual purpose.

The Court thus imputed to the framers an intent to place only the privileges and immunities of national citizenship under the protection of the Constitution; those of state citizenship, "whatever they may be, are not intended to have any additional protection by this paragraph of the [Fourteenth] Amendment."[47] Having distinguished between privileges and immunities of federal and state citizenship, the Court concluded that "the latter must rest for their security and protection where they have heretofore rested."[48] The practical intimation was that states, which traditionally had defined the incidents of state citizenship and whose abuses established the need for amendment, were minimally affected by constitutional change.

The majority's interpretation so eviscerated the meaning of the privileges and immunities clause that it remains an insignificant factor in Fourteenth Amendment jurisprudence.[49] As previously noted, the framers contemplated a more profound constitutional retooling. Although the Court's understanding reflected a concern expressed by many congressional supporters of the amendment, judicial reaction was excessive. It had been a commonly articulated aim that the restructuring of federal power not be so comprehensive or intrusive that it displaced or eclipsed the general affairs and interests of the states. Supporters and detractors alike, however, recognized how the Fourteenth Amendment altered the relationship between federal and state government insofar as necessary to account for a specified national interest. Typifying original understanding among congressional supporters was the sense that the amendment "plac[ed] personal liberty and personal rights . . . in the keeping of the nation."[50] Critics complained that it would enable Congress to enact "a civil and criminal code for every state in the Union [and thereby afford it] power to occupy the whole domain of local and state legislation."[51] Even if the warning was exaggerated and unwarranted, the Court responded to it.

Having established two variants of citizenship, which were independently significant, the Court considered the nature of their respective incidents. To determine the content of state privileges and immunities, it referred to Article IV, Section 2, which provides that "[t]he Citizens of each State shall be entitled to all Privileges and Immunities of Citizens in the several States."[52] Because this provision does not itemize what those incidents are, reference to it constituted an analytical departure rather than end point. The Court thus examined an antecedent in the Articles of Confederation and a federal court interpretation of Article IV, Section 2. The Articles of Confederation offered some specifics to the effect that "free inhabitants of each of these States . . . [had] all the privileges and immunities of free citizens in the several States; . . . free ingress and egress to and from any other State, and . . . all the privileges of trade and commerce, subject to the same duties, impositions and restrictions as the inhabitants thereof respectively."[53] Looking to Justice Washington's decision in *Corfield v. Coryell*, the Court found that the "privileges and immunities of citizens of the several States . . . [are those] which are *fundamental*; which belong of right to the citizens of all free governments, and which have at all times been enjoyed by citizens of the several States which compose this Union."[54] Detailing what those rights were would have been a treacherous exercise, because disagreement existed then as now over the nature and breadth of fundamental rights and liberties. The Court, therefore, merely restated the observation in *Corfield* that their enumeration

would be more tedious than difficult . . . [but] may all, however, be comprehended under the following general heads: protection by the government, with the right to acquire and possess property of every kind, and to pursue and obtain happiness and safety, subject, nevertheless, to such restraints as the government may prescribe for the general good of the whole.[55]

The depiction of privileges and immunities incidental to state citizenship specifically identified interests in property and personal security and intimated concern with material self-development. It thus tracked what was staked out originally by the Civil Rights Act of 1866 and by architects of the Fourteenth Amendment. As noted in the preceding chapter, their core concern was with contract and property rights, personal mobility and security, and standing before the law. The 1866 act and the Fourteenth Amendment supposedly had established a new federal accountability for those interests. The judicially crafted distinction between federal and state citizenship, however, effectively delimited the federal zone of interest. The Constitution's preexisting privileges and immunities clause had been understood to mean that whatever rights a state afforded its own citizens, "the same . . . shall be the measure of the rights of citizens of other States within your jurisdiction."[56] It descended from a like provision in the Articles of Confederation intended to ensure "mutual friendship and intercourse among the people of the different States."[57] The Fourteenth Amendment established an interest in equal rights not of citizens from different states but of citizens within the same state. Denial of that achievement delayed the actual shift in power contemplated by the framers and transformed the new privileges and immunities clause into a veritable redundancy.

To its own question, as to whether the Fourteenth Amendment by virtue of the privileges and immunities clause was "to transfer the security and protection of all the civil rights we have mentioned, from the States to the Federal Government," the Court answered negatively.[58] If a contrary conclusion were reached, it warned, state legislative power would be usurped by the Congress and the federal judiciary.[59] At least from the *Slaughter-House* majority's perspective, control of the incidents of citizenship was an all-or-nothing proposition, and it refused to preside over a transfer of the incidents of citizenship from state to federal authority.

By so perceiving the question and its role, the Court failed to recognize that the redistribution already had been ordained and the judiciary itself was impeding implementation. It essentially failed or refused to acknowledge an increased federal role in ensuring rights previously protected exclusively by the states. The Court could have acknowledged the federal interest and, because no question of race had been presented, reached the same result. Instead of a sensitive appraisal that recognized conjunctivity, the Court responded in disjunctive terms that also reflected evasion or misunderstanding. Despite a manifest intention to redefine governmental powers, the Court refused to admit it "in the absence of language which expresses such a purpose too clearly to admit of doubt."[60]

Characterization of the privileges and immunities at issue as incidents of state citizenship[61] predetermined a narrow reading of the meaning of federal citizenship. As depicted by the Court, the privileges and immunities of federal citizenship were notable for their relative lack of profundity. Although not purporting to provide an exhaustive recitation, the Court suggested that federal privileges and immunities included the right

"to come to the seat of government to assert any claim he may have upon that government, to transact any business he may have with it, to seek its protection, to share its offices, to engage in administering its functions . . . of free access to [the nation's] seaports, . . . to the sub-treasuries, land-offices, and courts of justice in the several States." . . . to demand the care and protection of the Federal Government over his life, liberty and property when on the high seas or within the jurisdiction of a foreign government. . . . to peaceably assemble and petition for redress of grievances, . . . [to assert] the writ of *habeas corpus*. . . . to use the navigable waters of the United States . . . and all rights secured to our citizens by treaties with foreign nations . . . [to] become a citizen of any State of the Union by a *bona fide* residence therein. . . . To these may be added the rights secured by the 13th and 15th articles of amendment, and by the other clause of the fourteenth. . . . [62]

Having already determined that the right asserted was an incident of state citizenship, the Court considered it unnecessary to pursue an extensive inquiry into federal privileges and immunities and their significance. The Court nonetheless identified some incidents of federal citizenship if only to defeat possible perception that it recognized none. In acknowledging the reality of federal privileges and immunities, however, the *Slaughter-House* Court further diminished them.

After finishing with the privileges and immunities provision, the Court turned its attention to the due process and equal protection clauses. It specifically rejected any notion that the due process guarantee might operate as a check on state legislative power. Noting that the clause paralleled a like provision in the Fifth Amendment, and was "found in some form of expression in the constitutions of nearly all the States,"[63] the Court refused to enhance due process beyond its traditional function as a guarantor of procedural fairness. It concluded that the due process clause had no new meaning "except so far as the [Fourteenth] Amendment may place the restraining power over the States in this matter in the hands of the Federal Government."[64] Even if reflecting a cautious explication, the Court acknowledged a federal interest in procedural fairness. It repudiated the intimation of *Scott v. Sandford* that the due process guarantee also operated substantively as a check upon legislative power. As the Fourteenth Amendment later evolved and became a source of unanticipated rights and liberties, the general vision of Taney rather than of Justice Miller would inspire the meaning of due process.

With respect to the equal protection clause, the Court had no difficulty discerning its central concern with the nation's new citizens and with devices such as the Black Codes that confounded their status. It observed that "[t]he existence of laws in the States where the newly emancipated negroes resided, which discriminated with gross injustice and hardship against them as a class, was the evil to be remedied by this clause, and by it such laws are forbidden."[65] The Court further acknowledged Congress's power to enforce the guarantee by suitable legislation.[66] It thus recognized a federal interest in prohibiting racially discriminatory legislation. The extent of that concern, however, was not amplified. Rather, the Court merely emphasized the narrow focus of equal protection and related its doubt as to "whether any action of a State not directed by way of discrimination against the negroes as a class, or on account of their race, will ever be held to come within the purview of this provision."[67] The development of equal protection jurisprudence from the middle of the twentieth century onward, invalidating classifications based on gender, alienage, and the marital status of parents and acts impacting fundamental rights, would have been a source of astonishment to the *Slaughter-House* majority. Such results have prompted the observation that "(t)he notion of equal protection as it spreads out tends to lift all to the level of the most favored."[68]

Viewing the Fourteenth Amendment as a whole, the Court asserted that from the republic's inception a line had separated federal and state power and, although never well defined, "continued from that day to this."[69] It noted that the first eleven amendments to the Constitution reflected a dominant concern with the exercise of federal power and that the Civil War revealed "the true danger to the perpetuity of the Union" presented by the states.[70] From that backdrop, Justice Miller gleaned an overarching principle "that the existence of the States with powers for domestic and local government, including the regulation of civil rights—the rights of person and of property—was essential to the perfect working of our complex form of government."[71] In a single paragraph, therefore, Miller disclosed the majority's failure or refusal to acknowledge the constitutional reality that had transpired.

Justice Field may have better perceived, but he still distorted the original vision of the Fourteenth Amendment. In his dissent, Field recognized that the amendment had established federal interests that previously were an exclusive concern of the states. He maintained that the privileges and immunities clause

recognizes in express terms, if it does not create, citizens of the United States, and it makes their citizenship dependent upon the place of their birth, or the fact of their adoption, and not upon the Constitution or laws of any State or the condition of their ancestry. A citizen of a State is now only a citizen of the United States residing in that State. The fundamental rights, privileges and immunities which belong to him as a free man and a free citizen, now belong to him as a citizen of the United States, and are not dependent upon his citizenship of any State.[72]

Field recognized the redistributive nature of the Fourteenth Amendment in securing rights against abridgment by the states.[73] Rather than identifying the designation and scope of civil rights as a state function unaffected by the Fourteenth Amendment, Field would have incorporated into the privileges and immunities clause the Civil Rights Act of 1866.[74] Instead of the mostly immaterial and peripheral concerns itemized by the majority, the incidents of federal citizenship as understood by Field included the right "to make and enforce contracts, to sue, be parties and give evidence; to inherit, purchase, lease, sell, hold, and convey real and personal property, and to full and equal benefit of all laws and proceedings for the security of person and property."[75] He also would have included as federal privileges and immunities the itemizations in *Corfield v. Coryell*, which the majority regarded as accoutrements of state citizenship.[76]

Insofar as he would have invalidated the slaughterhouse monopoly as a violation of the Fourteenth Amendment, Field offered an expansive sense of the provision that was as misplaced as the majority's narrow view. As construed by Field, the amendment was a proper source of the municipal law, which the majority feared.[77] Although acknowledging that states could enact reasonable regulation based on their police powers, his failure to defer to the nuisance considerations prompting the challenged law evidenced support for extensive displacement of traditional state concerns.

Justice Bradley, who had authored the lower court opinion, joined Field's dissent but also wrote separately to express his disagreement with the majority. Bradley offered an even more expansive listing of the privileges and immunities of federal citizenship that he considered protected by the Fourteenth Amendment. Referring to the Declaration of Independence, he asserted that the "[r]ights to life, liberty and the pursuit of happiness are equivalent to the rights of life, liberty and property ...[which] are fundamental...[and] can only be taken away by due process of law."[78] For Bradley, the federal privileges and immunities secured by the Fourteenth Amendment included the Bill of Rights.[79]

Both Bradley and Field were prepared to extend the Fourteenth Amendment beyond its original concern with race. Despite the absence of race-related state action, Field would have found the challenged monopoly an invasion of a federally secured privilege.[80] Bradley suggested violations of the due process guarantee, which he viewed in substantive terms, and of the equal protection clause.[81] The conclusions represented analysis as profound in its overreaching as the majority's was in its narrowness.

The competition of ideas reflected by the divergent opinions in the *Slaughter-House Cases* continues to characterize and influence Fourteenth Amendment jurisprudence to this day. Although Justices Field and Bradley were in the minority, their opinions predicted in significant part the Fourteenth Amendment's eventual meaning. Consistent with the dissenters' position, the Court soon recognized and protected economic rights unrelated to racial considerations. Because the privileges and immunities clause had been eviscerated, however, such reckoning was pursuant to Bradley's concept of due process rather than Field's notion of federal privileges.[82] Later in the twentieth century, the liberty component of the due process clause became the source of substantive personal rights including those of privacy and personal autonomy.[83] Equal protection, although largely ignored until the middle of the twentieth century, eventually functioned as a significant proscription against racial and other classifications.[84]

The dissenting justices thereby previewed the Fourteenth Amendment's future utility in accounting for interests beyond the framers' original expectation. Justice Miller emphasized the provision's central concern with race. By diminishing the privileges and immunities clause's essential significance, and leaving responsibility for civil rights and their enforcement with the states, the Court effectively delimited the possibility of federal remedies for state-caused deprivations. Between the dissenters' expansive interpretation that diluted attention to race and the majority's hypertechnical and restrictive reading, many racially based deprivations of basic rights subsequently escaped constitutional radar. Such a result may not have been disturbing to a society whose interest in racial justice had diminished in inverse proportion to its enhanced attention to national reunification and economic development. Subsequent decisions reflected the altered priorities but, like the *Slaughter-House* ruling, slighted the concerns of an amended constitution. Not until the middle of the twentieth century was the Fourteenth Amendment activated in terms that meaningfully reckoned with its core agenda. Until then, jurisprudence would reflect the distortions of the *Slaughter-House* majority and minority opinions which respectively complicated the quest for racial justice and established embryonic concepts of economic and other unenumerated liberties.

The Supreme Court in 1877 provided further doctrinal impetus to the eventual transformation of the Fourteenth Amendment into a guarantor of economic liberty. In *Munn v. Illinois*, it upheld a state law regulating the rates of grain elevators.[85] Despite upholding the enactment, the Court noted that it accounted for a special public interest and stressed that "in mere private contracts, . . . what is reasonable must be ascertained judicially."[86] The *Munn* decision thus previewed the future direction of substantive due process review, which by the early twentieth century had sanctified liberty of contract. A year before *Munn*, however, the Court disclosed how the Fourteenth Amendment's significance to issues of race would diminish in inverse proportion to the attention afforded general economic rights.

Jurisprudential minimization of the Fourteenth Amendment's significance with respect to race became manifest as pertinent claims for relief emerged. In *United States v. Cruikshank*, the Court vitiated Congress's power to enact laws making interference with another person's civil rights a criminal offense.[87] The *Cruikshank* case resulted from the aforementioned racially inspired Colfax Massacre.[88] Despite the backdrop of brutality and the absence of state control or intervention, the Court found that the interest at issue was a state rather than a federal concern.[89] It described the Fourteenth Amendment as a guarantee that "adds nothing to the rights of one citizen as against another...[but] simply furnishes an additional guaranty against any encroachment by the States upon the fundamental rights which belong to every citizen as a member of society."[90] Depreciation of a federal interest in criminal activity, as it related to Fourteenth Amendment considerations, reflected a sense that the provision was concerned only with state action and that regulation of crime was a local concern. The decision had profound consequences to the extent it eliminated any official check during ensuing decades on the terrorism and official segregation that would define racial reality especially in the South.

Several years later, in *United States v. Harris*, the Court considered a challenge to the Civil Rights Act of 1871.[91] The act was the basis for federal prosecution of state law enforcement officials charged with conspiracy to deny equal protection of the laws to a person who, while in custody, had been beaten to death.[92] Citing to *Cruikshank*, the Court reasserted that "[t]he duty of protecting all citizens in the enjoyment of an equality of rights was originally assumed by the States, and it remains there."[93]

The Fourteenth Amendment's imminent but selective devolution was not apparent in the first racially significant examination of its substantive meaning. To the contrary, its decision in *Strauder v. West Virginia* suggested the amendment had meaningful potential to reckon with discrimination.[94] In *Strauder*, the Court considered the constitutionality of a state law excluding blacks from juries.[95] That law directly implicated the Fourteenth Amendment, which, the Court observed, "cannot be understood without keeping in view the history of the times when [it] was adopted, and the general objects they plainly sought to accomplish."[96] According to Justice Strong, who wrote the majority opinion, the amendment was enacted to protect the interests of an exploited and disadvantaged race, which required special attention in order to prevent further oppression. Referring to experience immediately following abolition, Strong noted that

it required little knowledge of human nature to anticipate that those who had long been regarded as an inferior and subject race would, when suddenly raised to the rank of citizenship, be looked upon with jealousy and positive dislike, and that state laws might be enacted or enforced to perpetuate the distinctions that had before existed. Discriminations against them had been habitual. It was well known that, in some States, laws making such discriminations then existed, and others might be well expected. The colored race, as a race, was abject and ignorant, and in that condition was unfitted to command the respect of those who had superior intelligence. Their training had left them mere children, and as such they needed the protection which a wise government extends to those who are unable to protect themselves. They especially needed protection against unfriendly action in the States where they were resident. It was in view of these considerations the Fourteenth Amendment was framed and adopted.[97]

The *Strauder* Court thus discerned an original purpose to ensure equal enjoyment of civil rights and to provide "the protection of the general government, in that enjoyment, whenever it should be denied by the States."[98] This perception of the Fourteenth Amendment comported with the *Slaughter-House* Court's depiction of its "one pervading purpose" as accounting for "the freedom of the slave race."[99] The Court further determined that, given the amendment's remedial purpose, "it is to be construed liberally, to carry out the purposes of its framers."[100] Focusing specifically on the equal protection clause, Justice Strong construed it as "declaring that the law in the States shall be the same for the black as for the white; that all persons, whether colored or white, shall stand equal before the laws of the States."[101] Consistent with its standard of liberal construction, the Court found that equal protection not only operated as a prohibition against state action but also afforded "a positive immunity, or right, most valuable to the colored race."[102] It adduced "the right to exemption from unfriendly legislation against them distinctively, as colored; exemption from legal discriminations, implying inferiority in civil society, lessening the security of their enjoyment of the rights which others enjoy, and discriminations which are steps towards reducing them to the condition of a subject race."[103]

Official exclusion of blacks by law from juries resulted in the first finding of a racially significant violation of the Fourteenth Amendment.[104] Because the statute in question excluded citizens on the basis of race, the Court perceived it as "practically a brand upon [black persons], affixed by the law, an assertion of their inferiority, and a stimulant to that race prejudice which is an impediment to securing to individuals of the race that equal justice which the law aims to secure to all others."[105]

The *Strauder* decision represented the first invalidation of a racially discriminatory law under the Fourteenth Amendment specifically and under the Constitution in general. In a companion case, *Ex parte Virginia*, the Court determined that equal protection operated not only against legislative classifications but also against discrimination by state officials.[106] It thus discerned a constitutional violation when blacks were excluded from juries as a function of a judge's determination rather than of statutory prescription. The Court specifically determined that no agency of the State, or of the officers or agents by whom its powers are exerted, shall deny to any person within its jurisdiction the equal protection of the laws. Whoever, by virtue of public position under a State government deprives another of property, life, or liberty without due process of law, or denies or takes away the equal protection of the laws, violates the constitutional inhibition; and as he acts in the name and for the State, and is clothed with the State's power, his act is that of the State.[107]

As a consequence of *Ex parte Virginia*, equal protection operated not just against legislatures, whose enactment of the Black Codes had identified the need for the guarantee, but also against the states generally. The *Strauder* decision in particular suggested that the Fourteenth Amendment provided a direct action against racial discrimination. It acknowledged not only a proper federal interest but also a need on the part of the nation's new citizens for special constitutional attention. The Court also established a standard of review that, although soon moribund, eventually would provide a premise for defeating official segregation. The determination that categorical exclusion of blacks from juries "impl[ied] inferiority" anticipated the principle, subscribed to in 1954, that official segregation communicated a diminished worth and thus was inherently unequal.[108]

In the decades between *Strauder* and *Brown*, courts would be generally insensitive to racially significant connotations of official policy and actions. Special legislative or jurisprudential concern for the nation's new citizens also would be repudiated a few years hence. Even contemporaneous with *Strauder* and *Ex parte Virginia*, the Court disclosed that Fourteenth Amendment review would be qualified by significant limiting principles.

In *Virginia v. Rives*, the Court considered the indictments and convictions of two black defendants by all-white juries.[109] Unlike *Strauder* and *Ex parte Virginia*, evidence did not establish that the absence of black jurors was attributable to state law or action. It was argued that no black ever had served on a jury in the county.[110] Nevertheless, the Court distinguished between protection against actual discrimination and "a right to have the jury composed in part of colored men."[111] It thus established a significant qualification of the *Strauder* premise, not unlike what would limit the anti-discrimination principle that would evolve in the middle of the twentieth century. For the *Rives* Court, discrimination did not present a constitutional concern unless it was officially prescribed by law or official policy. Although acknowledging that a formal statute would implicate the Fourteenth Amendment, if denial of access to the judicial process was racially inspired, it refused to attach the same significance to ministerial acts of "subordinate officer[s]."[112] The Court failed to probe beyond outward appearances of racial neutrality. Because the law on its face did not discriminate and by its terms allowed and even required blacks to serve on juries,[113] the Court refused to inquire further into motive or effect.

The *Rives* case imposed on plaintiffs the heavy burden of demonstrating that discrimination was the actual function of official action. Because a tradition of exclusion and disproportionate impact was rejected as grounds for establishing discrimination, the result presaged the problem that would confound the desegregation mandate and the anti-discrimination principle a century later. As discussed in Chapters 5 and 6, modern discriminatory purpose criteria have cramped the equal protection guarantee in a similar fashion. The problem now, as then, is that wrongful intent may be hidden, and only the most obvious variants of discrimination are subject to identification. The *Rives* decision thus related a lesson that would become pertinent again a century later. Not until the late twentieth century did the Court finally reckon with tactics that continued to operate effectively in excluding blacks from juries.[114]

The *Strauder* decision, although contemporaneously qualified by *Rives*, made a forceful statement on the federal interest represented by the Fourteenth Amendment and the provision's special concern. It was reinforced by the observation, in *Ex parte Virginia*, that the Thirteenth and Fourteenth Amendments "were intended to be, . . . [and] really are, limitations of the power of the States and enlargements of the power of Congress."[115] Racial jurisprudence over the next three-quarters of a century, however, seldom reflected that fundamental realignment. Three years after finding the exclusion of black jurors unconstitutional, the Court rendered a decision challenging not the actual letter but the general spirit of *Strauder*. At issue in the *Civil Rights Cases* was the constitutionality of the Civil Rights Act of 1875,[116] which prohibited discrimination in public venues including "accommodations, advantages, facilities, and privileges of inns, public conveyances on land or water, theaters and other places of public amusement."[117] The cases concerned exclusions of black persons from hotels, theaters, and rail cars. Neither the decision nor the method of review reflected the liberal standard of interpretation advanced in *Strauder*. Rather, the reasoning and result disclosed a growing sense of fatigue with the demands of the Thirteenth and Fourteenth Amendments.

The *Civil Rights Cases* implicated squarely the nature and extent of Congress's enforcement power. In reviewing congressional authority to enact legislation pursuant to the Fourteenth Amendment, the Court determined that legislative power was bound by the terms of Section 1.[118] Noting that the first section of the amendment concerned itself only with state action, it concluded that congressional power was coextensive and thus limited to legislation correcting the effects of state law or action.[119] It did not include authority to create a code of municipal law for the regulation of private rights; but to provide modes of redress against the operation of state laws, and the action of state officers executive or judicial, when these are subversive of the fundamental rights specified in the Amendment.... [L]egislation must ... be predicated upon ... state laws or state proceedings, and be directed to the correction of their operation and effect.[120]

The Court's definition of congressional power thus disclosed the same reluctance, evidenced in the *Slaughter-House* decision, to sanction the redistribution of power provided for by the Fourteenth Amendment. Unlike the *Slaughter-House* Court, which expressed general resistance to the transfer, the *Civil Rights* Court's counteraction was selective. To the extent Fourteenth Amendment doctrine was evolving to account for general interests such as economic liberty, the limitation of legislative power effectively repudiated the amendment's central meaning.

The emerging double standard of Fourteenth Amendment review was denoted not only by contrasting analytical criteria but also by authorship of the majority opinion. As noted previously, Justice Bradley in the *Slaughter-House Cases* had advanced the most expansive vision of the Fourteenth Amendment. In contrast to the broad understanding he had articulated a decade before, Bradley's opinion for the Court in the *Civil Rights Cases* expressed concerns reminiscent of those that influenced the *Slaughter-House* majority. He warned that the legislation at issue, if approved, would

establish a code of municipal law regulative of all private rights between man and man in society. It would be to make Congress take the place of the State Legislatures and to supersede them.... In fine, the legislation which Congress is authorized to adopt in this behalf is not general legislation upon the rights of the citizen, but corrective legislation ... as may be necessary and proper for counteracting such laws as the States may adopt or enforce, and which, by the Amendment, they are prohibited from making or enforcing, or such acts and proceedings as the States may commit or take, and which, by the Amendment, they are prohibited from committing or taking.[121]

The articulated concern that Congress would create a comprehensive body of municipal law was overblown, as indicated by the Court's own observation that the Fourteenth Amendment proscribed only "state action of a particular character."[122] The circumscription of congressional power seemed at odds with settled criteria. Necessary and proper standards, purportedly employed, normally result in accommodation rather than limitation of congressional power.[123] The case for liberal construction was supported not only by *Strauder*'s command for a flexible rather than a technical interpretation but also by the constitutional assignment to Congress of an "affirmative power, by *legislation*, to *enforce* an express prohibition upon the States."[124] Still, the Court concluded that the law was fatally defective because it invaded "the domain of local jurisprudence" and was at odds with "the Tenth Amendment... which declares that powers not delegated to the United States by the Constitution, nor prohibited by it to the States, are reserved to the States respectively or to the people."[125]

Not only the Fourteenth Amendment itself but also congressional power to enforce it were restricted to instances of state action. The Court emphasized that

[t]he wrongful act of an individual, unsupported by any such authority, is simply a private wrong, or a crime of that individual; an invasion of the rights of the injured party, it is true, whether they affect his person, his property or his reputation; but if not sanctioned in some way by the State, or not done under state authority, his rights remain in full force, and may presumably be vindicated by resort to the laws of the State for redress. An individual cannot deprive a man of his right to vote, to hold property, to buy and to sell, to sue in the courts or to be a witness or a juror; he may, by force or fraud, interfere with the enjoyment of the right in a particular case; he may commit an assault against the person, or commit murder, or use ruffian violence at the polls, or slander the good name of a fellow citizen; but, unless protected in these wrongful acts by some shield of state law or state authority, he cannot destroy or injure the right; he will only render himself amenable to satisfaction or punishment; and amenable therefor to the laws of the State where the wrongful acts are committed.[126]

Because the federal law extended primarily and directly to activities within the traditional concern of the state, the Court determined that Congress had exceeded its constitutional grasp and wrongly arrogated powers not belonging to it. The Court's reasoning manifested continuing reservations over the extension of federal powers to areas of traditional state concern. Such resistance, however, did not reflect its evolving disposition toward displacement of state power affecting general economic activity. Critical to the increasingly bifurcated standard of review was a detectable sense of diminishing patience with the problems that had necessitated the Reconstruction amendments. Although perhaps less palpable in the Court's Fourteenth Amendment reasoning, race weariness was manifest in its Thirteenth Amendment analysis.

In considering whether passage of the Civil Rights Act of 1875 was justified under Thirteenth Amendment enforcement power, the Court acknowledged that Congress had authority to enact legislation necessary and proper for eradicating slavery and its badges and incidents.[127] It concluded, however, that national legislative power under the amendment did not extend to racial discrimination in public accommodations.[128] As the Court observed, "[i]t would be running the slavery argument into the ground, to make it apply to every act of discrimination which a person may see fit to make."[129] The point emphasized the Court's disinterest in the Thirteenth Amendment as a means for reckoning not only with slavery but also with its immediate legacy.

Although denying Congress the power to reach private discrimination, the Court suggested that a different result would be reached if the exclusion were a product of "unjust discrimination" by the states.[130] The distinction between private and official discrimination, however, was less precise than the Court may have assumed. As modern civil rights legislation has assumed, differentiation between sources of discrimination has less practical significance when the venue itself is public in nature. Even if the Court had been willing to forego the dubious distinction, it is doubtful that it was prepared to recognize a basis for constitutional attention. Reflecting society's general disposition toward the unfinished business of racial justice, the Court expressed its impatience and diminished interest. It accordingly observed that

[w]hen a man has emerged from slavery, and by the aid of beneficent legislation has shaken off the inseparable concomitants of that state, there must be some stage in the progress of his elevation when he takes the rank of a mere citizen, and ceases to be the special favorite of the laws, and when his rights, as a citizen or a man, are to be protected in the ordinary modes by which other men's rights are protected.[131]

This comment effectively indicated that, at least from the Court's perspective, the process of Reconstruction was finished, and the time for special attention had passed.

Compounding the impression of fatigue and impatience that the opinion disclosed was a sense that the contested exclusionary policies and practices simply were not significant. Noting that "thousands of free colored people" prior to abolition enjoyed basic rights, and "no one . . . thought" them compromised by discrimination in public accommodations or denial of certain privileges afforded whites,[132] the Court characterized the racial classifications as "[m]ere discriminations."[133] The depiction presaged the Court's insensitivity to the significance of exclusionary policies that would evidence themselves more profoundly a decade later when official segregation was challenged. Reduction of the contested policies and practices to a level of constitutional insignificance revealed that, even if basic civil rights and equality had been enshrined in the nation's charter document, society in general and the Court in particular had yet to pursue seriously the type of inquiry that would reveal the cultural impediments to meaningful application of the Fourteenth Amendment.

If left to Justice Harlan, who dissented from the judgment and opinion, Congress's enforcement power would have been delineated consistent with the liberal reading suggested by *Strauder* and eventually accepted by the Court in the late 1960s. Harlan regarded the burdens and disabilities of slavery broadly and as a legitimate object of congressional attention. Because slavery was what prompted the Thirteenth Amendment, and the institution was grounded in presumptions of racial inferiority, he argued that newly delineated freedoms were empty without immunity against and protection from all discrimination burdening civil rights.[134] Harlan argued that Congress, pursuant to its enforcement power, could enact laws protecting persons against "deprivation, *because of their race*, of any civil rights granted to other freemen in the same State."[135]

Significant for Harlan, at least with respect to the reach of congressional power, was the context of the challenged discriminatory policies and practices. From his perspective, distinguishing between public and private discrimination in the contexts at issue was an essentially procrustean exercise. He observed that railroads were created for a public purpose and access to them was critical to exercising personal liberty, which included "the power of locomotion, of changing situation or removing one's person . . . without restraint."[136] To the extent the right was impaired by racial discrimination, regardless of its source, Harlan perceived an imposition "which lay at the very foundation of the institution of slavery."[137] He described an innkeeper's function as "*quasi* public employment . . . [which] forbids him from discriminating against any person . . . on account of the race or color of that person."[138] With respect to regulated places of public amusement, Harlan maintained that government licensing "imports, in law, equality of right, at such places, among all members of that public."[139] To conclude otherwise would mean "that the common municipal government of all the people may, in the exertion of its powers, conferred for the benefit of all, discriminate or authorize discrimination against a particular race, solely because of its former condition of servitude."[140]

Harlan's inquiry into the nature of public carriers, inns, and theaters suggested that distinctions between state and private action were not especially significant. His insight was particularly relevant for future Fourteenth Amendment analysis, which, unlike Thirteenth Amendment analysis, requires determination of whether a challenged action is public or private. Jurisprudence eventually would comport more with Harlan's view, although even contemporary case law has refused to regard mere licensing or regulation as grounds for state action.[141] While suggesting that congressional power could reach quasi-public action, Harlan stopped short of the modern view that enables Congress to reach purely private conduct.[142]

Given Harlan's understanding that Congress could prohibit discrimination in public venues under the Thirteenth Amendment, his willingness to allow legislation pursuant to the "enlarged power under the Fourteenth Amendment" followed logically.[143] In delineating what he considered the proper ambit of legislative power, Harlan referred to the specific and unprecedented congressional charge "to enforce '*the provisions of this article*' of Amendment . . . — *all* of the provisions — affirmative and prohibitive."[144] Given this express assignment of legislative authority, he considered it unnecessary to correlate the enforcement powers of Section 5 to the substantive scope of Section 1. The charge to Congress indicated to him a broad mandate for enforcement "by means of legislation, operating throughout the entire Union, to guard, secure, and protect that right."[145]

Harlan offered a competing understanding of the Fourteenth Amendment in general. For him, the concept of privileges and immunities established constitutional security against racial discrimination. In considering the privileges and immunities conferred by the amendment, he maintained that

[t]here is one, if there be no other: exemption from race discrimination in respect of any civil right belonging to citizens of the white race in the same State. . . . Citizenship in this country necessarily imports at least equality of civil rights among citizens of every race in the same State. It is fundamental in American citizenship that, in respect of such rights, there shall be no discrimination by the State or its officers, or by individuals or corporations exercising public functions or authority, against any citizen because of his race or previous condition of servitude.[146]

Harlan thus related a constitutional vision that would not be actualized for several more decades. He also criticized the majority's cramped reading of congressional power and consequently "anomalous result."[147]

In accommodating slavery prior to the Civil War, Congress had enacted and the Court had upheld laws that operated directly on states and private persons. Fugitive slave legislation, discussed in Chapter 1, was sustained as a legitimate exercise of an implied albeit dubious power. As Harlan put it:

why shall the hand of Congress be tied, so that — under an express power, by appropriate legislation, to enforce a constitutional provision granting citizenship — it may not . . . bring the whole power of this Nation to bear upon States and their officers, and upon such individuals and corporations exercising public functions as assume to abridge, impair, or deny rights confessedly secured by the supreme law of the land?[148]

Finally, Harlan took issue with the Court's perception that the nation's new citizens no longer merited special legal attention.[149] He found the majority's sense of favoritism inapt, insofar as the civil rights legislation at issue protected "citizens of every race and color."[150] To the extent they might experience discrimination, Harlan noted, the law also accounted for them.[151] It would not be for nearly another century, as discussed in Chapter 6, that claims of reverse discrimination would clarify in the Court's mind that equal protection interests can cut in more than one way. For several decades after the *Civil Rights Cases*, however, courts largely refused to take seriously Harlan's admonition that "there cannot be, in this republic, any class of human beings in practical subjection to another class, with power in the latter to dole out to the former just such privileges as they may choose to grant."[152]

The *Civil Rights Cases* decision disclosed an enduring but increasingly convoluted tension in the Fourteenth Amendment's early operation. The majority opinion, like the *Slaughter-House Cases* decision, reflected fidelity to traditional premises and understandings of government power in the federalist system. It expressed discomfort with and resistance to a constitutional assignment of power perceived as the step toward a congressionally crafted "code of municipal law for the regulation of private rights."[153] Such reluctance to allow inroads into traditional state responsibilities and functions, when the context was racially significant, contrasted with the Court's evolution toward doctrine that displaced general state economic regulation. The federal interest reflected by the Fourteenth Amendment thus was defined expansively, but not broadly enough to reckon with racial discrimination and the consequent compromise of civil status and rights.

The first decade of racial jurisprudence pursuant to a revised constitution limited federal interest to discrimination that was indisputably official and gross. The possibility of establishing a Fourteenth Amendment violation would diminish further when, as discussed in the following chapter, official segregation was found reasonable and constitutional. The next seventy years would confirm the pertinence of Harlan's query as to whether "the recent Amendments be splendid baubles, thrown out to delude those who deserved fair and generous treatment at the hands of the Nation."[154]

NOTES

1. Civil Rights Cases, 109 U.S. 3, 25 (1883). The Court also determined that the legislation was not supported by the Fourteenth Amendment. *See infra* notes 116–54 and accompanying text.

2. *Id.* at 25.

3. *See* Hodges v. United States, 203 U.S. 1 (1906).

4. Jones v. Alfred H. Mayer Co., 392 U.S. 409 (1968).

5. *Id.* at 439–41.

6. Griffin v. Breckenridge, 403 U.S. 88 (1971).

7. *Id.* at 103–04.

8. *Id.* at 105–06.

9. *See id.* at 92–95 (citing Collins v. Handyman, 341 U.S. 651, 661 (1951)).

10. *Id.* at 104–06.

11. Runyon v. McCrary, 427 U.S. 160 (1976).

12. *Id.* at 170–71, 179.

13. *Id.* at 170–71.

14. 109 S. Ct. 2363 (1989).

15. *Id.* at 2370–72.

16. *Id.* at 2372–73.

17. Memphis v. Greene, 451 U.S. 100, 128–29 (1981).

18. *Id.* at 126–27.

19. General Building Contractors Association, Inc. v. Pennsylvania, 458 U.S. 375, 391 (1982).

20. 16 Stat. 170, 433 (1870).

21. *See* United States v. Cruikshank, 92 U.S. (2 Otto) 542 (1876); United States v. Reese, 92 U.S. (2 Otto) 214 (1876).

22. Giles v. Harris, 189 U.S. 475, 488 (1903).

23. *Id.*

24. *Id.*

25. *E.g.*, Breedlove v. Suttles, 302 U.S. 277 (1937).

26. Guinn v. United States, 238 U.S. 347 (1915).

27. *See* Nixon v. Herndon, 273 U.S. 536 (1927).

28. *See* Nixon v. Condon, 286 U.S. 73 (1932).

29. *See* Terry v. Adams, 345 U.S. 461 (1953); Smith v. Allwright, 321 U.S. 649 (1944); United States v. Classic, 313 U.S. 299 (1941).

30. Civil Rights Act of 1964, 42 U.S.C. §§ 2000a to 2000b–3 (public accommodations and facilities); §§ 2000d to 2000d–6(d) (public education); §§ 2000e to 2000e–2(j) (employment).

31. 71 Stat. 634.

32. 74 Stat. 86.

33. 42 U.S.C. § 1973 to 1973dd–6.

34. South Carolina v. Katzenbach, 383 U.S. 301 (1966).

35. *Id.* at 326 (quoting McCulloch v. Maryland, 17 U.S. (4 Wheat.) 316, 321 (1819)).

36. Slaughter-House Cases, 83 U.S. (16 Wall.) 36 (1873).

37. *See* C. Fairman, VII History of the Supreme Court of the United States, Reconstruction and Reunion, pt. 2, at 261–62 (1987).

38. Live-Stock Dealers & Butchers Association v. Crescent City Live-Stock Landing & Slaughterhouse Co., 15 Fed. Cas. 649, 652 (C.C.D. La. 1870).

39. *Id.* at 652–53.

40. Slaughter-House Cases, 83 U.S. (16 Wall.) at 71.

41. *Id.* at 72.

42. *Id.* at 73.

43. *Id.* at 74.

44. *Id.*

45. *Id.*

46. *Id.*

47. *Id.*

48. *Id.* at 75.

49. The privileges and immunities clause was relied on to invalidate a state law in Colgate v. Harvey, 296 U.S. 404 (1935). Even that single usage was repudiated, however, in Madden v. Kentucky, 309 U.S. 83 (1940).

50. Cong. Globe, 39th Cong., 1st Sess. (1866) (Rep. Garfield).

51. *Id.* at 1414–15 (Sen. Davis).

52. Slaughter-House Cases, 83 U.S. (16 Wall.) at 76–77; U.S. Const. art. IV, § 2, cl. 1.

53. Slaughter-House Cases, 83 U.S. (16 Wall.) at 75 (quoting Articles of Confederation, art. IV).

54. *Id.* at 76 (quoting Corfield v. Coryell, 6 F. Cas. 546, 551 (1823)) (emphasis in Slaughter-House opinion).

55. *Id.* (*quoting* Corfield v. Coryell, 6 F. Cas. at 551–52).

56. *Id.* at 77.

57. *Id.* at 75.

58. *Id.* at 77.

59. *Id.* at 77–78.

60. *Id.*

61. *Id.* at 80.

62. *Id.* at 79–80.

63. *Id.*

64. *Id.*

65. *Id.* at 81.

66. *Id.*

67. *Id.*

68. C. Fairman, *supra* note 37, at 134.

69. Slaughter-House Cases, 83 U.S. (16 Wall.) at 81–82. As a provision for that race and that emergency, the Court emphasized that "a strong case would be necessary for its application to any other." *Id.*

70. *Id.* at 82.

71. *Id.*

72. *Id.* at 95 (Field, J., dissenting).

73. *Id.* at 95–96 (Field, J., dissenting).

74. *Id.* at 96–97 (Field, J., dissenting).

75. *Id.* at 96 (Field, J., dissenting) (quoting Civil Rights Act of 1866, § 1).

76. *Id.* at 97 (Field, J., dissenting).

77. *Id.* at 77–78 (majority opinion).

78. *Id.* at 116 (Bradley, J., dissenting).

79. *Id.* at 118–19 (Bradley, J., dissenting).

80. *Id.* at 105–06 (Field, J., dissenting); *id.* at 122 (Bradley, J., dissenting).

81. *Id.* (Bradley, J., dissenting).

82. *E.g.,* Lochner v. New York, 198 U.S. 45 (1905).

83. *E.g.,* Zablocki v. Redhail, 434 U.S. 374 (1978); Moore v. City of East Cleveland, 431 U.S. 494 (1977); Roe v. Wade, 410 U.S. 113 (1973); Griswold v. Connecticut, 381 U.S. 479 (1965).

84. *See* Chapter 5.

85. Munn v. Illinois, 94 U.S. (4 Otto) 113 (1877).

86. *Id.* at 134.

87. United States v. Cruikshank, 92 U.S. (2 Otto) 542, 555 (1876).

88. *See supra* note 37 and accompanying text.

89. United States v. Cruikshank, 92 U.S. (2 Otto) at 555.

90. *Id.* at 554.

91. United States v. Harris, 106 U.S. 629 (1883).

92. *Id.* at 632.

93. *Id.* at 639 (quoting United States v. Cruikshank, 92 U.S. (2 Otto) at 555).

94. Strauder v. West Virginia, 100 U.S. (10 Otto) 303 (1879).

95. *See id.* at 304–05.

96. *Id.* at 306.

97. *Id.*

98. *Id.*

99. *Id.* at 307.

100. *Id.*

101. *Id.*

102. *Id.* at 307–08.

103. *Id.* at 308.

104. *See id.* at 310–12.

105. *Id.* at 308.

106. *Ex parte* Virginia, 100 U.S. (10 Otto) 339 (1879).

107. *Id.* at 347.

108. Brown v. Board of Education, 347 U.S. 483, 495 (1954) (discussed in Chapter 5).

109. Virginia v. Rives, 100 U.S. (10 Otto) 313 (1879).

110. *See id.* at 322.

111. *See id.* at 322–23.

112. *Id.* at 321–22.

113. *See id.* at 320–21.

114. *See* Batson v. Kentucky, 476 U.S. 79 (1986) (prosecutor may not use peremptory challenges in racially discriminatory fashion).

115. *Ex parte* Virginia, 100 U.S. (10 Otto) at 345.

116. *See* Civil Rights Cases, 109 U.S. 3 (1883).

117. *Id.* at 9–10.

118. *Id.* at 11.

119. *Id.* at 11–12.

120. *Id.* at 11.

121. *Id.* at 13–14.

122. *Id.* at 11.

123. *See* McCulloch v. Maryland, 17 U.S. (4 Wheat.) 316 (1819).

124. Civil Rights Cases, 109 U.S. at 45 (Harlan, J., dissenting) (emphasis in original).

125. *Id.* at 15 (majority opinion)

126. *Id.* at 17.

127. *Id.* at 20.

128. *Id.* at 21.

129. *Id.* at 24.

130. *Id.* at 25.

131. *Id.*

132. *Id.*

133. *Id.*

134. *Id.* at 36 (Harlan, J., dissenting).

135. *Id.* (Harlan, J., dissenting) (emphasis in original).

136. *Id.* at 39 (Harlan, J., dissenting) (quoting W. Blackstone).

137. *Id.* (Harlan, J., dissenting).

138. *Id.* at 41 (Harlan, J., dissenting).

139. *Id.* (Harlan, J., dissenting).

140. *Id.* (Harlan, J., dissenting).

141. *See* Jackson v. Metropolitan Edison Co., 419 U.S. 345 (1974); Moose Lodge No. 107 v. Irvis, 407 U.S. 163 (1972).

142. *See* United States v. Guest, 383 U.S. 745 (1966).

143. Civil Rights Cases, 109 U.S. at 43 (Harlan, J., dissenting).

144. *Id.* at 46 (Harlan, J., dissenting) (emphasis in original).

145. *Id.* at 47 (Harlan, J., dissenting).

146. *Id.* at 48 (Harlan, J., dissenting).

147. *Id.* at 53 (Harlan, J., dissenting).

148. *Id.* (Harlan, J., dissenting).

149. *Id.* at 61 (Harlan, J., dissenting).

150. *Id.* (Harlan, J., dissenting).

151. *Id.* at 62 (Harlan, J., dissenting).

152. *Id.* (Harlan, J., dissenting).

153. *Id.* at 11 (majority opinion).

154. *Id.* at 48 (Harlan, J., dissenting).

Chapter 4

Separate But Equal

Segregation by law has been a defining societal feature for the better half of the Fourteenth Amendment's existence. Official segregation of persons on the basis of race represented the formalization and institutionalization of social preferences that the Supreme Court had passed off in the *Civil Rights Cases* as "[m]ere discriminations."[1] State-mandated segregation, unlike the private action previously adjudicated, directly implicated government in the racial classification process. The *Strauder* Court, as discussed in Chapter 3, had indicated discriminations implying inferiority would merit constitutional attention. A few years later, in the *Civil Rights Cases*, the Court found private racial distinctions insignificant and consistent with societal norms. As jurisprudence evolved into the twentieth century, it became evident that the radiations of the *Civil Rights Cases* would be more predictive of segregation's constitutionality than would the intimations of *Strauder*.

Official segregation, as discussed in Chapter 1, was not an invention of the South. Prior to *Scott v. Sandford*, racial segregation of Boston public schools had been upheld.[2] Several years after the *Scott* decision, and consistent with the North's selective repudiation of Taney's opinion, the Ohio legislature also provided for racially separate schooling.[3] Although a northern creation, segregation was well suited to the needs of the South after the eradication of slavery and the displacement of the Black Codes. Florida enacted the first Jim Crow law in 1887, requiring racial separation in public transportation. By the end of the century, official segregation had become comprehensively established in and a defining feature of the South.

In *Plessy v. Ferguson*, the Supreme Court considered the constitutionality of state-enforced segregation.[4] The case presented a challenge to a Louisiana law, enacted in 1890, requiring racially separate rail cars. Specifically, the statute provided

that all railway companies carrying passengers in their coaches in this state shall provide equal but separate accommodations for the white and colored races, by providing two or more passenger coaches for each passenger train, or by dividing the passenger coaches by a partition so as to secure separate accommodations. . . .[5]

The petitioner in the case was described as a person of "seven eighths Caucasian and one eighth African blood . . . [and in whom] the mixture of colored blood was not discernible."[6]

The Court in *Plessy* rejected contentions that the law violated the Thirteenth and Fourteenth Amendments. Disclosing what a dead letter the Thirteenth Amendment had become, it observed that the provision's inaptness was "too clear for argument."[7] The Court depicted the amendment as concerned with involuntary servitude, only in the limited sense of "a state of bondage; the ownership of mankind as a chattel, or at least the control of the labor and services of one man for the benefit of another, and the absence of a legal right to the disposal of his own person, property, and services."[8] Having limited the Thirteenth Amendment's potential to reckon with the aftereffects of slavery, the Court concluded that

laws implying merely a legal distinction between the white and colored races— a distinction which is founded in the color of the two races, and which must always exist so long as white men are distinguished from the other races by color—has no tendency to destroy the legal equality of the two races, or reestablish a state of involuntary servitude.[9]

The Court's reading of the Thirteenth Amendment validated original concerns that its actual or potential reach was too limited. In the event any doubt remained, the *Plessy* decision confirmed that the amendment extended only to slavery and its most proximate incidents.

Turning to the Fourteenth Amendment, the Court acknowledged a purpose "to enforce the absolute equality of the two races before the law."[10] It maintained, however, that the amendment did not "intend to abolish distinctions based upon color, or to enforce social, as distinguished from political equality, or a commingling of the two races upon terms unsatisfactory to either."[11] The *Strauder* Court had suggested that official classifications implying inferiority were precluded by the Fourteenth Amendment.[12] With respect to laws requiring racial separation in public venues, the *Plessy* Court found that they did not connote inferiority and were "generally, if not universally, recognized as within the competency of the state legislature in the exercise of their police power."[13] As evidence of settled practice, the Court referred to officially sanctioned school segregation in the North and congressionally mandated racial separation in District of Columbia schools.[14]

The constitutionality of official segregation hinged for the Court on whether the state had exercised its police power reasonably, in good faith, and for the public good, rather than "for the annoyance or oppression of a particular class."[15] The majority, however, was unable to discern or unwilling to acknowledge that racial separation by law failed to satisfy those demands. Although finding the case reducible to whether the law was "a reasonable regulation," it determined that "with respect to this, there must necessarily be a large discretion on the part of the legislature."[16] Confirming how deferential its standard of review was, the Court noted that the state was "at liberty to act with reference to the established usages, customs, and traditions of the people, and with a view to the promotion of their comfort, and the preservation of the public peace and good order."[17] It thus accommodated and effectively validated the culture, including its racist conventions and impulses, of official segregation.

Responsive to the possibility that its decision was at odds with *Strauder*, the Court characterized as fallacious "the assumption that the enforced separation of the races stamps the colored race with a badge of inferiority."[18] Any such perception, it suggested, was "not by reason of anything found in the act, but solely because the colored race chooses to put that construction on it."[19] Further militating against displacement of state law was the Court's articulated sense that social prejudices were not to be defeated by legislation; nor would equal rights be secured "by an enforced commingling of the two races."[20] In closing, the Court emphasized what it considered to be the imprudence of tampering with what it previously had characterized as distinctions "in the nature of things."[21] It thus stressed that

legislation is powerless to eradicate social instincts or to abolish distinctions based upon physical differences, and the attempt to do so can only result in accentuating the difficulties of the present situation. If the civil and political rights of both races are equal, one cannot be inferior to the other civilly or politically. If one race is inferior to the other socially, the Constitution of the United States cannot put them on the same plane.[22]

Official segregation had been objected to, albeit unsuccessfully, on the grounds it was a methodology of race-dependent degradation, harassment, and humiliation. The next several decades would demonstrate that segregation responded to and facilitated precisely the evils disregarded or discounted in *Plessy*. In an essentially legalistic exercise, the Court nonetheless satisfied itself with the appearance of neat racial symmetry and blamed segregation's victims for any misunderstanding of the law. As critics have noted, it was the Court that failed to understand the meaning of segregation and avoided its constitutional significance. Official segregation was a cornerstone of white supremacy, and the notion that "blacks were inherently inferior was a conviction being stridently trumpeted by white supremacists from the press, the pulpit, and the platform, as well as from the legislative halls of the South."[23] Racial separation as a function of state decree communicated an official sense of unfitness for full civil status that effectively mocked the terms of *Strauder*.

The true nature and significance of official segregation were sensed and depicted by Justice Harlan, who warned in his dissent that the majority's decision eventually would prove "as pernicious as the decision made . . . in the *Dred Scott Case*."[24] For him, the law in question was at odds "not only with that equality of rights which pertains to citizenship, national and state, but with the personal liberty enjoyed by every one within the United States."[25] Harlan pierced segregation's veil of symmetry by stating the obvious. As he put it, "every one knows . . . its origin and the purpose was not so much to exclude white persons from railroad cars occupied by blacks, as to exclude colored people from coaches occupied or assigned to white persons."[26] From Harlan's perspective, and despite the majority's command that classifications must not be unreasonable, official segregation once established had no logical ending point. If the state could separate the races on rail coaches, he suggested, it could assign them to opposite sides of the street and distinguish also between "native and naturalized citizens . . . or . . . Protestants and Roman Catholics."[27]

Although a former slave owner, Harlan had reached the conclusion that "the destinies of the two races, in this country, are indissolubly linked together, and the interests of both require that the common government of all shall not permit the seeds of race hate to be planted under the sanction of law."[28] Challenging the majority's sense that official segregation promoted public harmony and order, he asserted that racial hatred and distrust were compounded by state laws premised on the notion "that colored citizens are so inferior and degraded that they cannot be allowed to sit in public coaches occupied by white citizens."[29] Harlan dismissed the notion that racial separation was a reasonable exercise of state police power, and asserted "the sure guarantee of the peace and security of each race is the clear, distinct unconditional recognition . . . of every right that inheres in civil freedom, and of the equality before the law of all citizens . . . without regard to race."[30]

Harlan's dissent effectively portrayed official segregation as a mechanism for protecting a dominant class and as a scheme that stigmatized blacks and fostered stereotypes. His own racial chauvinism nonetheless manifested itself in the observation that whites were "the dominant race in this country . . . in prestige, in achievements, in education, in wealth, and in power."[31] Furthermore, he "doubt[ed] not, it will continue to be for all time, if it remains true to its great heritage and holds forth to the principles of constitutional liberty."[32] Still, Harlan maintained that under the Constitution, "there is in this county no superior, dominant, ruling class of citizens . . . [and] no caste."[33] Rather, he emphasized, "our Constitution is color-blind."[34]

The *Plessy* Court, having denied that official segregation operated as a stamp of inferiority, fixed its imprimatur on legally mandated racial separation. The majority had depicted the Louisiana law somewhat euphemistically as "equal but separate." The next several decades would demonstrate that "separate but equal" was a more apt description and even then an exaggeration of reality. In *Plessy* itself, the Court deferred to formalized racial separation. What remained to be seen was whether it would insist on meaningful implementation of the equalization requirement. Within a few years, it became evident that, doctrinal appearances aside, official segregation was not subject to significant qualification.

The first test of the *Plessy* premise, in *Cumming v. Board of Education*, disclosed how thoroughly jurisprudence had revamped the Fourteenth Amendment into an instrumentality of the dominant culture.[35] In *Cumming*, the Court permitted a school board to close a black high school, even though it provided secondary education to whites.[36] Citing economic reasons, the board had shut the black school but continued to maintain a high school for white girls and helped fund a private high school for white boys.[37] From the board's perspective, closing the school may have seemed a sensible response to fiscal pressures and a societal context that did not afford black graduates meaningful opportunity to use their education. The decision, however, translated into an instance of inequality so profound as to constitute total deprivation.

Despite his dissent in *Plessy*, Harlan wrote for a unanimous Court and determined that allocation of tax monies was not governed by the Constitution and, in any event, "it is impracticable to distribute taxes evenly."[38] Instead of directing itself to the question of equality, the Court employed a balance-of-harm analysis favoring the school board. Officials had argued and Harlan agreed that if they were required to "maintain a separate school for the sixty children who wished to have a high school education," primary education would have to be denied to 300 black children.[39] The manifest inequality essentially was ignored. The holding instead was referenced to general utilitarian principles of being "in the interest of the greater number of colored children."[40]

The *Cumming* decision revealed the transparency of the separate but equal doctrine. It also fulfilled Harlan's prophecy, expressed in *Plessy*, that racial classifications eventually would be used to mete out and regulate rights and benefits.[41] The *Plessy* Court had conditioned separate on the requirement of equal. Even if the concepts were mutually exclusive, the qualifying principle still was constitutionally significant. Because the Court did not consider alternatives to closure, including a racially mixed school if no other options were practical, it was evident that standards were attuned primarily, and in *Cumming* exclusively, to the interest of segregation. The effective message was that doctrine would be more accommodating to separation than demanding of equality.

During the first decade of the twentieth century, the Court upheld official segregation in private colleges and public transportation. In *Berea College v. Kentucky*, it upheld a state law prohibiting corporations and persons from operating racially integrated schools.[42] Justice Harlan criticized the decision as evasive and hypocritical. Specifically, he considered "[t]he right to impart instruction" a protected liberty interest under the Fourteenth Amendment and meriting the same sentience the Court by then was affording general notions of economic freedom.[43] The *Berea College* decision illuminated the evolving duality of Fourteenth Amendment standards and how official management of race relations could be pervasive and intrusive without constitutional affront.

In *McCabe v. Atchison, Topeka & Santa Fe Railway Co.*, the Court again upheld separate train accommodations.[44] The *McCabe* case differed from *Plessy* to the extent it was necessary to consider whether dedicated eating and sleeping accommodations had to be provided in the absence of black patronage. The Court held that, regardless of demand or usage considerations, separate sleeping and dining cars had to be furnished.[45] The effect of its determination was diluted by the further conclusion that injunctive relief could not be ordered because the complainants themselves had never traveled on the railroad or specifically been denied service.[46] While an underused rail car may have been eloquent testimony of how thoroughly official racism denied opportunities to exercise basic rights secured by the Fourteenth Amendment, the *McCabe* decision merely polished the doctrinal veneer of equality.

During the first few decades of official segregation, the Court identified one instance in which state law was unreasonable and thus unconstitutional. In *Buchanan v. Warley*, it invalidated a municipal ordinance "requiring, as far as practicable, the uses of separate blocks for residences, places of abode and places of assembly by white and colored people respectively."[47] Although cast as a regulation to maintain public peace and promote the general welfare, the Court found it a "direct violation of the fundamental law enacted in the 14th Amendment of the Constitution preventing state interference with property rights except by due process of law."[48] Unlike in the *Berea College* case, in which blacks were not denied an education, the Court apprehended in *Buchanan* the deprivation of a fundamental right.

The *Buchanan* decision presented a significant irony and disclosed how substantially the Fourteenth Amendment had been transformed since its origin. Seminal jurisprudence had emphasized the amendment's concern with affording "a race recently emancipated, a race that through many generations had been held in slavery, all the civil rights that the superior race enjoy."[49] Soon after the *Plessy* decision, the Court developed and amplified the Fourteenth Amendment's meaning in a context entirely unrelated to race. Resultant court decisions enunciated principles of general economic liberty in expansive terms, as doctrine pertaining to the amendment's central concern cramped and contracted.

In *Allgeyer v. Louisiana*, one year after the *Plessy* decision, the Court advanced substantive due process theory to defeat a state law prohibiting the operation of insurance policies not issued in compliance with legislative requirements.[50] Construing the Fourteenth Amendment as a source of substantive rights and liberties, the Court found that due process guaranteed that a person may use "all his faculties ... [and was] free to use them in all lawful ways."[51] The *Allgeyer* decision extended previously qualified Fourteenth Amendment concepts, jurisprudentially introduced in the *Slaughter-House* dissents, to circumstances unrelated to race. It prefaced the *Lochner* era of substantive due process review which, although now criticized as an exercise in rampant activism,[52] nonetheless offered a convoluted way of finding some segregation unreasonable. The Court's decision in *Buchanan* reflected a sense of constitutional offense premised less on the law's racial significance than on its invasion of general contractual liberty. Such animation of the due process guarantee in substantive fashion, driven by rights designated by the judiciary rather than the Constitution itself, was the essence of Lochnerism.

In *Lochner v. New York* itself,[53] the Court elevated liberty of contract to the status of a fundamental right and for three decades persistently invoked it to thwart economic and social welfare legislation. The episode is widely regarded as a primary example of unrestrained subjectivism and judicial overreaching. The legacy of substantive due process analysis is so profoundly negative that, half a century after its repudiation, contemporary efforts to breathe life into the Fourteenth Amendment almost invariably engender allegations of Lochnerism.[54] Close attention to general economic liberty was especially dubious insofar as doctrine simultaneously retreated from the Fourteenth Amendment's original imperatives. The Supreme Court itself has repudiated Lochnerism on the grounds that the legitimacy of judicial review is contingent upon precepts clearly tied to constitutional text or design.[55] Even assuming the misdirected nature of Fourteenth Amendment analysis, invalidation of officially mandated segregation in *Buchanan* was connected albeit inartfully to the amendment's original but qualified concern with opportunity for material self-development. The opinion relied upon principles of embellishment and convenience to reach the same result that would have been dictated by attention to obvious design. Such analytical circuity thus offered a paradoxical example of how distorted doctrine had become.

As noted in Chapter 2, contractual liberty initially was regarded as an essential incident of citizenship. Considerations of economic freedom which influenced original understanding of civil rights, however, were consumed by more expansive and nonspecific notions of marketplace liberty. As the Supreme Court moved into the twentieth century, its composition was influenced significantly by Presidents Harrison, Cleveland and Taft, who were dedicated to advancing laissez-faire principles and used the judicial appointment process to facilitate broad notions of economic freedom.[56] Consistent with such inspiration, the Court tended vigorously to marketplace freedom[57] and interested itself in racial discrimination only when it intersected that liberty.

Contemporary criticism of Lochnerism focused less on its deviation from racially significant concerns than upon its function in achieving convenient results and impairing the operation of competing and democratically preferred philosophies of governance.[58] The *Lochner* decision itself, which found regulation of working hours at odds with liberty of contract,[59] identified no real nexus to the Fourteenth Amendment's inspiring concerns. In asserting that it would not "substitut[e] the judgment of the Court for that of the legislature,"[60] the Court suggested a standard of review akin to the deferential criteria of *Plessy*. The transparency of its claim and constitutional double standard were revealed, however, by the further pronouncement that "[w]e do not believe in the soundness of the views which uphold this law."[61]

What is especially striking about the Fourteenth Amendment's redirection is how vigorously the new agenda was pursued and how unfinished original business remained. If given a fraction of the jurisprudential consideration afforded economic liberty interests, the separate but equal doctrine at least might have accounted for equalization as well as separation. Lochnerism itself expired in the late 1930s, after political challenges to the Court's authority[62] and as a consequence of personnel changes.[63] The Court eventually announced that "[w]hether the legislature takes for its textbook Adam Smith, Herbert Spenser, Lord

Keynes or some other is no concern of ours."[64] Official segregation would survive, however, for nearly two more decades.

One measure of the difference between separate but equal in theory and in practice was the gross disparity in funding of black and white public schools. South Carolina in 1915, for example, spent ten times more money per white student than per black student.[65] Even by 1954, when southern states were pumping funds into black schools in an effort to rescue the separate but equal doctrine, the average expenditures were $165 per white student and $115 per black student.[66] Such discrepancies confirmed the acuity of Harlan's foresight in *Plessy* that endorsement of official segregation

will not only stimulate aggressions, more or less brutal and irritating, upon the admitted rights of colored citizens, but will encourage the belief that is possible, by means of state enactments, to defeat the beneficent purposes which the people of the United States had in view when they adopted the recent amendments of the Constitution, by one of which the blacks of this country were made citizens of the United States and of the states in which they respectively reside and whose privileges and immunities, as citizens, the states are forbidden to abridge.[67]

Official segregation and the jurisprudentially formulated separate but equal doctrine proved mutually reinforcing for more than half a century. The Supreme Court's deference to state legislative judgment contrasted with its standards of review that cramped congressional power to enforce the Fourteenth Amendment. Pertinent constitutional principle thus seemed largely consonant with antebellum understanding of federal and state interests. The Court's inclination to avoid confronting race-dependent practices and policies was acutely evidenced in the Fifteenth Amendment context, when officials in an Alabama community refused to register black voters.[68] Despite obvious state action at odds with the Fifteenth Amendment's indisputable mandate, the Court refused to intervene. In *Giles v. Harris*, it explained its inaction on the grounds that an injunction would be ignored by the white majority and its elected agents and so would be "pointless."[69] As Justice Holmes observed:

the court has little practical power to deal with the people of the State in a body. The bill imports that the great mass of the white population intends to keep the blacks from voting. To meet such an intent something more than ordering the plaintiff's name to be inscribed upon the [voting] lists ... will be needed.[70]

The Court advised that "relief from a great political wrong, if done, or alleged by the people of a state and the state itself, must be given them by the legislature and the political department of the United States."[71] Such a possibility was remote to say the least, because the state was the cause of deprivation rather than a source of amelioration. Congress within the preceding decade, moreover, had repealed voting rights legislation and blacks generally were unrepresented in a political process entirely unresponsive to their interests.

Although decided on Fifteenth Amendment grounds, the *Giles* case tested the Court's willingness to confront discrimination. The result was discouraging not only for specific equality interests associated with the Fifteenth Amendment but general equality concerns of the Fourteenth Amendment. The possibility of equal protection as a significant doctrinal source was further diminished by Justice Holmes' characterization of it as "the last resort of constitutional arguments."[72] Further evidencing the settled nature of segregation doctrine were how seldom it was challenged and the way it was contested. In *Gong Lum v. Rice*, a student of Chinese descent in Mississippi argued not that official segregation was wrong but that she was denied equal protection in being classified as "colored."[73] The case effectively illustrated how racial separation was a unique interest of whites. The Court found "that the question is [not] any different, or that any different result can be reached, assuming the cases to be rightly decided, where the issue is between white peoples and the peoples of the yellow race."[74]

Despite the entrenched status of official segregation, as a result of legislative enactment and judicial accommodation or endorsement, a legal strategy to defeat it eventually materialized. In the 1930s, Thurgood Marshall commenced the National Association for the Advancement of Colored People's two-decade long challenge of the separate but equal doctrine. The attack, under the litigative direction of Thurgood Marshall, targeted both the operation and the underlying premises of the *Plessy* principle. Marshall's aim was to contest segregation initially on grounds that equalization requirements were being slighted or ignored and ultimately on the basis that separate and equal were mutually inconsistent. Educating the courts with respect to that fundamental inconsonance would require nearly two decades. Given the embedded nature of policy and judicial doctrine, Marshall favored "an attack against the segregation system by law suits seeking absolute and complete equalization of curricula, faculty and physical equipment in white and black schools."[75] The tactical focus reflected a sense "that the extreme cost of maintaining two equal systems would eventually destroy segregation."[76]

The first opportunity to test the strategy before the Supreme Court was presented by *Missouri ex rel. Gaines v. Canada*.[77] The case arose when the state of Missouri denied a black applicant admission to its only public law school.[78] Because the state did not provide a separate institution for black students, it offered to fund a legal education elsewhere.[79] In spite of the offer to pay out-of-state tuition, the Court found a default of the Fourteenth Amendment obligation to maintain "the equality of legal rights to the enjoyment of the privilege which the state has set up."[80] The constitutional duty, as the Court put it, could not "be cast by one state upon another, and no state can be excused from performance by what another state may do."[81] Having considered whether the state had provided legal privileges for whites and denied them to blacks, the Court identified a discrimination that "if not relieved . . . would [be] a denial of equal protection."[82] Absent a state law school for black students, it found that the "petitioner was entitled to be admitted to the law school of the state university."[83]

The *Gaines* case represented the first successful challenge, at least in federal court,[84] to official segregation's underpinnings. It reflected a litigative strategy predicated on the assumption that while the separate but equal doctrine would not be displaced immediately, it would wither from persistent demonstration of its illogic. Reality at the time was that the *Plessy* principle was the norm, *Gaines* was the exception, and significant time and energy would have to be invested in showing that official segregation imprinted on its victims "a badge of inferiority."[85] By focusing on graduate and professional education, the NAACP targeted an accurately perceived point of vulnerability in the system of official segregation. Because the venues and numbers of persons affected were relatively small, deviations from the general rule of segregation seemed more achievable than if primary or secondary educational policy was challenged. As Marshall observed:

the university level was the best place to begin a campaign that had as its ultimate objective the total elimination of segregation in public institutions in the United States. In the first place, at the university level no provision for negro education was a rule rather than the exception. Then, too, the difficulties incident to providing equal educational opportunities even within the concept of the "separate but equal" doctrine were insurmountable. To provide separate medical schools, law schools, engineering schools, and graduate schools with all the variety of offerings available at most state universities would be an almost financial impossibility.[86]

The strategy in sum was that if segregation was pushed to the test of satisfying equal as well as separate, the policy eventually would implode as a result of its own weight.

Progress toward that ultimate objective was delayed by judicial caution and insensitivity to the realities of discrimination and by the determination of states to accept the challenge of equalization. In *Sipuel v. Board of Regents*, the Court considered the constitutional claim of a black student denied admission to the University of Oklahoma Law School and afforded no in-state opportunity for legal education.[87] The case essentially replayed the circumstances of *Gaines*. Unlike in the earlier litigation, however, the NAACP sought to demonstrate that a racially separate legal education was inherently unequal.[88] Marshall thus argued that

"segregation in public education helps to preserve a caste system which is based upon race and color. It is designed and intended to perpetuate the slave tradition. . . . 'Separate' and 'equal' can not be used conjunctively in a situation of this kind; there can be no separate equality."[89]

The argument in *Sipuel* previewed the premise that the Court eventually would subscribe to in 1954.[90] In *Sipuel* itself, however, the Court left the separate but equal doctrine intact. Because Oklahoma had neglected the equalization component, the Court demanded that it either provide a separate law school or allow blacks to enroll at the state university.[91]

The state's response was to cordon off a section of the state capitol building and characterize it as a law school.[92] As a manifest avoidance of meaningful equality, this act prompted another constitutional challenge. The Court in *Fisher v. Hurst* declined the invitation to reconsider the separate but equal doctrine's validity.[93] In refusing to find the separate arrangements constitutionally deficient, the Court also indicated a reluctance to manage the interests of equality. Inroads into the separate but equal doctrine thus did not advance beyond the relatively limited accomplishment of *Gaines*. From the NAACP's perspective, the result even suggested regression. If a state was obligated to provide a separate institution, but not to invest significant resources in it, a black student actually might be better off accepting a state's offer to fund his or her education elsewhere. The *Gaines* decision had indicated that the separate but equal principle at least had to live up to its stated premise. The *Sipuel* and *Fisher* rulings appeared consonant, however, with the doctrine's less demanding tradition.

Given the result in *Sipuel*, the NAACP refocused on the deficiencies of separate graduate education and attempted to enhance the Court's sensitivity to those realities. In *Sweatt v. Painter*[94] and *McLaurin v. Oklahoma State Regents for Higher Education*,[95] expert testimony was presented to the effect that segregated education would remain unequal even if tangible differences were eliminated. Given the nature of the challenge to established law and the promise of states to equalize within the context of segregation, the constitutional issue inevitably was reducing itself to the separate but equal doctrine's general fitness. The *Sweatt* and *McLaurin* cases thus represented the most significant challenge yet of the *Plessy* principle.

The *Sweatt* case concerned the University of Texas' refusal to admit a black law student.[96] Unlike the circumstances in *Gaines* and *Sipuel*, the school's decision was based on the availability of a black institution.[97] Despite the separate opportunity and the state's assurance that it promptly would equalize any deficiencies in physical facilities, the Court found the school unequal for constitutional purposes.[98] By directing the university to admit the petitioner,[99] it effectively integrated the school.

The Court's reasoning indicated that, at least in the context of graduate or professional education, it considered separate inimical to equal. The Court noted that the white school had a stronger faculty, a better library, a larger student body, and more extensive student activities.[100] Its analysis did not terminate, however, with identification of physical or readily palpable differences. Rather, the Court identified intangible factors, such as faculty reputation, alumni position and influence, institutional traditions and prestige, and linkage to professional opportunities,[101] which were "incapable of objective measurement."[102]

Consideration of factors disproving the validity of separate but equal prompted like results in the *McLaurin* decision. The case arose when a state university admitted a black applicant to an all-white graduate program, pursuant to court order, but segregated him within the institution itself. Initially, the student was required to attend classes in a side room, study at a desk on the library's upper floor, and use a designated section of the cafeteria at a special time.[103] The rules were altered in the course of litigation so that he could sit in the classroom, albeit in a special row; use the main floor of the library; and eat at regular hours, although at a special table.[104] The Court concluded that the racially determined arrangements impaired the "ability to study, to engage in discussions, and exchange views with other students, and in general, to learn [one's] profession."[105] To the extent it impeded the "pursuit of effective graduate instruction," such internal segregation was found constitutionally impermissible.[106]

The *Sweatt* and *McLaurin* decisions represented significant movement toward general doctrinal upheaval. In *McLaurin*, the Court considered but was unimpressed by arguments that, even without state-mandated restrictions, racial separation would persist. Of particular significance to future rulings, it distinguished between official proscription of commingling and refusal to associate as a function of personal preference.[107] The Court in both decisions emphasized intangible factors that could never be equalized. Although the separate but equal doctrine's broad operation was not reassessed or invalidated, the Court's analysis prefaced its finding a few years later that such "considerations apply with added force to children in grade and high schools."[108] The *Sweatt* and *McLaurin* decisions had immediately significant consequences but were doubly profound insofar as they previewed the impending demise of official segregation in *Brown v. Board of Education*.[109]

Wholesale reformulation of equal protection doctrine had to await the transformation of the Vinson Court into the Warren Court. Although having animated the separate but equal doctrine so that equalization interests were no longer entirely dismissed, the Vinson Court had evidenced its reluctance to jettison the *Plessy* principle altogether. The appointment of Earl Warren as chief justice altered institutional dynamics and resulted in leadership more receptive to the possibility of doctrinal redesign. A challenge to segregated primary and secondary education required not exception from but vitiation of the general rule. As Marshall recognized, elementary and high schools were distinguishable from graduate and professional "specialized institutions with national or even statewide reputations."[110]

Further complicating a challenge to segregated education was the reality that Fourteenth Amendment history seemed to support the established order. An examination of the record reveals that the framers did not contemplate the prospect of racially mixed education.[111] Precisely the opposite intent was suggested insofar as District of Columbia schools were segregated by the same Congress that adopted the Fourteenth Amendment. What history denied eventually would be reclaimed (1) by social science data indicating that official segregation stigmatized black students and denied them equality of educational opportunity, and (2) by a sense that public schooling was more crucial to Fourteenth Amendment interests in 1954 than in 1868.[112]

The Court's eventual repudiation of official segregation, although largely a responsive to the NAACP's challenge, was attributable also to a general evolution of equal protection theory. In the late 1920s, the Court had dismissed the equal protection guarantee as the tool of a desperate litigant.[113] At the same time, it was vitalizing the due process guarantee in substantive terms that created a panoply of basic liberties unspecified by the Constitution. In contrast to its uncharitable readings of equal protection, the Court at the apex of Lochnerism identified fundamental rights and freedom in terms that included not only

freedom from bodily restraint, but the right of the individual to contract, to engage in any of the common occupations of life, to acquire useful knowledge, to marry, to establish a home and bring up children, to worship God according to the dictates of his own conscience, and generally to enjoy those privileges long recognized . . . as essential to the orderly pursuit of happiness by free men.[114]

In closing out the *Lochner* era in 1937, the Court announced a major change in Fourteenth Amendment thinking. In *West Coast Hotel v. Parrish*, it depicted substantive due process analysis as a deviation "from the true application of the principles governing the regulation by the State of the relation of employer and employed."[115] The next year, in *United States v. Carolene Products Co.*, the Court advanced a revised, albeit preliminary, view of future Fourteenth Amendment analysis.[116] Although allowing that "the existence of facts supporting . . . legislative judgment are to be presumed, for regulation affecting ordinary commercial transactions,"[117] it suggested that special circumstances might justify stricter review. The Court specifically noted that more rigorous examination may be apt when legislation implicates a specific constitutional prohibition "such as those of the first ten amendments."[118] For equal protection purposes, the Court found it unnecessary to inquire "whether prejudice against discrete and insular minorities may be a special condition, which tends seriously to curtail the operation of those political processes ordinarily to be relied upon to protect minorities, and which may call for a correspondingly more searching judicial inquiry."[119]

The *Carolene Products* decision, if not actually setting a new equal protection standard when racial discrimination was at issue, at least ventured the possibility that the Fourteenth Amendment might be animated in terms more responsive to its original purpose. The reality of a new analytical model was evidenced when the Court reviewed an equal protection challenge to the relocation of Japanese Americans during World War II.[120] For reasons of national security, President Roosevelt had authorized their detention in remote camps.[121] In examining the plan, the Court introduced a standard to the effect

that all legal restrictions which curtail the civil rights of a single racial group are immediately suspect. That is not to say that all such restrictions are unconstitutional. It is to say that courts must subject them to the most rigid scrutiny. Pressing public necessity may sometimes justify the existence of such restrictions; racial antagonism never can.[122]

The notion that racial classifications were suspect and thus must be strictly scrutinized by the courts, although not disruptive of the wartime relocation scheme, eventually would prove critical to dismantling the nation's system of official discrimination.

Equal protection until the middle of the twentieth century was reviewed by the courts on the basis of reasonableness standards,[123] which largely translated as judicial deference to legislative judgment. Strict scrutiny, as conceived in *Korematsu v. United States*, provided analytical weaponry for identifying the "racial antagonism" underlying official segregation. Before such rigorous review eventuated, the separate but equal doctrine survived pursuant to outward appearances of symmetrical application. The appearance of parallelism was perhaps best projected by the Supreme Court's allowance of state prohibitions against interracial intimacy or marriage. The Court in 1875 had upheld a state law that enhanced the penalties for fornication if the offenders were of different races and prohibited miscegenation altogether. Reviewing the provision in *Pace v. Alabama*, the Court found no constitutionally significant discrimination because the law applied equally to both races.[124] Not until 1967 did it fully repudiate the notion that equal application of the law was not necessarily synonymous with equal protection of the law. In *Loving v. Virginia*, the Court recognized that antimiscegenation laws were an extension of racist ideology and impaired the freedom to marry.[125]

Arrival at that point of understanding represented a significant passage from the notion that official racial classifications were reasonable and could be considered harmful only if misunderstood. Erosion of the separate but equal doctrine in response to the NAACP's challenge to official segregation suggested that the principle was living on borrowed time. General reconstruction of Fourteenth Amendment standards in the post-*Lochner* era afforded analytical methodology for closely examining the nature, premises, and effects of segregation. When leadership of the Court changed in 1953, circumstances had ripened for what has been described as the "Second American Revolution."[126]

NOTES

1. Civil Rights Cases, 109 U.S. 3, 25 (1883).
2. Roberts v. City of Boston, 59 Mass. (5 Cush.) 198 (1850).
3. State v. McCann, 21 Ohio St. 198 (1872).
4. Plessy v. Ferguson, 163 U.S. 537, 540 (1896).
5. *Id.* at 540–41 (*quoting* Louisiana statute).
6. *Id.* at 541.
7. *Id.* at 542.
8. *Id.*
9. *Id.* at 543.
10. *Id.* at 544.
11. *Id.*
12. Strauder v. West Virginia, 100 U.S. (10 Otto) 303, 308 (1880).
13. Plessy v. Ferguson, 163 U.S. at 544.
14. *See id.* at 544–45.
15. *Id.* at 550.
16. *Id.*
17. *Id.*
18. *Id.* at 551.
19. *Id.*
20. *Id.*
21. *Id.* at 544.
22. *Id.* at 551–52.
23. Levy, *Plessy v. Ferguson*, in Civil Rights and Equality 174 (K. Karst ed. 1989).
24. Plessy v. Ferguson, 163 U.S. at 559 (Harlan, J. dissenting).
25. *Id.* at 555 (Harlan, J., dissenting).
26. *Id.* at 557 (Harlan, J., dissenting).
27. *Id.* at 558 (Harlan, J., dissenting).
28. *Id.* at 560 (Harlan, J., dissenting).
29. *Id.* (Harlan, J., dissenting).

30. *Id.* (Harlan, J., dissenting).

31. *Id.* at 559 (Harlan, J., dissenting).

32. *Id.* (Harlan, J., dissenting).

33. *Id.* (Harlan, J., dissenting).

34. *Id.* (Harlan, J., dissenting).

35. Cumming v. Board of Education, 175 U.S. 528 (1899).

36. *Id.* at 544–45.

37. *Id.* at 530–33.

38. *Id.* at 542.

39. *Id.* at 544.

40. *Id.*

41. *See* Plessy v. Ferguson, 163 U.S. at 562–63 (Harlan, J., dissenting).

42. Berea College v. Kentucky, 211 U.S. 45, 57–58 (1908).

43. *Id.* at 67–68 (Harlan, J., dissenting). The jurisprudentially enhanced breadth of the Fourteenth Amendment, at least when race was not concerned, is discussed *infra* at notes 50–64 and accompanying text.

44. McCabe v. Atchison, Topeka & Santa Fe Railway Co., 235 U.S. 151, 163–64 (1908).

45. *Id.* at 161–62.

46. *Id.* at 161–63.

47. Buchanan v. Warley, 245 U.S. 60, 70 (1917).

48. *Id.* at 82.

49. Strauder v. West Virginia, 100 U.S. (10 Otto) at 306.

50. Allgeyer v. Louisiana, 165 U.S. 575, 592–93 (1897).

51. *Id.* at 589.

52. For a general discussion of the *Lochner* era of substantive due process review and criticisms of it, see L. Tribe, American Constitutional Law 567–86, 769–72 (2d ed. 1988).

53. 198 U.S. 45 (1905).

54. *See, e.g.,* Zablocki v. Redhail, 434 U.S. 374, 407 (1978) (Rehnquist, J., dissenting) (criticizing recognition of fundamental right to marry); Vlandis v. Kline, 412 U.S. 441, 467–68 (1973) (Rehnquist, J., dissenting) (criticizing recognition of fundamental right to travel); Griswold v. Connecticut, 381 U.S. 479, 514–15 (1965) (Black, J., dissenting) (criticizing recognition of fundamental right of privacy). Justice Brennan noted that the lesson of Lochnerism for the Court was that it could "actively intrude into...economic and policy matters only if ...prepared to bear enormous institutional and social costs." United States Trust Co. v. New Jersey, 431 U.S. 1, 62 (1978) (Brennan, J., dissenting).

55. *See, e.g.,* Bowers v. Hardwick, 478 U.S. 186, 194 (1986).

56. *See* A. Mason, William Howard Taft—Chief Justice 157–58 (1964).

57. *See id.*

58. Lochner v. New York, 198 U.S. at 74–76 (Holmes, J., dissenting).

59. *Id.* at 53.

60. *Id.* at 56–57.

61. *Id.* at 61.

62. For a discussion of President Roosevelt's Court-packing plan, *see* H. Abraham, Justices and Presidents 292–93 (1974).

63. *See id.*

64. Ferguson v. Skrupa, 372 U.S. 726, 731–32 (1963).

65. *See* A. Lewis, Portrait of a Decade: The Second American Revolution 29 (1964).

66. *See id.*

67. Plessy v. Ferguson, 163 U.S. at 560 (Harlan, J., dissenting).

68. *See* Giles v. Harris, 189 U.S. 475, 482 (1903).

69. Id. at 488.

70. *Id.*

71. *Id.*

72. Buck v. Bell, 274 U.S. 200, 208 (1927).

73. Gong Lum v. Rice, 275 U.S. 78, 80 (1927).

74. *Id.* at 87.

75. Marshall, *An Evaluation of Recent Efforts to Achieve Racial Integration in Education through Resort to the Courts*, 21 J. Negro Educ. 316, 318 (1952).

76. *Id.*

77. 305 U.S. 337 (1938).

78. *Id.* at 342.

79. *Id.* at 346.

80. *Id.* at 349–50.

81. *Id.* at 350.

82. *Id.* at 345.

83. *Id.* at 352.

84. A similar order, requiring admission of a black student to the only public law school in Maryland, had been achieved in state court litigation. *See* Pearson v. Murray, 182 A. 590, 594 (Md. 1936).

85. Brown v. Board of Education, 347 U.S. 483, 494 (1954).

86. Marshall, *supra* note 75, at 319.

87. *See* Sipuel v. Board of Regents, 332 U.S. 631, 632 (1948).

88. *See* K. Ripple, Constitutional Litigation § 4–4, at 127 (1984).

89. *Id.* (quoting Brief for Appellant as quoted in R. Kluger, Simple Justice 259 (1975)).

90. *See* Chapter 5.

91. Sipuel v. Board of Regents, 332 U.S. at 633.

92. *See* K. Ripple, *supra* note 88, at 127.

93. *See* Fisher v. Hurst, 333 U.S. 147 (1948).

94. 339 U.S. 629 (1950).

95. 339 U.S. 637 (1950).

96. *See* Sweatt v. Painter, 339 U.S. at 631.

97. *See id.* at 633.

98. *See id..* at 635.

99. *Id.* at 635–36.

100. *Id.* at 632–34.

101. *Id.* at 634.

102. *Id.*

103. McLaurin v. Oklahoma State Regents for Higher Education, 339 U.S. at 640.

104. *See id.*

105. *Id.* at 641.

106. *Id.*

107. *Id.* 641–42.

108. Brown v. Board of Education, 347 U.S at 494.

109. 347 U.S. 483 (1954).

110. Marshall, *supra* note 75, at 322.

111. *See* Chapter 2.

112. *See* Brown v. Board of Education, 347 U.S. at 494 and n.11.

113. *See* Buck v. Bell, 274 U.S. at 208, discussed *supra* at note 72 and accompanying text.

114. Meyer v. Nebraska, 262 U.S. 390, 399 (1923).

115. West Coast Hotel v. Parrish, 300 U.S. 379, 397 (1937).

116. United States v. Carolene Products Co., 304 U.S. 144 (1938).

117. *Id.* at 152.

118. *Id.* at 152 n.4.

119. *Id.*

120. Korematsu v. United States, 323 U.S. 214, 219 (1944).

121. *Id.* at 218.

122. *Id.* at 216.

123. *See* Plessy v. Ferguson, 163 U.S. at 550–51.

124. Pace v. Alabama, 106 U.S. 583, 585 (1882).

125. Loving v. Virginia, 388 U.S. 1, 11–12 (1967).

126. A. Lewis, *supra* note 65.

Chapter 5

Desegregation and the Anti-Discrimination Principle

Displacement of official segregation represented a fundamental redirection of equal protection jurisprudence. In both its formulation and its operation, however, the principle that separate inherently was unequal reflected abiding tension between the imperatives of civil equality and societal reality. Dramatic as it was in nature, the desegregation mandate was cautiously introduced. The Supreme Court heard initial arguments in *Brown v. Board of Education* in its 1952 term, invited reargument for its 1953 term, rendered a decision in 1954, and ordered relief in 1955. Within two decades, the desegregation mandate was qualified by limiting principles that significantly reduced its potential for securing equal educational opportunity. From the mid-1950s to early 1970s, however, the Court activated the equal protection guarantee in forceful and unprecedented terms.

The *Brown* decision itself resolved four cases consolidated for purposes of review that challenged segregated public education in Kansas, Delaware, Virginia, and South Carolina. The lower courts had upheld official segregation with varying degrees of enthusiasm. Although the separate but equal doctrine was sustained in Delaware, for instance, educational disparities prompted an order requiring white schools to admit black students.[1]

The South Carolina case[2] was especially notable insofar as it involved two personalities whose careers, before and after *Brown*, symbolized the emerging and dying orders. Thurgood Marshall, who argued the plaintiffs' case, would be appointed to the Supreme Court in another decade.

John J. Parker, who as Chief Judge of the U.S. Court of Appeals for the Fourth Circuit authored the district court panel's split decision upholding segregation, had narrowly missed appointment to the Supreme Court in 1930.[3] Critical to the Senate's rejection of his nomination by one vote was a perception that Parker was anti-labor and anti-black.[4] Refusal to confirm him thus was influenced by a sense that he was "obviously incapable of viewing with sympathy the aspirations of those who are aiming for higher and better places in the world."[5]

As a member of the three-judge panel hearing the challenge to South Carolina's segregated schools, Parker diverted the challenge to the *Plessy* principle into an assessment of whether facilities at black and white schools were being equalized.[6] Consequent analysis led to the conclusion that segregation was "grounded in reason and experience" and consistent with the Fourteenth Amendment.[7] A dissenting opinion criticized the Court for "avoid[ing] the primary purpose of the suit."[8] It objected to a "method of judicial evasion" that would ensure that "these very infant plaintiffs . . . will probably be bringing suits for their children and grandchildren decades . . . hence."[9] Subsequent events confirmed the accuracy of that forecast. After the desegregation mandate was rendered, Judge Parker was prominent in resisting it. Among other things, he asserted that the Constitution, even if forbidding official discrimination, "does not require integration."[10] Such reasoning accepted new doctrine in a legalistic sense only, as it repudiated the need to dismantle segregation. The "frustrating effects"[11] of such analysis reflected a persisting challenge to the federal interest in civil rights and equality and a doctrinal twist calculated to preserve the established order.

The Supreme Court in *Brown* squarely confronted the issue of whether segregated schools were or ever could be made equal for purposes of the Fourteenth Amendment. Having requested and heard reargument on the question of what the framers had contemplated, the Court concluded that the purpose of Congress and the ratifying states was indeterminate.[12] Depiction of the historical record as uncertain is at least debatable. Although inquiry into motive can be a treacherous exercise, since official intent can represent the convergence of varying purposes or be concealed,[13] the actions and aims of the framers were not equivocal. A general consensus existed, as noted in Chapter 2, that the Fourteenth Amendment accounted for a narrow range of rights and equality. Especially pertinent to the question of whether racially mixed schools were contemplated was the fact that the same Congress responsible for the Fourteenth Amendment also provided for segregated schools in the District of Columbia.[14] Some ratifying states, moreover, mandated segregation of public schools or prohibited education of blacks altogether.

As the Court properly noted, public education in the immediate post-Civil War period was a nonexistent or underdeveloped reality in many states.[15] Public schooling, although eventually considered crucial to economic opportunity and personal development, was not so regarded when the Fourteenth Amendment was conceived. The Court concluded that "it is not surprising that there should be so little in the history of the Fourteenth Amendment relating to its intended effect on public education."[16] Such a determination may have been misleading insofar as it suggested an empty record, but it was apt in indicating that education had become connected to original aims in a way the framers themselves never had an opportunity to contemplate.

Having resolved that original intent was essentially unfathomable, the Court allowed that it could not in any event "turn the clock back to 1868 when the Amendment was adopted, or even to 1896 when *Plessy v. Ferguson* was written."[17] Characterizing education as "perhaps the most significant function of state and local governments," the Court stressed its "present place in American life" and its "importance . . . to our democratic society."[18] It thus noted that education

is required in the performance of our most basic public responsibilities, even service in the armed forces. It is the very foundation of good citizenship. Today it is a principal instrument in awakening the child to cultural values, in preparing him for later professional training, and in helping him to adjust normally to his environment. In these days, it is doubtful that any child may reasonably be expected to succeed in life if he is denied the opportunity of an education.[19]

The Court's analysis thus proceeded from the premise that original purpose was not discernible or pertinent but that education was critical for individual development and opportunity. Having identified that nexus, the Court considered the effect of segregation on public education.[20] In assessing the consequences of segregated elementary and secondary schools, it determined that the impairments identified a few terms earlier with respect to graduate education applied with even greater force.[21] The Court found that separation of children solely because of race "generates a feeling of inferiority as to their status in the community that may affect their hearts and minds in a way unlikely ever to be undone."[22] Quoting findings of the Kansas court, which considered itself bound by *Plessy*, the Court reiterated that

[s]egregation of white and colored children in public schools has a detrimental effect upon the colored children. The impact is greater when it has the sanction of the law; for the policy of separating the races is usually interpreted as denoting the inferiority of the negro group. A sense of inferiority affects the motivation of a child to learn. Segregation with the sanction of law, therefore, has a tendency to [retard] the educational and mental development of Negro children and to deprive them of some of the benefits they would receive in a racial[ly] integrated school system.[23]

Sensing the insufficiency of original support for racially mixed schools, the NAACP had introduced extensive social science data confirming the effect of segregation on black children. The extent to which such evidence influenced the *Brown* decision remains uncertain. The Court itself observed that, regardless of the nature or extent of psychological knowledge in 1896, the harmful effects of segregation were now amply documented, and any contrary indications in *Plessy* were inapplicable.[24] The notion that perceptions of inferiority were the fault of the victim[25] rather than the law thus was repudiated. Reference to social science research has engendered criticism that the *Brown* decisions rest on an unacceptable predicate.[26] Despite the opinion's reference to such data, Chief Justice Warren later would deny that it was the actual premise for the ruling.[27]

The thrust of the decision, regardless of the considerations influencing it, was certain and direct. The Court concluded

that in the field of public education the doctrine of "separate but equal" has no place. Separate educational facilities are inherently unequal. Therefore, we hold that the plaintiffs and others similarly situated for whom the actions have been brought are, by reason of the segregation complained of, deprived of the equal protection of the laws guaranteed by the Fourteenth Amendment.[28]

The challenge to segregated public schools had been presented on equal protection and due process grounds. Because the Court discerned an equal protection violation, analysis of the due process claim was bypassed.[29] Although irrelevant to *Brown*, due process considerations were critical to defeating segregation in the District of Columbia.

The Fifth Amendment, unlike the Fourteenth Amendment, does not include an explicit equal protection guarantee. If not subject to identical constitutional demands, federally segregated schools in the District of Columbia might have survived the desegregation mandate as a legal anomaly. In *Bolling v. Sharpe*, the Court concluded that concepts of equal protection and due process emanate from the "American ideal of fairness."[30] It depicted the equal protection guarantee as "a more explicit safeguard of prohibited unfairness" and, for purposes of decisional analysis, subsumed by the due process clause.[31] Operating from the premise that racial classifications must be scrutinized closely, the Court found school segregation in the District of Columbia "not reasonably related to any proper governmental objective and ... an arbitrary deprivation of ... liberty in violation of the Due Process Clause."[32]

The determination that separate education was inherently unequal represented a bold jurisprudential stroke but, compared to the challenge of implementation, a relatively simple step. The desegregation principle required radical cultural change and moral redefinition. Recognizing the unsettling demands it was making and the potential for resistance, the Court's consideration of relief was characterized by caution and appeals for state and local cooperation. It immediately sought to dispel concern that constitutional imperatives would be the function of auto-cratic and inflexible standards for relief. The Court accordingly observed that the decision had "wide applicability" in a "great variety of local conditions" and that the formulation of relief presented "problems of considerable complexity."[33] The decision thus stopped at the point of determining that segregation in public schools was constitutionally im-permissible. Determination of relief was postponed for another term. Consistent with the Court's objective of minimizing opposition and se-curing cooperation, it invited the input of affected states for purposes of assisting in the fashioning of appropriate relief.[34]

In its next term, the Court delineated the terms for relief and re-manded the cases to the lower courts for implementation.[35] Reflecting further an effort to secure the support of state and local officials, the ruling was couched somewhat deferentially. The Court acknowledged that school authorities had primary responsibility for solving educational problems.[36] To further minimize its role in the process, the Court vested federal district courts with the responsibility of determining whether desegregation was being effected in "good faith."[37] The charge recog-nized the district courts' "proximity to local conditions," and presumed they could better assess remedial needs and options.[38] Although the Court had announced a uniform constitutional demand, the implemen-tation process was to be inspired by local calculation and influence.

For purposes of actually framing decrees, the lower courts were re-minded of their traditional equitable powers. In exercising that author-ity, they were to be mindful of the plaintiffs' interests in obtaining relief as soon as practicable and the public's interest in eliminating "obstacles in a systematic and effective manner."[39] At minimum, the Court insisted on "a prompt and reasonable start toward full compliance" and imposed on states the burden of showing that additional time was necessary for effective remediation.[40] Jurisdiction for purposes of assessing the ade-quacy of desegregation plans thus was assigned to local federal courts. They were directed, however, to ensure that the affected schools de-veloped racially nondiscriminatory admissions policies "with all delib-erate speed."[41]

The sharing of remedial duties represented a strategy calculated to defuse resistance and minimize repudiation. The tactic reflected sensi-tivity to the historically sharp and unsettled dispute over the zones of federal and state interest under the Fourteenth Amendment. Although the Court announced a uniform constitutional demand that cut deeply into established state law, custom, and power, its assignment of primary responsibility for implementation at least appeared to cushion the impact and created a basis for self-determined cooperation.

Reaction to the desegregation mandate was "electric."[42] In states and communities manifestly affected by *Brown*, it also was decidedly negative. In spite of the Court's effort to make desegregation a collaborative enterprise, the general response was characterized by widespread resistance, evasion, and delay. Typical desegregation plans were shams, subterfuges, or inactions that effectively maintained segregation as a function of custom rather than official dictate. Some states passed laws intended to preclude actual desegregation or at least cripple the process.

Arkansas, for instance, enacted legislation intended to free students from compulsory attendance at biracial schools. The statute was rooted in a state constitutional amendment requiring the legislature to approve "in every Constitutional manner the Unconstitutional desegregation decisions . . . of the United States Supreme Court."[43] It eventually was struck down, as discussed later, although desegregation itself required intervention by federal armed forces.[44] The state of Virginia, attempting to deter litigative initiative, activated a regulation providing for disbarment of attorneys representing groups with no pecuniary interest in the litigation.[45] Enforcement was directed primarily at the NAACP but eventually defeated as offensive to the First Amendment.[46] Deferring to local idiosyncrasies, sensing the need for grass-roots support, and aiming to minimize the divisive potential of its decision, the Court originally structured desegregation with an eye to enhancing its acceptability. Reality, however, quickly defeated anticipation. The Court, which had calibrated implementation in terms designed to distance itself from the process, thus was forced to reformulate its strategy.

The first major test of the *Brown* principle presented itself in Little Rock, Arkansas. Although local authorities had devised a desegregation plan, the state legislature, as previously noted, enacted a law purporting to relieve students from compulsory attendance at racially mixed schools.[47] When the governor summoned the National Guard to prevent black students from entering the city's all-white high school,[48] President Eisenhower responded by dispatching federal troops to enforce desegregation.[49] The intensity of public reaction to the events prompted the school board to move for a delay in the implementation of its plan.[50] In support of postponement, the board cited impairment of the educational process attributable to demonstrable tension and conflict. Although acknowledging that the educational process might suffer, and without doubting the board's good faith, the Court in *Cooper v. Aaron* denied the requested delay.[51]

The *Cooper* case was an extension of the persisting debate over federal and state interests reckoned with in *Brown* but for practical purposes still unresolved. Commencing with the premise that the Constitution is supreme and the judiciary has the power to "say what the law is,"[52] the Court characterized the desegregation mandate as "the supreme law of the land and binding on the states."[53] The self-drawn profile of function and effect continues to elicit criticism as an example of judicial over-reaching. For purposes of determining the supreme law of the land, detractors would distinguish between the Constitution itself and the Court's interpretation of it.[54] The decision in *Cooper* was prompted by the sense that "[t]he constitutional rights of respondents are not to be sacrificed or yielded to the violence and disorder which have followed upon the actions of the Governor and Legislature."[55] Given the linkage between official action and public antagonism in Little Rock, the Court determined that "law and order are not here to be preserved by depriving the Negro children of their constitutional rights."[56] It also warned that the desegregation mandate was not to be compromised either directly by legislative, executive, or judicial officers or indirectly by official evasion.[57]

In spite of the Court's insistence that constitutional duties were not to be avoided, desegregation plans commonly evolved in terms that appeared to comport with the *Brown* mandate but actually skirted it. Common methods of evasion included policies of gradual implementation, school closures, freedom of choice, gerrymandering of district lines, and remedial limitations. In *Rogers v. Paul*, the Court considered a desegregation plan that expanded at the rate of one grade per year.[58] Because it effectively denied relief to the plaintiffs, who would graduate before desegregation reached their level, the Court determined that the policy did not satisfy constitutional demands.[59]

Some school districts, instead of desegregating, simply stopped operating. To the extent such action was combined with public financial assistance to private schools, however, the Court discerned a constitutional failure. In *Griffin v. County School Board of Prince Edward County*, it determined that the schools were closed solely to avoid desegregation.[60] Supporting that finding was the fact that the public education system had been shut down and a system for funding private schools established after the county had been ordered to desegregate.[61]

Freedom of choice plans projected the image of racial neutrality by enabling students to select the school they would attend. In *Green v. County School Board of New Kent County, Virginia*, however, the Court determined that such a scheme did not satisfy the requirement of "admission to the public schools on a nonracial basis."[62] Significant factors influencing the determination of constitutional infirmity were the plan's adoption after *Brown*, the absence of any white applicants seeking admission to the previously all-black school, and the scarcity of black students seeking transfer to the traditionally all-white school.[63] From those circumstances, the Court inferred an effort to avoid rather than comply with the desegregation mandate.[64] It did not foreclose the possibility that freedom of choice plans might be permissible in other contexts but characterized them generally as ineffective and "unacceptable . . . if there are reasonably available other ways . . . promising speedier and more effective conversion to a unitary, nonracial school system."[65]

The Court in the aftermath of *Brown* also foiled manipulation of school district lines calculated to evade desegregation. In *Wright v. City Council of Emporia*, it found a school district's subdivision to be an impermissible scheme for insulating a predominantly white community from constitutional demands.[66] The Court also invalidated the partition of a single school district into two districts.[67] The suspect nature of both schemes was enhanced by the timing of the boundary changes, which occurred immediately after the prospect of desegregation arose.[68]

The success of the *Brown* principle ultimately was dependent on its effective enforcement. While state and local officials resisted and evaded the mandate, federal action in the mid–1960s significantly bolstered the cause and process of desegregation. By authorizing the United States attorney general to bring desegregation actions, Congress expanded the possibility of constitutional challenges beyond the range of private and often limited resources. The Department of Health, Education, and Welfare, moreover, promulgated rules denying federal funding to districts not complying with the imperatives of *Brown*.

States nonetheless persisted with strategies and devices designed to cramp operation of the desegregation mandate. Obstructionist efforts resulted in laws that did not contest the validity of *Brown* but curtailed the nature and scope of remedies for effecting desegregation. In *North Carolina State Board of Education v. Swann*, the Court struck down a state law precluding pupil assignments on the basis of race and prohibiting busing.[69] Its ruling was grounded on the supremacy clause, requiring "state policy [to] give way when it operates to hinder vindication of federal constitutional guarantees."[70]

In subsequent years, anti-busing measures were upheld to the extent they were not perceived as an evasion of *Brown*. The Court, in *Crawford v. Board of Education*, determined that a California constitutional amendment denying state courts any option to order busing except to remedy official and purposeful segregation, did not offend the Fourteenth Amendment.[71] In *Washington v. Seattle School District No. 1*, it found that redistribution of the power to make race-dependent assignments or to order busing effected a substantial and unique racial burden.[72] The pertinent law, approved by voters, transferred such authority from local school boards to the state legislature. Arguably, such a removal of power had been effected when state court authority was reduced. The Court in *Crawford*, however, did not find the circumstances comparable.

By the end of the 1960s, the changes contemplated by *Brown* had bypassed an entire generation of public school students. The Court was thus prompted to reexamine the premises for effectuating the *Brown* mandate. Reality was that conditions in the region most affected by the desegregation principle for practical purposes had remained largely unchanged. One of the districts subject to the original desegregation order in *Brown* remained "totally segregated" a decade later.[73] Given such unvaried circumstances, compounded by persisting evasion and intransigence, the Court eventually asserted that "[t]he time for mere 'deliberate speed' has run out."[74] It accordingly demanded that school boards come forward with a desegregation "plan that promises realistically to work, and promises realistically to work *now*."[75]

Movement from a standard of "all deliberate speed" to one of immediate relief fortified the Court's role in the desegregation process. The *Griffin* decision had suggested that equitable powers might be used prohibitively and affirmatively to halt public funding of private schools and to reopen and operate public schools.[76] In *Swann v. Charlotte-Mecklenburg Board of Education*, the Court elaborated on the subject of remedial authority and defined the possibilities for relief expansively.[77]

As the *Swann* opinion noted, a district court's power to prescribe the terms of desegregation was broad and extensive but conditioned on proof of a constitutional violation and failure of school officials to adopt an effective plan.[78] In *Green*, the Court had defined "an affirmative duty to take whatever steps might be necessary to convert to a unitary system in which racial discrimination would be eliminated root and branch."[79] Consistent with that premise, the *Swann* Court identified eradication of all official discrimination as a school board's first duty.[80]

Perceiving that faculty assignments could effect swift and meaningful change in a segregated system, the Court approved fixed ratios of white and black teachers.[81] Such allowance, as jurisprudence in other remedial contexts has disclosed, was a rare departure from the Court's usual animus toward quotas.

The Court regarded construction policies as critical in maintaining or undoing school segregation. Because school siting prior to *Brown* had been rooted in segregation, and since 1954 had been used to avoid desegregation, the Court warned that patterns of building and abandonment would be "a factor of great weight."[82] Local courts thus were to be attentive to the possibility that "construction and abandonment are not used and do not serve to perpetuate or re-establish [a] dual system."[83]

With respect to student assignments, the Court contemplated and accepted the possibility of "bizarre" results, inconvenience, and burden as an inevitable but necessary incident of desegregation.[84] It observed that "[a]ll things being equal," assignment of students to schools nearest their homes was sensible, but further noted that "all things are not equal in a system that has been deliberately constructed and maintained to enforce racial segregation."[85] Attendance policies thus were to be the function of discretionary judgment, checked only by the requirement that relief must be keyed toward the objectives of dismantling a dual school system.[86]

In reviewing the district court's demand for racial balance among students, the Court rejected the notion of fixed quotas as a constitutional imperative.[87] This limitation was a preview of standards that, as discussed in Chapter 6, eventually defined analysis of affirmative action and other remedial policies. In *Swann*, the Court refused to translate the desegregation principle into a command "that every school in every community must always reflect the racial composition of the school system as a whole."[88] Although required to purge their districts of discrimination, authorities were not subject to a "per se rule" against one-race schools.[89] As a departure point in the process of remediation, but not an inflexible requirement, the Court approved the limited use of numerical ratios as a legitimate exercise of a court's discretion.[90]

Despite refusing to provide rigid student transportation guidelines, the Court recognized that busing "has been an integral part of the public education system for years."[91] It thus endorsed busing for desegregation purposes,[92] at least to the extent travel time and distance were not so excessive that they presented a health risk to students or impaired the educational process.[93]

The *Swann* ruling represented the desegregation mandate's apex but also prefaced its devolution. Even before the decision was rendered, signs of popular discomfort with the implications of *Brown* had appeared on the political landscape. Widespread opposition to busing translated into significant support during 1968 for the presidential candidacy of George Wallace. An ardent segregationist at the time, Wallace attracted significant backing in the North and West, where major cities appeared vulnerable to the desegregation mandate's extension. A central theme in Richard Nixon's campaign was the reconstruction of the Supreme Court with personnel who not only would be responsive to law and order concerns but also would blunt the operation of the equal protection guarantee. Nixon won with less than a majority of the total vote. His appeal, coupled with Wallace's, suggested renewed tension akin to what characterized public sentiment in the decade after the Fourteenth Amendment was enacted. Although the amendment reflected a commitment to racial justice, its potential soon was qualified by societal resistance and fatigue. Mounting discomfort with the desegregation mandate suggested a like conflict between general aims and inclination to persevere with and accept the consequences of doctrinal change. Actual delimitation of the desegregation principle was prefaced by the *Swann* Court's observation that once a unitary school system was established, barring resegregation as a function of official action, constitutional responsibilities had been fulfilled.[94] The *Swann* decision, while delineating desegregative remedial powers in broad terms, thus established a foundation for doctrinal limitation.

Consistent with invalidation of dual school systems in 1954, the Court in quick order had struck down official segregation in numerous public venues.[95] Within several years, judicial output pursuant to *Brown* had exceeded the volume of cases decided over six decades of separate but equal jurisprudence. Given the aforementioned political trends of the late 1960s, it is not surprising that when the Warren Court became the Burger Court, equal protection jurisprudence soon began to reflect equivocation.

Central to *Brown* was the objective of abolishing racially identifiable schools. The Court perceived racial separation as a system which officially connoted inferiority and adversely affected the self-image and educational opportunities of its victims. Consistent with the Court's understanding are observations that formal segregation causes psychological injury "by assaulting a person's self-respect and human dignity, and [by] brand[ing]... with a sign that designates inferior status to others."[96] Without belittling the significance of *Brown*, it is necessary to recognize what the Court accomplished in 1954 and how the principle then enunciated was later qualified. The desegregation mandate, as it evolved, required liquidation of educational systems segregated by law or by overtly discriminatory official action.[97] Left unaffected by constitutional demands, however, has been pervasive and extensive segregation in the North and West attributable to patterns of residential settlement. Critics have asserted that whether a "child perceives his separation as discriminatory and invidious, he is not... going to make fine distinctions about the source of particular separation."[98] Whatever concern originally existed for the impact of segregation on self-image and opportunity therefore was lost in the translation of the doctrine in the 1970s.

The desegregation mandate was articulated at the same time society was experiencing unprecedented individual mobility and significant demographic changes. Enhanced opportunities for personal movement coalesced with suburban development to expand and redefine metropolitan areas. By the 1970s, new school districts had been established in communities that recently had not even existed. Given their lack of history, identifying a record of overt, much less subtle, discrimination was a virtual impossibility. As Justice Powell observed, "[t]he type of state-enforced segregation that *Brown I* properly condemned no longer exists in this country."[99] Notwithstanding the opportunity to craft doctrine that would reach segregation regardless of cause, the Court, instead of reckoning with the underlying dynamics of racially separate education, stopped at elimination of its overt manifestations.

As the 1970s unfolded, it became apparent that the outer limits of equal protection had been reached. Confinement of the *Brown* mandate to instances where segregative intent was identified checked the process of desegregation as it threatened to expand into heavily populated areas of the North and West.[100] Reflecting dominant public concern with the potential scope of desegregation, the Court invalidated a remedial plan covering a major northern city and its suburbs.[101] Having demarcated the spatial scope of desegregation remedies, the Court next fixed temporal limitations on desegregation obligations. It held that resegregation of a school district, following implementation of a desegregation decree, was not constitutionally offensive absent proof of discriminatory motive.[102] The trilogy of limiting principles, enunciated in three separate decisions, preserved opportunities for white flight and effectively immunized suburban communities from the demands of *Brown*.

The first qualification of the desegregation principle, in *Keyes v. School District No. 1*, conditioned the duty to desegregate on demonstration of officially discriminatory action.[103] For a constitutional responsibility to exist, it was necessary to establish first a *prima facie* case of segregative intent, which authorities had the opportunity to rebut.[104] To the extent segregation could be attributed to factors other than what the Court would consider purposeful state action, no duty to desegregate would exist. Desegregation thus would be a selective rather than a comprehensive duty, imposed only when a formal system of segregation had existed or a palpable discriminatory intent could be identified.

By failing to acknowledge a link between government action and housing patterns, the Court overlooked or discounted the legacy of official policies and practices that facilitated residential segregation. As the Court noted, "the differentiating factor between *de jure* segregation and so-called *de facto* segregation . . . is *purpose* or *intent* to segregate."[105] The line between the two concepts, however, is more illusory than real. Segregated housing was a function in many communities of officially enforced restrictive covenants.[106] Racially separated neighborhoods were an extension of not only state but national policy. The Federal Housing Administration's lending policies, for instance, protected residential loans from "adverse influences" that included the mixing of "inharmonious racial groups."[107] Further contributing to racially discrete neighborhoods have been decisions concerning the construction and closing of schools, employment of faculty and staff, assignment of students, siting of public housing, and distribution of urban development funds.[108]

Rather than exploring those ties to state action, the Court opted for bright but not necessarily precise boundaries between permissible and impermissible segregation. The consequent dividing line formally distinguishes race-dependent and race-neutral action but is useful in discerning and defeating overt rather than subtle discrimination. Even if officially determined racial separation was more evident in the South, where it was patently systematized, segregation in education was a pervasive national phenomenon.[109] Arguably, it was more insidiously rooted in the North where racial segregation became more spatial than ceremonial.[110] Despite required change in the South, as Justice Powell observed, no comparable progress would be realized in the North and West because "of the *de jure–de facto* distinction."[111] Powell suggested a hypocrisy in the Court's formulation insofar as it was "accepted complacently by many of the same voices which denounced the evils of segregated schools in the South."[112] Characterizing the severability of segregation as "a legalism rooted in history rather than present reality," which also was irrational insofar as cause did not alter adverse effect on such educational opportunity, he would have abolished the *de jure/de facto* distinction.[113]

The differentiation survived Powell's challenge and profoundly diminished the Court's responsiveness to and concern with modern segregation. It announced or at least prefaced a reluctance to adjust equal protection doctrine to the new demographic realities of the post-*Brown* era. Comprehensive realization of equal educational opportunity and elimination of all racially identifiable schools were placed beyond the reach of the desegregation mandate. Motive-referenced criteria thus exempted from constitutional attention much racially separate and unequal education.

The duty to desegregate, as limited by the *de jure* requirement, imposed a substantial burden upon plaintiffs seeking to establish a constitutional violation. That a school system was intentionally segregated could be easily proved insofar as the law spoke for itself, as it did during the Jim Crow era. Discriminatory purpose when not overt may be elusive, however, and its discernment a "tortuous effort."[114] Even the most routine decisions, as Powell noted, may affect segregation. A panoply of opportunities exists for influencing the racial mix of public schools, including

action or nonaction with respect to school building construction and location; the timing of building new schools and their size; the closing and consolidation of schools; the drawing or gerrymandering of student attendance zones; the extent to which a neighborhood policy is enforced; the recruitment, promotion and assignment of faculty and supervisory personnel; policies with respect to transfers from one school to another; whether, and to what extent, special schools will be provided, where they will be located, and who will qualify to attend them; the determination of curriculum, including whether there will be "tracks" that lead primarily to college or to vocational training, and the routing of students into these tracks; and even decisions as to social, recreational and athletic policies.[115]

Further complicating the inquiry is the problem of varying, mixed or disguised motive.[116] In those parts of the country which did not have laws requiring dual schools, proof of segregation was elusive or non-existent. Segregation of primary and secondary education in the North and West, not surprisingly, remains more profound and resistant than in the South.[117]

The *de jure* principle operates in effect as a liability-limiting concept akin to the tort principle of proximate cause. The standard, which requires a nexus between act and injury that is not too attenuated, ensures that liability for a negligent act will not be limitless. Although the cutoff point is not precisely defined, responsibility for consequential harm abates as actual injury becomes more distant and less foreseeable. Like the concept of proximate cause, the *de facto* notion is vulnerable to subjective perceptions that influence the etching of legally significant dividing lines. The liability-reducing criteria, chosen to qualify the desegregation principle, seem notable more for their capacity to restrain than for their precision.

Investment in such limiting principles for desegregation provoked sharp debate within the Court itself. As noted previously, Justice Powell would have avoided the *de jure/de facto* distinction altogether. Justice Marshall observed that school district boundaries yielding racially distinct systems, whether proximately or more remotely caused by official action, communicate the same negative message that concerned the *Brown* Court. The premise that a child's constitutional rights are not implicated because he or she is "born into a *de facto* society"[118] struck Marshall as facile and capricious.[119] To the extent racial separation suggests a systematic pattern, breeds a sense of inferiority, and impairs educational development and opportunity, causation-based distinctions from his perspective seemed more a function of convenience than principle. This perception conformed with Powell's sense that causation-referenced limiting principles serve no purpose other than to "perpetuate a legalism rooted in history rather than present reality."[120]

Further bounding the duty to desegregate was the Court's determination that, in the event of purposeful segregative design, any remedy must be tailored to the scope of the constitutional violation. Such a qualification radiated from the *de facto* distinction and ensured that demands would not be imposed in communities where official wrong was not discernible. As demonstrated by the circumstances from which *Milliken v. Bradley* arose, the limiting principle precluded interdistrict remedies in major urban centers.[121] Even if the city school system itself had a history of discrimination, any attempt to desegregate was a generally vain exercise if a court order could not reach adjacent and mostly white suburban communities that had evolved in the meantime.

In the *Milliken* case, it was established that the Detroit school board purposely had created and maintained a segregated system.[122] The trial court determined that the state had contributed significantly to that result. With respect to the city's role, the trial court specifically found that the school board had created and maintained optional attendance zones, bused students to distant schools for purposes of perpetuating segregation, and gauged construction policies to minimize mixing.[123] It determined that the state had facilitated segregation by nullifying a voluntary desegregation plan, overseeing construction, implementing a transportation program that was racially steered and unequally funded, and sanctioning race-dependent attendance plans.[124]

Despite the trial court's findings, the Supreme Court disagreed with the nature and extent of illegal state action. Although not foreclosing the use of interdistrict remedies as a matter of theory, the Court limited their operation to constitutional violations transcending a single district. Area-wide relief was unavailable as a practical matter, therefore barring a finding that district lines had been established or adjusted to foster segregation or that the racially discriminatory acts of one district had a segregative effect in another.[125] Without such a determination, the Court found that the scope of relief exceeded the nature of the constitutional violation.[126]

In emphasizing local autonomy in education and minimizing the possibilities for cross-district relief, the Court effectively shielded most metropolitan areas from constitutional demands. As Justice White saw it, however, deliberate segregative acts and consequences were left unremedied, and similar results would follow elsewhere to the extent states vested "sufficient power over [their] public schools in [their] local school districts."[127] He thus emphasized findings "that over a long period of years those in charge of the Michigan public schools engaged in various practices calculated to effect the segregation of the Detroit school system."[128] Even if the state was implicated in fostering segregation, the Court was unwilling to impute the wrong to specific suburban districts.

The desegregation principle, having been circumscribed in *Keyes* by the *de jure/de facto* distinction, thus was narrowed further in *Milliken*. Reversal of the trial court decision communicated an attitude contrary to what the Court had radiated for nearly two decades. Federal courts, which had been rebuked for not going far enough in facilitating desegregation, were admonished for going too far. In contrast to the demand in *Green* for plans that work now, the circumscription of remedial potential in *Milliken* suggested the possibility that effective relief might not even be an option.

Exemption of suburban districts from remedial obligations reflected another significant doctrinal change. Previously, the Court had insisted on elimination of the vestiges of segregation, "root and branch."[129] Without the possibility of interdistrict relief, it was evident that eradication processes might be partial rather than comprehensive. Such consequences have elicited criticism on the grounds that the Court has not only relaxed remedial obligations but also disregarded *Brown*'s concern with equal educational opportunity. As Justice Marshall put it, the denial of a meaningful remedy afforded "no remedy at all . . . guaranteeing that Negro children . . . will receive the same separate and inherently unequal education in the future as they have been unconstitutionally afforded in the past."[130]

The *Keyes* and *Milliken* decisions showed the Court's reluctance to adapt the desegregation principle to diverse circumstances of racial separation. Further indicating that the *Brown* mandate would not be a doctrine for all segregative seasons was a third limiting principle emphasizing that the duty to desegregate was not enduring. In *Milliken*, the Court had determined that constitutional obligations were subject to spatial restrictions. Its decision in *Pasadena City Board of Education v. Spangler* established qualifications also with respect to duration.[131]

In *Spangler*, the Court determined that desegregation duties abated when a unitary system was established.[132] "[H]aving once implemented a racially neutral attendance pattern in order to remedy . . . perceived constitutional violations," new duties would not be imposed simply as a function of demographic change.[133] Termination of remedial obligations, upon severance of the linkage between official act and segregative result was presented as an extension of the *de facto* concept. Further constitutional responsibility would not be imposed absent a showing of segregative action attributable to state or local authorities.[134] The indication of *Spangler* was that when a system becomes unitary, barring evidence of official tampering, school officials need not respond if the community resegregates. It is not a universally accepted premise, however, that population redistribution after a desegregation order is constitutionally insignificant. The Court in *Spangler* attributed demographic consequences affecting the racial composition of schools to the "quite normal pattern of human migration."[135] Despite that characterization, it has been argued that a connection to official action exists, which the Court simply ignores. Justice Marshall maintained that insofar as a state has "created a system where whites and Negroes were intentionally kept apart so that they could not become accustomed to learning together, [it] is responsible for the fact that many whites will react to the dismantling of that segregated system by attempting to flee to the suburbs."[136]

The limiting principle enunciated in *Spangler* denied any such responsibility. To the extent resegregation follows desegregation efforts and a linkage to official action is not discerned, equal protection is not implicated. The promise of "a unitary school system in which racial segregation [was] eliminated root and branch"[137] thus does not operate as a permanent guarantee of racially mixed education. Removal of resegregation from a chain of events commenced by discriminatory practices and policies was consistent with the liability-limiting nature of the *de facto* concept itself and likewise reminiscent of how proximate causation principles operate. The practical consequence was further expansion of constitutionally permissible segregation. Desegregation in such cities as Boston, Detroit, Dayton, and San Francisco was followed by declining white enrollment at rates ranging from 15 to 22 percent during the implementation years themselves.[138] Such an exodus, without the opportunity for interdistrict remedies, has helped make meaningful desegregation in urban centers a mathematical impossibility.

Further diminishing the potential of the desegregation principle was the determination that education was not a fundamental right. The *Brown* Court had described education as "importan[t] . . . to our democratic society," and at least intimated that it was of fundamental significance.[139] That impression was reinforced in *Bolling v. Sharpe*, when the Court referred to a "deprivation of . . . liberty."[140] In *San Antonio Independent School District v. Rodriguez*, however, the Court declared that education was not a fundamental right and thus rejected the proposition that it must be equally funded in all of a state's districts.[141] The irony of the *Rodriguez* decision was that disparities in educational quality, which theoretically might have been repaired pursuant to the separate but equal doctrine, were no longer subject to constitutional regulation.

For some, the devolution of the desegregation mandate in the 1970s was reminiscent of Fourteenth Amendment jurisprudence a century earlier. Responding to what he perceived as unwarranted doctrinal retreat, Justice Marshall reminded that "[d]esegregation is not and was never expected to be an easy task."[142] What he saw in principles limiting *Brown*'s operation was a general sense that the desegregation process "ha[d] gone far enough."[143] Such an observation hints that, as in the *Civil Rights Cases*,[144] constitutional principle had reached the margins of societal tolerance and interest had given way to fatigue. The narrowing of the desegregation principle also suggests that, at least with respect to its premise that the law "is powerless to eradicate social instincts,"[145] the *Plessy* Court did not entirely miscalculate.

The Court, especially during the late 1950s and throughout the 1960s, invoked the equal protection guarantee. Such jurisprudence was contrary to doctrinal antecedents notable for accommodation of state power and cultural norms. As equal protection doctrine assumed the risk of social disruption, abiding tensions associated with the Fourteenth Amendment invariably were exacerbated. Justice Powell thus observed that "in city after city [forced integration has fostered] . . . [t]he process of resegregation, stimulated by resentment against judicial coercion."[146] For many years, the Court refused to factor in resentment of and resistance to desegregation as mitigating considerations in the crafting of constitutional policy.[147] Yet it was the Court itself during the 1970s that, while not overtly deferring to separatist instincts, afforded them constitutional living space.

Powell also characterized modern school segregation as the consequence of "familiar segregated housing patterns . . . caused by social, economic, and demographic forces for which no school board is responsible."[148] This depiction reflects perceived limits of constitutional responsibility and suggests perhaps that residential segregation is normative. Consistent with that vision is Justice Rehnquist's observation that "[e]ven if the Constitution required it, and it were possible for federal courts to do it, no equitable decree can fashion an 'Emerald City' where all races, ethnic groups, and persons of various income levels live side by side."[149]

The desegregation mandate originally assumed that educational policy should be race-neutral rather than race-dependent. It is ironic but perhaps not surprising, given lingering race-consciousness, that interest in preserving constitutional gains has induced contemporary policy attentive to race. Burdens imposed on minorities to maintain integration, however, have refocused attention on the feasibility of *Brown*'s aims in a society that, if no longer segregated as a matter of law, nonetheless remains functionally disposed toward racial separation.

Preserving the accomplishments of *Brown* thus has presented a challenge to school boards, which, in attempting to avoid resegregation, have reverted to policies that previously would have been unthinkable. In the name of integration maintenance, school boards have discontinued or substantially modified busing plans and reintroduced neighborhood school concepts that would have been unacceptable during the first decade of *Brown*. Contrary to the original aim of eliminating racially identifiable schools, single-race facilities define some modern integration maintenance plans. Such reversion reflects an official sense that controls on racial mixing are necessary to stem an otherwise accelerated movement of white students from public schools.[150]

In Brooklyn, New York, for instance, where the white student population had declined from 94.2% in 1957 to 36.4% in 1981, school officials adopted a freedom of choice plan, which allowed students from an all-minority high school to attend other high schools in Queens and later anywhere in New York.[151] Because white students continued to exit city schools and thereby destabilize desegregation efforts, official policy increasingly factored in white sensitivities.[152] The pursuit of racial balance thus became hostage to white perceptions that, if sensing too much or too quick of a minority increase, might prompt further disenrollment.[153]

By imposing controls on the rate and extent of racial change at critical schools, officials contemplated metered minority transfers that would minimize white flight and resegregation.[154] Restricted entry into racially diverse schools, however, effectively locked many minorities into racially identifiable schools. Black and Hispanic students were not allowed to enroll in schools where their attendance would cause white enrollment to drop below 50 percent.[155] The plan thus assumed the continuation of at least some single-race schools and established a system of racial preferences that effectively burdened minorities to preserve a semblance of racial balance.[156]

A system of racially identifiable schools also was central to an integration maintenance plan adopted in Norfolk, Virginia.[157] Unlike New York, where school integration was mandated by state policy, Norfolk schools had been desegregated by judicial decree in 1971—fifteen years after litigation had commenced.[158] Four years after being ordered to desegregate, the school system was declared unitary.

Consistent with the experience of other cities forced to desegregate, the population of Norfolk itself diminished and white enrollment in the school system declined substantially. To minimize white flight, the school board reestablished neighborhood schools for elementary students[159] in anticipation that they eventually would be fed into racially mixed junior and senior high schools.[160] The trial court noted that public sentiment could not obstruct or dilute the obligation to dismantle an officially segregated dual school system.[161] Nonetheless, it concluded that white flight might be factored into voluntary efforts to improve racial balance.[162] Concern for the dominant race's reaction, which was a source of the *Plessy* principle[163] but unacceptable as a basis for evading desegregation responsibilities,[164] thus was reintroduced as a predicate for integration maintenance. Constitutional achievement accordingly had been reduced to a determination that limited segregation was needed to preserve some racial diversity.

The desegregation process by the 1990s resembled to some extent a ritual performed as a condition for reversion to the societal norm. Consistent with such imagery, the Court in *Board of Education of Oklahoma City Public Schools v. Dowell* emphasized that school desegregation decrees "are not intended to operate in perpetuity."[165] In so doing, the Court distinguished permanent decrees in the antitrust context where a "continuing danger of unlawful[ness] still existed"[166] and modification was impermissible if litigative aims "have not been fully achieved."[167] Despite the reemergence of racially identifiable schools, even if ultimately chargeable to past, albeit abandoned, discriminatory policy,[168] the *Dowell* Court reiterated that inquiry will be confined to whether school officials have "complied in good faith with [a] desegregation decree . . . , and whether the vestiges of past discrimination hav[e] been eliminated to the extent practicable."[169] As for the tension that still defines Fourteenth Amendment jurisprudence, the resolution is more accommodating than disruptive of a society functionally disposed toward, if no longer officially governed by, racial distinctions.

General equal protection doctrine since 1954 has mirrored changes in the desegregation principle. Consistent with the *de jure* requirement grafted on the *Brown* principle, constitutional reckoning during the 1970s became captive to the "discriminatory purpose" standard. The Court determined that claims of disproportionate impact in employment, housing, and criminal justice were constitutionally insignificant because disproportionate impact by itself did not satisfy the requirement of purposeful discrimination.[170] Motive-based inquiry, as noted previously, is notoriously unfavorable to constitutional claims because subjective intent is easily concealed or otherwise difficult to discern.[171] For precisely such reasons, the Court has refused to apply purpose criteria in the freedom of speech context.[172] Motive-referenced inquiry was inapt, it observed, because constitutional "stakes are sufficiently high... to eschew guesswork."[173]

Despite its repudiation and futility in other constitutional contexts, purpose criteria have been jurisprudentially established for equal protection purposes. As explained by the Supreme Court, a focus on disproportional impact alone would disrupt the political process by jeopardizing "a whole range of tax, welfare, public service, regulatory, and licensing statutes."[174] Critics maintain that such concern is overblown because the Court must attend only to effects that have racial significance.[175] Investment in discriminatory purpose criteria for practical purposes has established an effective foil to equal protection claims. Although the Court has suggested a historical pattern of segregation would count as evidence that an illegal motive infected a challenged action, it turned a blind eye to substantial disparities in the operation of a state's death penalty and the legacy of a dual justice system. Research offered in *McCleskey v. Kemp* showed that Georgia prosecutors "sought the death penalty in 70% of the cases involving black defendants and white victims; 32% of the cases involving white defendants and white victims; 15% of the cases involving black defendants and black victims; and 19% of the cases involving white defendants and black victims" during a ten-year period.[176] Georgia courts, moreover, assessed the death penalty "in 22% of the cases involving black defendants and white victims; 8% of the cases involving white defendants and white victims; 1% of the cases involving black defendants and black victims; and 3% of the cases involving white defendants and black victims."[177] Responding to those disparities, the Court dismissed duality in capital punishment as a mere "discrepancy that appears to correlate with race... [and] an inevitable part of our criminal justice system."[178] Such a conclusion, as Justice Brennan suggested, was possible only to the extent the Court ignored the history of a dual criminal justice system and the different advice an attorney would be obligated to provide white and black clients.[179] Even if probably not understood by the Court as constitutionally significant, an execution in 1991 represented the first time in nearly half a century that a white defendant was put to death in the United States for a crime against a black victim.[180]

Consistent with its forceful expoundment of the equal protection guarantee during the 1960s, the Court simultaneously read Congress's power to enforce the Fourteenth Amendment in broad terms. As a consequence, post-*Brown* civil rights legislation prohibiting discrimination in employment, education, voting, housing, and public contracting became possible.[181] As equal protection jurisprudence approached the final decade of the twentieth century, however, the Court narrowed the operative reach of two legislative enactments.

In *Wards Cove Packing Co. v. Atonio*, it increased the burden upon claimants alleging discrimination under Title VII of the Civil Rights Act of 1964.[182] Plaintiffs consequently were obligated, in establishing a *prima facie* case, to identify the specific employment practice allegedly responsible for any observed statistical disparities.[183] A previous requirement, that an employer justify a challenged practice by showing "business necessity," was relaxed in favor of "a reasoned review" of its justification.[184]

The Court in *Patterson v. McLean Credit Union* narrowed 42 U.S.C. §1981, the modern descendant of the Civil Rights Act of 1866, so that it prohibited racial discrimination in contracts but did not cover post-formation harassment.[185] Responding to concern about its direction, the Court observed that "[n]either our words nor our decisions should be interpreted as signaling one inch of retreat from...forbid[ding] discrimination in the private, as well as the public sphere."[186]

Both decisions, however, delimited the scope of anti-discrimination standards. The *Patterson* decision retreated from even the early command of *Strauder* that remedial legislation was to be construed liberally and flexibly.[187] The Court's drift prompted some justices to "wonder whether the majority still believes that race discrimination—or, more accurately, race discrimination against nonwhites—is a problem in our society, or even remembered that it ever was."[188]

Even though eventually qualified, the *Brown* decision remains unsettling to some legal theorists still unable to square it with principles of judicial restraint. Perceptions of the desegregation mandate as an essentially anti-democratic exercise are rooted in an original record that did not contemplate racially mixed schools. Some critics endeavor to reconcile the desegregation principle with apolitical demands by suggesting that the *Brown* case required investment in methodology disfavored by the Fourteenth Amendment's framers or abandonment of equal protection altogether.[189] The notion that the Court was caught between two alternatives, each at odds with original understanding, may be a somewhat procrustean and unnecessary effort at reconciling the imperatives of review with the requirements of democratic consent. The same history that discloses early provision for racially segregated schools also reveals original flexibility in accounting for civil rights. When the Fourteenth Amendment was framed, for instance, it was considered politically suicidal to advocate black suffrage. What was unrealistic in 1868 proved not only feasible but also essential in 1869 when Republicans, concerned with the influence of a politically resurgent South and seeking security for recently established civil status and rights, championed the notion. The redirection of policy showed an inclination to reexamine and even abandon an initial position if necessary to realize overarching aims. It at least is credible if not certain that, upon recognizing how closely related education would be to economic opportunity, the framers might have made similar adjustments in their thinking.

The devolution of *Brown* has disclosed a coursing of the law to a point that actually may be closer to initial expectations than the either-or choice identified by many professed originalists. Distinctions between *de jure* and *de facto* segregation and consequent constriction of the duty to desegregate, compounded by reversion of judicial review from strict scrutiny to mere rationality when discriminatory purpose is not established, indicate repudiation of a broadly defined anti-discrimination principle. Such qualification at least comports with the reality that original equalization concerns themselves were limited. As discussed in Chapter 7, however, resultant doctrine still underserves original and consensual expectations.

NOTES

1. *See* Brown v. Board of Education, 347 U.S. 483, 486 n.1 (1954) (citing Gebhart v. Belton, 87 A.2d 862 (Del. 1952)).

2. Briggs v. Elliott, 98 F. Supp. 529 (E.D.S.C. 1951).

3. *See* Lively, *The Supreme Court Appointment Process: In Search of Constitutional Roles and Responsibilities*, 59 S. Cal. L. Rev. 551, 567–72 (1986).

4. *See id.* at 567.

5. 72 Cong. Rec. 8,037 (1930) (Sen. Wagner).

6. *See* Briggs v. Elliott, 98 F. Supp. at 538–40 (Waring, J., dissenting).

7. *Id.* at 536.

8. *Id.* at 540 (Waring, J., dissenting).

9. *Id.* (Waring, J., dissenting).

10. Briggs v. Elliott, 132 F. Supp. 776, 777 (E.D.S.C. 1955).

11. United States v. Jefferson County Board of Education, 372 F.2d 836, 863 (5th Cir. 1966), *corrected*, 380 F.2d 385 (5th Cir.), *cert. denied*, 389 U.S. 840 (1967).

12. Brown v. Board of Education, 347 U.S. at 489.

13. *See supra* notes 17–19 and accompanying text.

14. *See* Chapter 2, note 30 and accompanying text.

15. Brown v. Board of Education, 347 U.S. at 489–90.

16. *Id.* at 490.

17. *Id.* at 492.

18. *Id.* at 492–93.

19. *Id.* at 493.

20. *Id.*

21. *Id.* at 494.

22. *Id.*

23. *Id.*

24. *Id.*

25. See Plessy v. Ferguson, 163 U.S. 537, 551 (1896), discussed in Chapter 4.

26. *See, e.g.*, R. Bork, The Tempting of America 82–83 (1990).

27. *See* R. Kluger, Simple Justice 706 (1976).

28. Brown v. Board of Education, 347 U.S. at 495.

29. *See id.*

30. Bolling v. Sharpe, 347 U.S. 497 (1954).

31. *Id.* at 499.

32. *Id.* at 500.

33. Brown v. Board of Education, 347 U.S. at 495.

34. *Id.* at 495–96.

35. Brown v. Board of Education, 349 U.S. 294 (1955).

36. *See id.* at 299.

37. *Id.*

38. *Id.*

39. *Id.* at 300.

40. *Id.*

41. *Id.* at 301.

42. A. Mason, The Supreme Court from Taft to Warren 207–08 (1968).

43. Ark. Const. amend. 44 (quoted in Cooper v. Aaron, 358 U.S. 1, 8–9 (1958)).

44. *See* Cooper v. Aaron, 358 U.S. at 12.

45. NAACP v. Button, 371 U.S. 415, 422 (1963).

46. *Id.* at 444–45.

47. *See* Cooper v. Aaron, 358 U.S. at 8–9.

48. *See id.* at 11.

49. *See id.* at 12.

50. *See id.* at 12–13.

51. *Id.* at 16–17.

52. Marbury v. Madison, 5 U.S. (1 Cranch) 137, 177 (1803).

53. Cooper v. Aaron, 358 U.S. at 18.

54. *See, e.g.*, R. Bork, *supra* note 26, at 120, 176; Meese, *The Law of the Constitution*, 61 Tul. L. Rev. 979, 982 (1987).

55. Cooper v. Aaron, 358 U.S. at 16.

56. *Id.*

57. *Id.* at 18.

58. Rogers v. Paul, 382 U.S. 198 (1965).

59. *Id.* at 200.

60. Griffin v. County School Board of Prince Edward County, 377 U.S. 218, 232 (1964).

61. *See id.* at 225.

62. Green v. County School Board of New Kent County, Virginia, 391 U.S. 430 (1968).

63. *See id.* at 438, 441.

64. *Id.* at 438.

65. *Id.* at 441.

66. Wright v. City Council of Emporia, 407 U.S. 451 (1972).

67. United States v. Scotland Neck City Board of Education, 407 U.S. 484 (1972).

68. Wright v. City Council of Emporia, 407 U.S. at 456; United States v. Scotland Neck City Board of Education, 407 U.S. at 486–87.

69. North Carolina State Board of Education v. Swann, 402 U.S. 43 (1971).

70. *Id.* at 45.

71. Crawford v. Board of Education, 458 U.S. 527 (1982).

72. Washington v. Seattle School District No. 1, 458 U.S. 457, 484 (1982).

73. A decade after *Brown*, barely two percent of black students in southern states attended schools where they were not in a racial majority. *See* Bureau of the Census, U.S. Dept. of Commerce, Statistical Abstract of the United States 124 (1974).

74. Green v. County School Board of New Kent County, Virginia, 391 U.S. at 438 (quoting Griffin v. County School Board of Prince Edward County, 377 U.S. at 234.

75. *Id.* at 439 (emphasis in original).

76. *See* Griffin v. County School Board of Prince Edward County, 377 U.S. at 233–34.

77. Swann v. Charlotte-Mecklenburg Board of Education, 402 U.S. 1 (1971).

78. *See id.* at 15–16.

79. Green v. County School Board of New Kent County, Virginia, 391 U.S. at 437–38.

80. Swann v. Charlotte-Mecklenburg Board of Education, 402 U.S. at 15.

81. *Id.* at 19–20.

82. *Id.* at 21.

83. *Id.*

84. *Id.* at 28.

85. *Id.*

86. *Id.* at 28–29.

87. *Id.* at 24.

88. *Id.*

89. *Id.* at 26.

90. *Id.* at 25.

91. *Id.* at 29.

92. *Id.* at 29–30.

93. *Id.* at 30–31.

94. *Id.* at 31–32.

95. *E.g.*, New Orleans City Park Improvement Association v. Detiege, 358

U.S. 54 (1958) (parks); Gayle v. Browder, 352 U.S. 903, 903 (1956) (buses); Mayor and City Council of Baltimore City v. Dawson, 350 U.S. 877, 877 (1955) (beaches).

96. Lawrence, *The Id, the Ego and Equal Protection: Reckoning with Unconscious Racism*, 39 Stan. L. Rev. 317, 350–51 (1987).

97. Columbus Board of Education v. Penick, 443 U.S. 449, 458–60 (1979).

98. A. Bickel, The Supreme Court and the Idea of Progress 119 (1970).

99. Columbus Board of Education v. Penick, 443 U.S. at 481 (Powell, J., dissenting).

100. *See* Keyes v. School District No. 1, 413 U.S. 189 (1973).

101. *See* Milliken v. Bradley, 418 U.S. 717 (1974).

102. *See* Pasadena City Board of Education v. Spangler, 427 U.S. 424 (1976).

103. Keyes v. School District No. 1, 413 U.S. at 208.

104. *Id.* Put simply, a *prima facie* case exists when a plaintiff establishes facts that, absent any contradictory evidence, would entitle him or her to prevail.

105. *Id.* (emphasis in original).

106. *See id.* at 216 (Douglas, J., concurring).

107. *See* P. Jacobs, Prelude to Riot: A View of Urban America from the Bottom 140 (1967).

108. Keyes v. School District No. 1, 413 U.S. at 216 (Douglas, J., concurring).

109. *See* U.S. Department of Health, Education and Welfare, School Enrollment Survey (1971), 118 Cong. Rec. 563–66 (1972).

110. G. Myrdal, An American Dilemma 621 (1944).

111. Keyes v. School District No. 1, 413 U.S. at 218–19 (Powell, J., concurring and dissenting).

112. *Id.* at 219 (Powell, J., concurring and dissenting).

113. *Id.*

114. *Id.* at 234–35 (Powell, J., concurring and dissenting).

115. *Id.* at 234–35; *see* Goodman, *De Facto School Segregation: A Constitutional and Empirical Analysis*, 60 Calif. L. Rev. 275, 284–85 (1972).

116. *See* Edward v. Aguillard, 482 U.S. 578, 636–37 (1987) (Scalia, J., dissenting); United States v. O'Brien, 391 U.S. 367, 383–84 (1969); Lawrence, *supra* note 96, at 319.

117. *See* U.S. Commission on Civil Rights, Desegregation of the Nation's Public Schools: A Status Report 18–27 (1979).

118. Cisneros v. Corpus Christi Independent School District, 467 F.2d 142, 148 (5th Cir. 1972) (en banc) (quoting United States v. Jefferson County Board of Education, 380 F.2d at 397 (Gewin, J., dissenting)).

119. Milliken v. Bradley, 418 U.S. at 782, 804–05 (Marshall, J., dissenting).

120. Keyes v. School District No. 1, 413 U.S. at 219 (Powell, J., concurring and dissenting).

121. Milliken v. Bradley, 418 U.S. at 717.

122. *Id.* at 725–26.

123. *Id.*

124. *Id.* at 734–35 n.16; *id.* at 770–71 (White, J., dissenting).

125. *Id.* at 746–47.

126. *Id.*

127. *Id.* at 763 (White, J., dissenting).

128. *Id.* at 762 (White, J., dissenting).

129. Green v. County School Board, 391 U.S. at 438.

130. Milliken v. Bradley, 418 U.S. at 782 (Marshall, J., dissenting).

131. Pasadena City Board of Education v. Spangler, 427 U.S. at 437.

132. *Id.* at 436.

133. *Id.* at 436–37.

134. *Id.* at 435–36. *See* Swann v. Charlotte-Mecklenburg Board of Education, 402 U.S. at 32 (absent showing of deliberate official action to manipulate demographics and thereby affect racial composition of schools, further judicial action unnecessary).

135. 427 U.S. at 436.

136. Milliken v. Bradley, 418 U.S. at 806 (Marshall, J., dissenting).

137. Swann v. Charlotte-Mecklenburg Board of Education, 402 U.S. at 15 (*quoting* Green v. County School Board of New Kent County, 391 U.S. at 437–38).

138. Marek, *Education by Decree*, New Perspectives, Summer 1985, at 36, 39.

139. Brown v. Board of Education, 347 U.S. at 492–93.

140. Bolling v. Sharpe, 347 U.S. at 500.

141. San Antonio Independent School District v. Rodriguez, 411 U.S. 1, 33–37 (1973).

142. Milliken v. Bradley, 418 U.S. at 814 (Marshall, J., dissenting).

143. *Id.* (Marshall, J., dissenting).

144. In striking down federal civil rights legislation prohibiting racial discrimination in public accommodations, as discussed in Chapter 3, the Court observed that "there must be some stage in the progress of [one's] elevation when he takes the rank of a mere citizen, and ceases to be the special favorite of the laws, and when his rights ... are to be protected in the ordinary mode by which other men's rights are protected." Civil Rights Cases, 109 U.S. 3, 25 (1883).

145. Plessy v. Ferguson, 163 U.S. at 551.

146. Columbus Board of Education v. Penick, 443 U.S. at 483 (Powell, J., dissenting).

147. *See, e.g.,* Alexander v. Holmes County Board of Education, 396 U.S. 19, 20 (1969); Cooper v. Aaron, 358 U.S. at 16.

148. Columbus Board of Education v. Penick, 443 U.S. at 483 (Powell, J., dissenting).

149. Cleveland Board of Education v. Reed, 445 U.S. 935, 938 (1980) (Rehnquist, J., dissenting from denial of certiorari).

150. *See, e.g.,* Riddick v. School Board of Norfolk, 784 F.2d 521, 527 (4th Cir.), *cert. denied,* 479 U.S. 938 (1986); Parent Association of Andrew Jackson High School v. Ambach, 598 F.2d 705 (2d Cir. 1979).

151. *See* Parent Association of Andrew Jackson High School v. Ambach, 598 F.2d at 710–11.

152. Parent Association of Andrew Jackson High School v. Ambach, 738 F.2d 574, 576 (2d 1984).

153. *Id.*

154. *Id.*

155. *Id.* at 577.

156. *Id.* at 581 n.9.

157. *See* Riddick v. School Board of Norfolk, 627 F. Supp. 814 (E.D. Va. 1984), *aff'd*, 784 F.2d 521 (4th Cir.), *cert. denied*, 479 U.S. 938 (1986).

158. *Id.* at 816–17.

159. *Id.* at 818.

160. *Id.*

161. *Id.* at 823.

162. *Id.* at 824.

163. *Id.* Segregation, as discussed in Chapter 4, was upheld on the grounds that it reflected established custom, promoted public comfort, and preserved peace and order.

164. *See supra* note 147 and accompanying text.

165. Board of Education of Oklahoma City Public Schools v. Dowell, 111 S. Ct. 630, 632 (1991).

166. *Id.* at 636.

167. *Id.* (quoting United States v. United Shoe Machinery Corp., 391 U.S. 244, 248 (1968)).

168. *Id.* at 644 (Marshall, J., dissenting).

169. *Id.* at 638.

170. *See* McCleskey v. Kemp, 481 U.S. 279, 298 (1987) (death penalty); Village of Arlington Heights v. Metropolitan Housing Development Corporation, 429 U.S. 252, 265 (1977) (housing); Washington v. Davis, 426 U.S. 229, 240 (1976) (public employment).

171. *See supra* note 116 and accompanying text.

172. *See* United States v. O'Brien, 391 U.S. at 383–84.

173. *Id.* at 384.

174. Washington v. Davis, 426 U.S. at 248.

175. *See* Lawrence, *supra* note 96, at 355–58.

176. McCleskey v. Kemp, 481 U.S. at 287.

177. *Id.* at 286.

178. *Id.* at 312.

179. *Id.* at 321, 329 (Brennan, J., dissenting).

180. *See* Rarity for U.S. Executions: White Dies for Killing Black, New York Times, Sept. 7, 1991, § 1, at 1, col. 1.

181. *See* Civil Rights Act of 1964, 42 U.S.C. §§2000a to 2000b–3 (public accommodations and facilities); §§2000d to 2000d–6(d) (public schools); § 2000e to 2000e–2(j) (employment).

182. Wards Cove Packing Co. v. Atonio, 109 S. Ct. 2115 (1989).

183. *Id.* at 2124.

184. *Id.* at 2126.

185. Patterson v. McLean Credit Union, 109 S. Ct. 2363, 2373 (1989).

186. *Id.* at 2379.

187. Strauder v. West Virginia, 100 U.S. 303 (1879).

188. Wards Cove Packing Co. v. Atonio, 109 S. Ct. at 2136 (Blackmun, J., dissenting, joined by Brennan and Marshall, J.J.).

189. R. Bork, *supra* note 26.

Chapter 6

Color Blindness Revisited

The concept of a color-blind Constitution was introduced by Justice Harlan in the late nineteenth century.[1] Harlan's assertion that "[t]here is no caste here"[2] essentially was dismissed by the *Plessy* Court pursuant to distinctions between civil and social equality. Eventual determination that separate was inherently unequal in education and in other public contexts reflected investment in color blindness as a broad spectrum principle of equal protection. The subsequent addition of discriminatory purpose criteria, however, effectively narrowed and confounded the possibilities of establishing constitutional violations. By requiring proof of illegal motive and discounting the significance of disproportionality, the Supreme Court fashioned doctrine responsive to overt discrimination but poorly adapted to recognizing and accounting for subtle or unconscious prejudice.

As equal protection jurisprudence coursed toward the end of the twentieth century, traditional manifestations of discrimination, such as prescriptive segregation, essentially had been eradicated. Racism and discrimination primarily had become unconscious or a function of hidden motive.[3] To the extent patently race-conscious policies existed, they generally manifested themselves as initiatives or programs accounting for past discrimination. For modern purposes, therefore, color-blind criteria have become more instrumental in defeating the remediation rather than the reality of discrimination against minorities.

Affirmative action is a concept susceptible to diverse understandings that are not always clarified before debate commences. The notion, for instance, may include institutional initiatives to identify impediments to minority recruiting, advancement or retention. It also may denote an effort to seek out qualified minority candidates and thus broaden a selection pool. Affirmative action also may describe a program of minority preferences. Such policies, especially in employment and education contexts, have been the source of significant constitutional controversy.

The debate over racial preferences discloses abiding tension between society's commitment to racial justice and its willingness to absorb associated costs. The Court first reckoned substantively with the issue of minority set asides in 1978. A few years earlier, in *De Funis v. Odegaard*, it had denied review of a preferential admission program at a state-supported law school.[4] Dismissal of the action as moot elicited criticism that the Court was "transform[ing] principles of avoidance of constitutional decisions into devices for side-stepping resolution of difficult cases."[5] The denial of review also prompted dissenting justices to note the pressing nature of the issue and that "few constitutional questions in recent history have stirred as much debate."[6] The controversy magnified rather than abated, and the Court a few years later rendered its lengthiest and most fractionated decision on race since *Scott v. Sandford*.

In *Regents of the University of California v. Bakke*, the Court examined a preferential admissions program at a state medical school.[7] The institution had established criteria which set aside positions for designated racial or ethnic minorities. The respondent, a white male, maintained that he was denied admission as a consequence of the policy.[8] The California Supreme Court, finding the program at odds with the state constitution, Title VI of the Civil Rights Act of 1964, and equal protection, accordingly ordered the school to admit the respondent.[9] The U.S. Supreme Court affirmed the decision[10] but did so on grounds that did not conclusively answer the constitutional question. Four justices determined that the special admissions program breached neither the equal protection guarantee nor Title VI of the Civil Rights Act of 1964.[11] Four justices avoided the constitutional issue altogether and discerned a violation of Title VI.[12] Justice Powell concluded that the program was generally at odds with the equal protection guarantee and Title VI.[13] Unlike the four justices who discerned a statutory violation, Powell maintained that neither Title VI nor the Constitution barred all race-conscious programs.[14] His refusal to foreclose such classifications entirely was significant because it was the one constitutional point in the decision that commanded majority support.[15]

On the critical question of what the appropriate standard of review should be, Powell refused to join the four justices who found the program constitutionally permissible. Instead of a bifurcated level of review contingent on the nature of the classification, he asserted that any racial favoritism, even if characterized as benign, should be subject to strict review.[16] The level of judicial scrutiny employed in evaluating a policy or action is critical to the outcome of a case. To the extent a mere rationality standard operates, as in the assessment of general economic regulation, review is highly deferential and the contested law generally is upheld. When the Court engages in strict scrutiny, the challenged enactment or provision must be justified by compelling reasons and must minimally burden constitutional interests. Such exacting review, characterizing analysis of racial classifications, tends to be unforgiving. In between strict and rationality criteria is an intermediate standard of review, used when gender and other classifications are implicated, which is reducible to a balancing of constitutional and governmental interests. In advocating rigorous judicial scrutiny of the special admissions program, Powell did not make clear whether he meant review that, as applied since 1954, was "strict in theory, and fatal in fact."[17] Confusing the issue somewhat was his mixing of "compelling interest" language of an intermediate standard.[18] Because a less rigorous level of review was urged by other justices whom he did not join, it may be logical to infer that Powell intended all racial classifications to be reviewed pursuant to the most exacting standards.

Having identified what he considered the appropriate level of scrutiny, Powell determined whether a compelling reason existed for the special admissions program. The university had offered four justifications that included enrolling a minimum number of students from certain racial or ethnic groups, eliminating discrimination, improving health care in disadvantaged communities, and maintaining a diverse student body.[19] Powell considered each point seriatim. First, he determined that the objective of admitting a fixed proportion of designated minorities, whether identified in terms of quotas or goals, was "facially invalid."[20] Although acknowledging a valid state interest in accounting for "identified discrimination," he concluded that remediation requires legislative or judicial findings of prior wrongdoing by the pertinent institution or program.[21] Such determinations had not been made, nor did he consider the school itself authorized to make them on its own.[22] Third, Powell criticized the assumption that minority students necessarily would practice in and thereby improve the quality of health care in disadvantaged communities.[23] Even if that goal might reflect a profound interest, he found no evidence that the "special admissions program is either needed or geared to promote that goal."[24] Finally, Powell determined that the aim of general diversification represented a compelling interest. Although disapproving of diversification based on racial or ethnic considerations exclusively, he concluded that "students with a particular background—whether it be ethnic, geographic, culturally advantaged or disadvantaged—may bring to a professional school of medicine experiences, outlooks and ideas that enrich the training of its student body and better equip its graduates to render with understanding their vital service to humanity."[25]

Given four votes for a manifestly race-conscious policy and Powell's approval of race as a factor within a general diversification policy,[26] majority support existed at least for the latter premise. The Court did not exempt any racial classification from close scrutiny for compliance but left open the possibility of limited consideration of race. Although the policy itself was deficient under the Fourteenth Amendment, the state had a constitutional "interest that legitimately may be served by a properly devised admissions program involving the competitive consideration of race and ethnic origin."[27]

Justice Brennan, joined by Justices White, Marshall, and Blackmun, urged a more relaxed standard of review on the grounds that the Court should not impede initiatives calculated to eliminate discrimination against minorities.[28] For Brennan, the process defect rationale of strict scrutiny was inapt because whites were neither traditionally excluded from nor underrepresented in the political process and their interests were thus unlikely to be slighted.[29] Because even benign-appearing classifications might stereotype or stigmatize a discrete group, and because race constituted an immutable characteristic, Brennan did not advocate entirely deferential review.[30] Rather, he proposed an intermediate standard that would have required a careful examination of but a more favorable disposition toward racial preferences. As Brennan put it:

to justify such a classification an important and articulated purpose for its use must be shown. In addition, any statute must be stricken that stigmatizes any group or that singles out those least well represented in the political process to bear the brunt of a benign program. Thus our review under the Fourteenth Amendment should be strict—not " 'strict' in theory and fatal in fact," because it is stigma that causes fatality—but strict and searching nonetheless.[31]

Brennan thus proposed a version of "strict" review friendlier to remedial policy and aims but not insensitive to possible abuse or misuse of racial classifications. Specifically, any preferential policy would have to be justified by an important interest outweighing its burdens and narrowly tailored to avoid stigmatizing consequences. From Brennan's perspective, remediation of societal discrimination was a significant interest that outweighed any harm to members of the majority race.[32] Nor did he consider the special admissions policy a source of stigma insofar as the respondent would not "in any sense [be] stamped as inferior by [his] rejection."[33]

In a separate opinion, Justice Marshall noted the nation's legacy of racial discrimination, which from his viewpoint justified race-dependent attention.[34] Noting that the Court a century earlier had foreclosed "several affirmative action programs after the Civil War," he expressed his "fear that we have come full circle."[35] Justice Blackmun maintained that racial discrimination could not be effectively reckoned with absent policies that directly and explicitly confronted its consequences. He accordingly observed that "[i]n order to get beyond racism, we must first take account of race."[36]

A third analysis was provided by a plurality of four justices who, focusing solely on the statutory permissibility of the program, asserted that federal law required strict neutrality.[37] In an opinion joined by Chief Justice Burger and Justices Rehnquist and Stewart, Justice Stevens opined that Title VI and its legislative history required strict colorblindness.[38]

Justice Blackmun had expressed the hope that the "time will come when an 'affirmative action' program is unnecessary . . . [and] . . . we could reach this stage within a decade at the most."[39] It has become evident after nearly two decades of litigation that, to say the least, Blackmun was overly optimistic. Two years after the *Bakke* case, the Court confronted the question of federal set-asides for minority contractors in public works projects. The resultant decision in *Fullilove v. Klutznick* reflected further fragmentation of opinion.[40] The program at issue, requiring 10 percent minority participation in all covered work, was upheld. Three justices, in an opinion written by Chief Justice Burger, found it a proper exercise of congressional power.[41] Three others, headed by Justice Marshall, advocated a standard of review akin to what Brennan had asserted in *Bakke*.[42] Justices Stewart and Rehnquist articulated absolute opposition to all racial classifications,[43] and Justice Stevens expressed his general disfavor of them.[44]

Burger specifically avoided any of the analytical formulas advanced in *Bakke*.[45] His opinion did not disclose clearly, however, what standard of review was appropriate. He considered whether the program's objectives were within Congress's power and found sufficient authority under the commerce, spending, and necessary and proper clauses and the Fourteenth Amendment.[46] Burger, however, did not indicate whether legislative means must be justified by an important or a compelling interest and thus whether scrutiny should be rigorous or relaxed. Further muddying the standard of review was his observation that deference must be extended to congressional policy choices, but that legislative means must be subject to "careful judicial evaluation."[47] It appears that, because the program implicated congressional authority, Burger favored judicial inquiry of "limited scope."[48] He also found the policy reasonably designed to accomplish its end.[49] Contributing to the program's reasonableness, at least from Burger's perspective, were the absence of fixed quotas, its remedial operation in a prospective fashion, the availability of waivers for contractors who could not secure minority participation despite their best efforts, and safeguards against participation by front groups and firms unaffected by discrimination.[50]

Justice Powell in a concurring opinion reasserted his previously articulated strict scrutiny standard and concluded that the set-aside program passed constitutional muster. In his view, the policy represented remediation of specific discrimination identified by a body capable of making such findings.[51] Redressing the effects of discrimination, at least to the extent such practice was established, represented to Powell a compelling interest.[52] He also recognized the Thirteenth and Fourteenth Amendments as sources of authority affording Congress discretion to choose a suitable remedy for redressing racial discrimination.[53]

Also concurring were Justices Marshall, Brennan, and Blackmun. They found the policy constitutional because it repaired the effects of discrimination and thus was substantially related to achieving an important governmental objective.[54]

Justice Stewart, joined by Justice Rehnquist, authored a dissent that invoked Harlan's depiction of the Constitution as color-blind. Stewart maintained that "any official action that treats a person differently on account of his race or ethnic origin is inherently suspect."[55] Whether Harlan actually would have endorsed such an undifferentiating presumption against all racial classifications is unclear. His vision of a color-blind constitution was articulated in response not to remedial initiatives but to classifications favoring a "dominant race—a superior class of citizens."[56] Regardless of how Harlan actually would have regarded modern affirmative action programs, adopted by democratic processes to account for consequences of historical discrimination against minorities, Stewart and Rehnquist insisted that racial classifications generally should be prohibited, regardless of whom they benefited and why.

Justice Stevens was willing to "assume that the wrong committed against the Negro class is both so serious and so pervasive that it would constitutionally justify an appropriate classwide recovery measured by a sum certain for every member of the injured class."[57] Stevens, however, found Congress's interest in support of "favored access . . . a plainly impermissible justification for this racial classification."[58] With respect to the historical realities of the construction industry, he discerned inadequate evidence of past discrimination against any particular minority.[59] Unlike Stewart and Rehnquist, Stevens indicated that preferential policies may be apt for "victims of unfair treatment in the past" or for groups less able to compete in the future.[60]

The *Bakke* and *Fullilove* decisions established a limited constitutional tolerance for remedial classifications. Still uncertain, however, were standards of review and adequate justification. By the mid-1980s, even though a majority position had yet to evolve, at least two trends had manifested themselves. First, it was evident that remedial classifications would elicit enhanced judicial attention. Second, general societal discrimination, despite its reality and legacy, would not be a permissible reference point for race-conscious remedies. Such truths manifested themselves when the Court invalidated a preferential layoff scheme for teachers in *Wygant v. Jackson Board of Education.*[61]

The policy at issue in *Wygant* had been collectively bargained for and adopted following a history of racial tension and problems in the affected school system. It responded specifically to the underrepresentation of minority faculty members, reflected a sensed need for minority role models, and was described by the court of appeals "as an attempt to alleviate the effects of societal discrimination."[62] A plurality of four, in an opinion written by Justice Powell, determined that societal discrimination by itself was "too amorphous a basis for imposing a racially classified remedy."[63] Even a limited remedial policy could not survive, pursuant to the plurality position, absent "some showing of prior discrimination by the governmental unit involved."[64] Also rejected was the role model theory as a justification for preferential status. As Powell put it:

[t]he role model theory allows the Board to engage in discriminatory hiring and layoff practices long past the point required by any legitimate remedial purpose. ... [B]ecause the role model theory does not necessarily bear a relationship to the harm caused by prior discriminatory hiring practices, it actually could be used to escape the obligation to remedy such practices by justifying the small percentage of black teachers by reference to the small percentage of black students. Carried to its logical extreme, the idea that black students are better off with black teachers could lead to the very system the Court rejected in [1954].[65]

The plurality cautioned that before implementing an affirmative action program, a public official or entity "must have sufficient evidence to justify the conclusion that there has been prior discrimination...so that remedial action is warranted."[66] Such an inquiry was crucial, from Powell's perspective, for purposes of eliminating vestiges of discrimination and avoiding new racial distinctions.[67] Without specific evidence of past discrimination, at least as indicated by four justices, policy was bound by principles of racial neutrality.

The plurality also determined that the "reasonableness" test used by the court of appeals was the wrong standard of review.[68] Strict scrutiny, which had been advocated singularly by Powell in *Bakke*, thereby attracted broader support in *Wygant*. As described by Powell, strict review required that "the means chosen to accomplish the state's asserted purpose must be specifically and narrowly framed to accomplish that purpose."[69] Although advocating rigorous review, the plurality did not foreclose all race-conscious remedies. It acknowledged "that in order to remedy the effects of prior discrimination, it may be necessary to take race into account. As part of this Nation's dedication to eradicating racial discrimination, innocent persons may be called upon to bear some of the burden of the remedy."[70]

Concern with what were indentified as innocent victims, and the context in which burdens were imposed as a consequence of remedial policies, was significant to the outcome in *Wygant*. Powell distinguished preferential hiring and layoff provisions on the grounds that the latter resulted in more profound harm.[71] He observed that

[i]n cases involving valid *hiring* goals, the burden to be borne by innocent individuals is diffused to a considerable extent among society generally. Though hiring goals may burden some innocent individuals, they simply do not impose the same kind of injury that layoffs impose. Denial of a future employment opportunity is not as intrusive as loss of an existing job.[72]

Because the impact of preferential layoffs was considered too severe, and because less burdensome remedies such as hiring goals were available, the plurality concluded that the policy could not "satisfy the demands of the Equal Protection Clause."[73]

Justice O'Connor wrote separately to emphasize that a finding of prior discrimination should not be an absolute prerequisite for voluntary affirmative action plans by public employers.[74] Although noting that such a finding ensures policy responsive to identified illegality, rather than general societal discrimination, she cautioned that the requirement "would severely undermine public employers' incentive to meet voluntarily their civil rights obligations."[75] Despite the divergence of opinions and the absence of a clear majority position, O'Connor suggested that significant common ground existed among the various justices. She thus ventured that

the Court is at least in accord in believing that a public employer, consistent with the Constitution, may undertake an affirmative action program which is designed to further a legitimate remedial purpose and which implements that purpose by means that do not impose disproportionate harm on the interests, or unnecessarily trammel the rights, of innocent individuals directly and adversely affected by a plan's racial preference.[76]

Even if suggesting an evolving majority position, O'Connor's sentiment did not represent a consensus.

In a dissenting opinion, Justice Marshall criticized the Court for disregarding key facts and circumstances and for relying on an underdeveloped factual record.[77] Although agreeing that "layoffs are unfair," he distinguished the harm from constitutional injury.[78] Marshall suggested that dislocation was a function of economic realities rather than the challenged process.[79] From his perspective, a general proscription of preferential layoffs denied the community of "hard-won benefits of its integration efforts" and elevated seniority to a fundamental and indefeasible status.[80] He further noted that the prioritization of seniority was selective because qualifications and needs unrelated to race traditionally have been allowed to trump it.[81]

Marshall was influenced by the source of the layoff provision and manner in which it had been established. The policy had emerged from the collective bargaining process and, as he described it, thus had been "forged in the crucible of clashing interests.... [in which] the economic powers of the predominantly white teachers' union were brought to bear against those of the elected Board, and the process yielded consensus."[82] Given a procedure described as "a legitimate and powerful vehicle for the resolution of thorny problems," over which the judiciary normally exercises "minimal supervision," he suggested that

[t]he perceived dangers of affirmative action being misused, therefore, are naturally averted by the bilateral process of negotiation, agreement, and ratification. [When] an elected school board and a teachers' union collectively bargain a layoff provision designed to preserve the effects of a valid minority recruitment plan by apportioning layoffs between two racial groups, as a result of a settlement achieved under the auspices of a supervisory state agency charged with protecting the civil rights of all citizens, that provision should not be upset by this Court on constitutional grounds.[83]

Justice Stevens offered a separate dissent and an alternative line of inquiry. Instead of debating whether such classifications could be justified by general or specific discrimination in the past, Stevens advocated a forward-looking perspective. He thus suggested attention to whether promoting "the public interest in educating children for the future ... justifies any adverse effects on the disadvantaged group."[84] At least for purposes of public education, he concluded that

one of the most important lessons that the American public schools teach is that the diverse ethnic, cultural, and national backgrounds that have been brought together in our famous "melting pot" do not identify essential differences among the human beings that inhabit our land. It is one thing for a white child to be taught by a white teacher that color, like beauty, is only "skin deep"; it is far more convincing to experience that truth on a day-to-day basis during the routine, ongoing learning process.[85]

He thus found "a rational and unquestionably legitimate basis" for recruiting and retaining minority teachers.[86]

Stevens also suggested that the trend toward race-neutral standards, regardless of a classification's purpose, was misdirected. Unlike the plurality, he advocated distinguishing between policies that excluded minorities and those that were designed to include them. As Stevens related it, an

exclusionary decision rests on the false premise that differences in race, or in the color of a person's skin, reflect real differences that are relevant to a person's right to share in the blessings of a free society. As noted, that premise is "utterly irrational," and repugnant to the principles of a free and democratic society. Nevertheless, the fact that persons of different races do, indeed, have differently colored skin, may give rise to a belief that there is some significant difference between such persons. The inclusion of minority teachers in the educational process inevitably tends to dispel that illusion whereas their exclusion could only tend to foster it. The inclusionary decision is consistent with the principle that all men are created equal; the exclusionary decision is at war with that principle. One decision accords with the Equal Protection Clause of the Fourteenth Amendment; the other does not. Thus, consideration of whether the consciousness of race is exclusionary or inclusionary plainly distinguishes the Board's valid purpose in this case from a race-conscious decision that would reinforce assumptions of inequality.[87]

Stevens acknowledged that preferential policies may cause constitutionally unacceptable harm. Instead of the generally prohibitive standards established by the majority to protect innocent victims, however, Stevens proposed a two-part inquiry into whether consequent burdens were excessive or inimical to the public interest. Such analysis would focus first on the procedures used to establish the classification and second on the nature and extent of the actual harm.[88] Looking at the first consideration, Stevens described the collective bargaining procedure as "scrupulously fair."[89] He noted that the union representing all teachers "negotiated the provision and agreed to it; the agreement was put to a vote of the membership, and overwhelmingly approved."[90] Stevens characterized the injury itself as the consequence of economic conditions and the policy of preserving the faculty's integrated character.[91] Such harm to him was indistinguishable from the results of a decision to protect a teacher with special skills.[92] Because the layoff provision effected "a valid public purpose," was the output of "fair procedures," had "a narrow breadth," transcended "the harm to petitioners," and represented a step toward eliminating "entirely from governmental decision-making such irrelevant factors as a human being's race," Stevens discerned no constitutional offense.[93]

Justice Powell's opinion in *Bakke* had disclosed an animus toward racial quotas that for practical purposes since has defined the possibilities for affirmative action. A plurality decision supported by Powell departed from that general rule, however, in a case characterized by exigent circumstances. At issue in *United States v. Paradise* was a lower court order requiring the Alabama state police to set aside for qualified black troopers at least fifty percent of the promotions to the rank of corporal.[94] The quota system was framed as a temporary remedy and had been preceded by twelve years of noncompliance, litigation, and delay.[95]

The plurality opinion, authored by Justice Brennan, did not set a specific standard of review but determined that the order was narrowly tailored to effect a compelling government interest and at least would survive strict scrutiny.[96] The compelling justifications included the elimination of past and present discrimination and the enforcement of federal court judgments.[97] Given the need for flexible and temporary relief, the ineffectiveness of alternative remedies, the availability of waiver provisions, the relationship of the numerical goals to the relevant labor market, and the impact of relief on the rights of third parties, the plurality apprehended a sufficiently tight fit between the means and the ends.[98]

The Brennan plurality also found that the 50 percent standard did not impose undue burdens on innocent persons. Rather,

the temporary and extremely limited nature of the requirement substantially limits any potential burden on white applicants for promotion.... Nor has the Court imposed an "absolute bar" to white advancement.... The one-for-one requirement does not require the layoff and discharge of white employees and therefore does not impose burdens of the sort that concerned the plurality in Wygant.... Because the one-for-one requirement is so limited in scope and duration, it only postpones the promotions of qualified whites.[99]

Although joining the opinion, Justice Powell separately emphasized the "persistent violation of constitutional rights and repeated failure to carry out court orders," which, if unaccounted for, would have subverted the judiciary's remedial power.[100] Referring also to the state's past and persistent disobedience, Justice Stevens suggested that it should have the burden of proving that relief exceeded the bounds of reasonableness.[101]

Justice O'Connor, joined by Chief Justice Rehnquist and Justice Scalia, dissented. They maintained that evidence did not support "such an extreme quota" because it "far exceeded the percentage of blacks in the trooper force," was prompted solely by "in terrorem" considerations, and thus could not "survive strict scrutiny."[102] She also suggested several alternatives, such as the appointment of a trustee to develop promotion procedures and the issuance of citations, fines, or other penalties for contempt of court decrees.[103] O'Connor emphasized that racial classifications "must fit with greater precision than any alternative remedy," and concluded that the order failed strict scrutiny.[104]

The first decade of affirmative action jurisprudence was characterized by doctrinal competition and uncertainty. In *City of Richmond v. J. A. Croson Co.*, analysis was substantially clarified and hardened against race-conscious remedies.[105] For the first time, a majority agreed not only that societal discrimination was an inapt premise but also that remedial policies should be subject to strict scrutiny.[106] Justice Scalia urged an especially rigorous model of review that would translate into a virtually absolute proscription of all racial classifications.[107] Dispute within the majority thus was reducible to whether strict scrutiny should be exacting or unforgiving.

At issue in *Croson* was a municipal set-aside program for minority contractors that essentially replicated the policy adopted by Congress and upheld in the *Fullilove* case.[108] Local government officials had based the program on congressional findings of nationwide discrimination in the construction industry and on a local study. The latter showed that while blacks constituted 50 percent of Richmond's population, minority businesses received only .67 percent of the city's building contracts.[109] Despite the congruence with congressional action, Justice O'Connor distinguished state and local remedial initiatives on the grounds that they are not a function of the "specific constitutional mandate to enforce the dictates of the Fourteenth Amendment."[110] Characterizing the equal protection guarantee as an explicit check on state power, the Court resolved the tension in favor of a proscriptive constitutional interest. At least in the context of remediation, the Court diverted from a Fourteenth Amendment legacy of deference to state concern.

Forceful use of the equal protection guarantee to curb state authority, as demonstrated in preceding chapters, is not a historical norm. Except for a short interval commencing with *Brown* and expiring with the introduction of motive-based criteria, equal protection review largely has yielded to state interests and imperatives. The Court in *Croson*, however, maintained that "[t]o hold otherwise would be to cede control of the [guarantee] to the 50 state legislatures and their myriad political subdivisions."[111] Nor was remedial latitude affected by the nature of the classification. As the Court noted:

[t]he mere recitation of a benign or compensatory purpose for the use of a racial classification would essentially entitle the States to exercise the full power of Congress under §5 of the Fourteenth Amendment and insulate any racial classification from judicial scrutiny under §1. We believe that such a result would be contrary to the intentions of the Framers of the Fourteenth Amendment, who desired to place clear limits on the States' use of race as a criterion for legislative action, and to have the federal courts enforce those limitations.[112]

Turning to the operative standard of review, O'Connor asserted that racial classifications, regardless of how they are characterized, must be closely examined. She maintained that

[a]bsent searching judicial inquiry into the justification for such race-based measures, there is simply no way of determining what classifications are "benign" or
"remedial" and what classifications are in fact motivated by illegitimate notions
of racial inferiority or simple racial politics. Indeed, the purpose of strict scrutiny
is to "smoke out" illegitimate uses of race by assuring that the legislative body
is pursuing a goal important enough to warrant use of a highly suspect tool.
The test also ensures that the means chosen "fit" this compelling goal so closely
that there is little or no possibility that the motive for the classification was
illegitimate racial prejudice or stereotype.[113]

Refusal to differentiate among classifications, regardless of "the race
of those burdened or benefited,"[114] reflected a sense that group-
referenced policies are categorically pernicious. O'Connor accordingly
observed that remedial "[c]lassifications based on race carry a danger of
stigmatic harm. Unless they are strictly reserved for remedial settings,
they may in fact promote notions of racial inferiority and lead to a politics
of racial hostility."[115] In repudiating a more relaxed standard of review
proposed by the dissent, she emphasized that "without first engaging in
an examination of the factual basis for [the] enactment and the nexus
between its scope and that factual basis," it would be impossible to determine whether a classification was truly remedial.[116] What O'Connor
depicted as a "watered-down version of equal protection review," from
her perspective, would ensure "that race will always be relevant in American life."[117] Further militating in favor of close scrutiny, at least for
O'Connor, was the fact that blacks constituted half of the city's population
and held a majority of the council seats.[118] Such political dynamics suggested to her a possibility that the legislative process might be misused
and a need for exacting review of its output.

Also fatal to the set-aside plan were what O'Connor considered inadequate findings of actual discrimination in the local construction industry. Although acknowledging "the sorry history of both private and
public discrimination in this country," O'Connor renounced the notion
that societal discrimination by itself was sufficient to support a race-
dependent policy.[119] Without a showing of actual discrimination, she
asserted, a legislative body could not determine the precise scope of the
injury it needed to redress.[120] Amorphous claims, O'Connor cautioned,
would engender policies with no logical stopping point.[121] Noting that
the remedial policy at issue defined "minority" in broad terms, including
Aleuts and Eskimos, who probably never even resided in Richmond, she
discerned a "gross overinclusiveness . . . [which] strongly impugns the
city's claim of remedial motivation."[122]

Characterizing the plan as insufficiently linked to identified discrimination, O'Connor suggested that it was impossible to assess whether it
was narrowly tailored to remedy past wrongs.[123] She nonetheless found
no evidence that race-neutral methodologies, such as city financing of

small firms, had been considered.[124] Consistent with the Court's general hostility toward fixed quotas, at least absent exigent circumstances, O'Connor opined that the plan could not be tailored to achieve any goal other than unadorned racial balancing.[125] Despite acknowledging that legislative factfinding ordinarily is accorded a presumption of regularity and usually deferred to, she concluded that mere recitation of a benign purpose, generalized reference to remedial goals, and identification of disparities were inadequate to survive strict scrutiny.[126]

Although having foreclosed the possibility of race-conscious remedies in response to general societal discrimination, O'Connor noted that "[n]othing we say today precludes a state or local entity from taking action to rectify the effects of identified discrimination within its jurisdiction."[127] As possibilities for an adequate remedial premise, she suggested significant statistical disparity between the number of qualified minority contractors willing and able to perform and the number of them actually engaged by the city or its prime contractors.[128] In an extreme case, she acknowledged that "some form of narrowly tailored racial preference might be necessary to break down patterns of deliberate exclusion."[129] O'Connor reminded, however, that

[p]roper findings in this regard are necessary to define both the scope of the injury and the extent of the remedy necessary to cure its effects. Such findings also serve to assure all citizens that the deviation from the norm of equal treatment of all racial and ethnic groups is a temporary matter, a measure taken in the service of the goal of equality itself.[130]

In closing, O'Connor further repudiated the notion, already rejected by the *Wygant* plurality, that remediation might be referenced to general historical reality. She warned that

[t]o accept Richmond's claim that past societal discrimination alone can serve as the basis for rigid racial preferences would be to open the door to competing claims for "remedial relief" for every disadvantaged group. The dream of a Nation of equal citizens in a society where race is irrelevant to personal opportunity and achievement would be lost in a mosaic of shifting preferences based on inherently unmeasurable claims of past wrongs. . . . We think such a result would be contrary to both the letter and spirit of a constitutional provision whose central command is equality.[131]

Discerning no sufficient basis for remediation, O'Connor determined that the city's "treatment of its citizens on a racial basis violates the dictates of the Equal Protection Clause."[132]

Justice Stevens, concurring separately and in part, reiterated his preference for the criteria he advanced in *Wygant*. He found the Richmond program deficient because it (1) made "no claim that the public interest in the efficient performance of its construction contracts will be served by granting a preference to minority-business enterprises," (2) represented a legislative rather than judicial remedial effort, and (3) was a function of racial stereotyping.[133]

Justice Scalia, concurring only in the judgment and thus not the reasoning supporting it, challenged "the Court's dicta suggesting that... state and local government may in some circumstances discriminate on the basis of race...."[134] Scalia proposed a standard that, absent extraordinary circumstances unrelated to remediation, would prohibit any official racial classification. He observed that

[t]he difficulty of overcoming the effects of past discrimination is as nothing compared with the difficulty of eradicating from our society the source of those effects, which is the tendency—fatal to a nation such as ours—to classify and judge men and women on the basis of their country of origin or the color of their skin. A solution to the first problem that aggravates the second is no solution at all.[135]

For Scalia, color blindness was a fixed rule that could be deviated from only to dismantle an officially segregated school system or to deal with "a social emergency rising to the level of imminent danger to life and limb."[136] As an example of exigent circumstances sufficient to justify a departure from strict neutrality, he suggested a prison riot necessitating temporary segregation.[137] Expressing further his general antipathy toward remedial classifications, he asserted that "[w]here injustice is the game, ... turn-about is not fair play."[138] From Scalia's perspective, and excepting school desegregation processes, policy designed to undo the effects of identifiable discrimination would have to be race-neutral.

Resistance to race-conscious remedies, even in response to specifically identified discrimination, distinguished Scalia's position from that of the O'Connor plurality. He stressed, however, that nothing precluded a state from implementing a racially neutral remedial "preference to identified victims of discrimination. While most of the beneficiaries might be black, neither the beneficiaries nor those disadvantaged by the preference would be identified *on the basis of their race*."[139]

Although acknowledging "that in our society blacks have suffered discrimination immeasurably greater than any directed at other racial groups," Scalia maintained that race-dependent policy reinforces "a manner of thinking by race that was the source of the injustice and that will, if it endures within our society, be the source of more injustice still."[140] In closing, he cautioned that

racial preferences appear to "even the score" (in some small degree) only if one embraces the proposition that our society is appropriately viewed as divided into races, making it right that an injustice rendered in the past to a black man should be compensated for by discriminating against a white. Nothing is worth that embrace. Since blacks have been disproportionately disadvantaged by racial discrimination, any race-neutral remedial program aimed at the disadvantaged *as such* will have a disproportionately beneficial impact on blacks. Only such a program, and not one that operates on the basis of race, is in accord with the letter and the spirit of our Constitution.[141]

The alternative of policy focused on general rather than racial disadvantage has elicited criticism that it diverts attention from the unique harm of racial discrimination and is unresponsive to its legacy. Proponents of race-conscious measures maintain that, if remediation was referenced to need rather than historical discrimination, indigent whites would receive most of the benefits.[142] Justice Marshall, joined by Justices Brennan and Blackmun, authored an especially strident dissent, depicting the decision as "a deliberate and giant step backward in this Court's affirmative action jurisprudence."[143] Marshall noted the significance of the majority investment in strict scrutiny but found it ironic that the decision "second guess[ed]" the judgment of a city which as "the former capital of the Confederacy . . . knows what racial discrimination is."[144]

Marshall criticized the Court for "down-play[ing] the fact that the City Council had before it a rich trove of evidence that discrimination in the Nation's construction industry had seriously impaired the competitive position of businesses owned or controlled by members of minority groups."[145] He would have shifted the presumption in favor of remediation because Richmond had not demonstrated itself to be an exception to the comprehensive pattern of exclusion identified by Congress. From the Court's opinion, Marshall apprehended a sense of "cynicism" responsible for "a grapeshot attack on race-conscious remediation," blindness to the reality of national discrimination, and, a consequent lack of perspective infecting its analysis of the entire case.[146]

Marshall discerned two interests sufficient to justify the set-aside program. The first was the city's general aim of eradicating the effects of racial discrimination.[147] The second premise was "the prospective one of preventing the city's own spending decisions from reinforcing and perpetuating the exclusionary effects of past discrimination."[148] Contrary to O'Connor's reading of the record, Marshall was satisfied that extensive evidence existed to establish a record of discrimination. He referred specifically to presidential and congressional studies, the miniscule proportion of city contracts awarded to minority enterprises, and the absence of any testimony challenging the reality of pervasive racial discrimination.[149] Such reference points, Marshall maintained, were "a far cry from the reliance on generalized 'societal discrimination' which the majority decries as a basis for remedial action."[150] For him, the

Court's failure to apprehend a real history of specifically identifiable discrimination "simply blinks credibility"[151] and reflected "an unwillingness to come to grips with why construction contracting was" essentially a whites-only enterprise.[152]

Pursuing further his critique of the Court's pluralistic sensitivity, Marshall described invalidation of the set-aside program as a function of the majority's "armchair cynicism."[153] He suggested that if it had

paused for a moment on the facts of the Richmond experience, it would have discovered that the city's leadership is deeply familiar with what racial discrimination is. The members of the Richmond City Council have spent long years witnessing multifarious acts of discrimination, including, but not limited to, the deliberate diminution of black residents' voting rights, resistance to school desegregation, and publicly sanctioned housing discrimination. Numerous decisions of federal courts chronicle this disgraceful recent history.[154]

Marshall also objected to the lack of significance attached to findings by the federal government. To the extent that state and local authorities could not rely on such data, he perceived an onerous and formalistic documentary obligation even when "the reality of past discrimination was apparent."[155] Marshall intimated that the Court's hard line against remedial classifications, although couched in vigorous equal protection terms, actually forestalled a reckoning with discrimination.

In place of strict scrutiny, Marshall suggested a standard of review that would be attentive to abuse or misuse of classifications but also function more hospitably toward race-conscious remedies. For him it was sufficient that the program at issue was (1) substantially related to the city's aims of remedying past discrimination and (2) narrowly tailored insofar as it afforded waivers, did not interfere with vested interests, and operated prospectively.[156]

Although claiming that he "would ordinarily [end] his analysis at this point," the majority's investment in strict scrutiny "compelled [him] to add more."[157] Marshall observed that

[t]oday, for the first time, a majority of this Court has adopted strict scrutiny as its standard of Equal Protection Clause review of race-conscious remedial measures. This is an unwelcome development. A profound difference separates governmental actions that themselves are racist, and governmental actions that seek to remedy the effects of prior racism or to prevent neutral governmental activity from perpetuating the effects of such racism.[158]

He thus found troubling the Court's refusal to differentiate racial classifications for constitutional purposes.[159] For him, a sensible distinction existed between classifications reflecting a presumption of racial inferiority and those designed to remedy the effects of discrimination.

Marshall expressed concern that, just as many communities were electing minority leaders inclined to rectify past discrimination, the Court was harnessing them in a "strict scrutiny straitjacket."[160] Failure to accommodate remedial initiatives, he suggested, evaded or discounted "the tragic and indelible fact that discrimination against blacks and other racial minorities in this Nation has pervaded our Nation's history and continues to scar our society."[161] Marshall's sense was that the *Croson* decision compounded rather than deviated from a jurisprudential legacy that largely had accommodated discrimination. He expressed concern that

[i]n concluding that remedial classifications warrant no different standard of review under the Constitution than the most brute and repugnant forms of state-sponsored racism, a majority of this Court signals that it regards racial discrimination as largely a phenomenon of the past, and that government bodies need no longer preoccupy themselves with rectifying racial injustice. I, however, do not believe this Nation is anywhere close to eradicating racial discrimination or its vestiges. In constitutionalizing its wishful thinking, the majority today does a grave disservice not only to those victims of past and present racial discrimination in this Nation whom government has sought to assist, but also to this Court's long tradition of approaching issues of race with the utmost sensitivity.[162]

As depicted by Marshall, the Court's response was reminiscent of sentiment a century before that victims of discrimination should "cease[ ] to be the special favorite of the laws . . . [and] be protected in the ordinary modes by which other men's rights are protected."[163]

Finally, Marshall regarded the Court's invigoration of the equal protection guarantee as an exercise in convenience rather than principle. The selective significance of equal protection, at least for him, was evidenced by doctrine that confounded policies for reckoning with discriminatory realities.[164] Such analysis struck Marshall as procrustean and inconsistent with the original concern "that States would *not* adequately respond to racial violence or discrimination against newly freed slaves."[165] For him, interpretation of the Reconstruction amendments in a way that cramps remedial attention "turns the[m] . . . on their heads."[166] He argued that "nothing in the Amendments themselves, or in our long history of interpreting or applying those momentous charters, suggests that States, exercising their police power, are in any way constitutionally inhibited from working alongside the Federal Government in the fight against discrimination and its effects."[167] His suggestion that the Court had transformed the original meaning of the Fourteenth Amendment was notable because the premises he challenged were fashioned by justices closely associated with concepts of judicial restraint and fidelity to framer's intent.

Justice Marshall, who had helped guide the Court out of the separate but equal era, offered pointed criticism for what he perceived as doctrinal regression. In so doing, he illuminated an ironic spin of equal protection jurisprudence. A century earlier, the Court had deferred to the exercise of state police power and effectively accommodated the white majority.[168] In the affirmative action context, Marshall objected because the Court had curbed state power but again accommodated the dominant culture.[169] Compounding Marshall's message of despair was Blackmun's expression of disappointment that "this Court, the supposed bastion of equality, . . . [had acted] as though discrimination had never existed or was not demonstrated."[170] His perception, like Marshall's, was that "the Court today regresses."[171]

Subsequent jurisprudence has disclosed that, even if constitutional standards have hardened against racially preferential policies, they are not yet entirely proscriptive or necessarily limited to the narrow premises approved in *Croson*. In *Metro Broadcasting, Inc. v. Federal Communications Commission*, the Court upheld the policies that afforded minorities an advantage in comparative broadcast licensing proceedings and offered an incentive for financially distressed licensees to sell their radio or television properties to minorities.[172] The Federal Communications Commission, prompted by Congress, had adopted both policies on the grounds that minorities were underrepresented in broadcasting and that increased minority participation would enhance programming diversity.[173]

The Court, in reviewing the policies, determined that they did not offend the Fifth Amendment. It assigned overarching significance to the fact that the minority ownership programs had been not only congressionally approved but mandated.[174] The Court determined, moreover, that the preferences were permissible without regard to whether they were remedial or not. Specifically, it

h[e]ld that benign race-conscious measures mandated by Congress—even if those measures are not "remedial" in the sense of being designed to compensate victims of past governmental or societal discrimination—are constitutionally permissible to the extent that they serve important governmental objectives within the power of Congress and are substantially related to the achievement of those objectives.[175]

The Court concluded that the provisions were within Congress's power and sufficiently related to important aims.[176]

More specifically, it determined that enhancement of broadcast diversity constituted at least "an important governmental objective."[177] Justice Brennan, who wrote the majority opinion, analogized the challenged preferences to the "constitutionally permissible goal on which a race-conscious university admissions program may be based."[178] Promotion of program diversity in particular, he noted, "serves important First Amendment values."[179]

In finding the policies substantially related to permissible governmental aims, the Court referred to "long study and painstaking consideration of alternatives"[180] that established the policies as "critical means of promoting broadcast diversity" and to which it "must give great weight."[181] It anticipated

that expanded minority ownership of broadcast outlets will, in the aggregate, result in greater broadcast diversity. A broadcasting industry with representative minority participation will produce more variation and diversity than will one whose ownership is drawn from a single racially and ethnically homogeneous group. The predictive judgment about the overall result of minority entry into broadcasting is not a rigid assumption about how minority owners will behave in every case but rather is akin to Justice Powell's conclusion in *Bakke* that greater admission of minorities would contribute, on average, "to the robust exchange of ideas."[182]

Besides agreeing with the policies' premises, the Court rejected arguments that the preferences ran afoul of established equal protection doctrine.[183] It thus was unpersuaded that the challenged policies would result in impermissible stereotyping.[184] Responding to contentions that the rules would create unending preferences based on race, the Court found them "appropriately limited in extent and duration, and subject to reassessment and revaluation by Congress prior to any extension or re-enactment."[185] The majority also depicted the provisions as means rather than ends, which would expire on their own when the goal of diversification had been realized.[186] With respect to arguments that the preferences victimized nonminorities, the Court found that the burden upon them was "slight."[187] Contributing to the Court's sense of insubstantial injury was the broadcast licensing process itself, which offers no settled expectation that an application will be granted without consideration of multiple public interest factors that include minority ownership.[188]

Justice O'Connor, joined by Chief Justice Rehnquist and Justices Scalia and Kennedy, dissented on the grounds that the policy impermissibly distributed "benefits and burdens among individuals based on the assumption that race or ethnicity determines how they act or think."[189] O'Connor perceived a policy rooted in stereotype and at odds with what she considered the settled demands of strict scrutiny. Because the Court did not require a compelling justification for the preferences, she found a "renewed toleration of racial classifications and a repudiation of our recent affirmation that the Constitution's equal protection guarantees extend equally to all citizens."[190]

Although she acknowledged broad congressional latitude in the exercise of remedial power under the Fourteenth Amendment, O'Connor maintained that such power was not implicated by a federal program, as opposed to a congressional "act respecting the States."[191] She found the policies constitutionally defective because they were inadequately grounded in the Fourteenth Amendment, not pitched toward remedying identified past discrimination, and indefensible pursuant to strict scrutiny.[192] For O'Connor, the policies represented neither a proper remedial purpose nor a proper exercise of power.[193] In sum, she found the standard of review too relaxed, the justification too insubstantial and impertinent, and the rules inadequately tailored.

Justice Kennedy wrote a separate dissent, suggesting that the relaxed standard of review ignored the lessons of earlier jurisprudential ignominies. He warned that "a fundamental error of the *Plessy* Court was its similar confidence in its ability to identify "benign discrimination.""[194] Referring to South African apartheid law's disclamation of any unflattering premises, Kennedy noted that "[p]olicies of racial separation and preference are almost always justified as benign, even when it is clear to any sensible observer that they are not."[195] He concluded that

perhaps the Court can succeed in its assumed role of case-by-case arbiter of when it is desirable and benign for the Government to disfavor some citizens and favor others based on the colors of their skin. Perhaps the tolerance and decency to which our people aspire will let the disfavored rise above hostility and the favored escape condescension. But history suggests much peril in this enterprise, and so the Constitution forbids us to undertake it. I regret that after a century of judicial opinions we interpret the Constitution to do no more than move us from "separate but equal" to "unequal but benign."[196]

In response to the warning, the majority expressed its inability to "understand how Justice Kennedy can pretend that examples of 'benign' race-conscious measures include South African apartheid, the 'separate but equal' law at issue in *Plessy v. Ferguson*, and the internment of American citizens of Japanese ancestry upheld in *Korematsu v. United States*."[197] The Court voiced "confiden[ce] that an 'examination of the legislative scheme and its history' . . . will separate benign measures from other types of racial classifications."[198]

The *Metro Broadcasting* decision commanded the narrowest possible majority. It galvanized four dissenting justices into an opposing position that seemed especially unbending. Respectively authoring and supporting the judgment and opinion were Justices Brennan and Marshall. Given their subsequent resignations and replacement by Justices Souter and Thomas, the future vitality of the ruling is uncertain.

The debate over racial preferences, in the course of its evolution, has enkindled increasingly sharp and at times ill-tempered argument on both sides. The case against affirmative action is forcefully stated in the *Croson* decision and the *Metro Broadcasting* dissents, which identify concerns about limitless racial preserves, harm to innocent victims, stereotyping and stigmatization, racial politics, and judicial ineptitude in distinguishing harmful from benign classifications.[199] Such reasoning has elicited criticism from both within and beyond the Court. Doctrinal resistance to racial preferences comports with dominant attitudes, which strongly disfavor them.[200] It also reflects the persisting dilemma of the Fourteenth Amendment, which, although framed primarily with a systematically disadvantaged minority in mind, historically has been implemented in terms that accommodate majoritarian priorities. Principles unfriendly to race-conscious remediation thus have been criticized as convenient rationalizations rather than convincing rationales.

Concern that advantages granted to racial minorities will be overbroad and operate indefinitely, for instance, has been characterized as unfounded.[201] Because a popular majority elects the personnel who formulate and implement preferential programs, critics maintain that resultant policy is vulnerable to and conditioned anyway by the limits of self-sacrifice.[202] Consistent with the argument is the challenge of a preferential layoff policy that was collectively bargained for but contested when its terms were implemented.[203] Such reaction suggests a remedial policy susceptible to inherent limits of self-denial and to superseding interest.

The Court also has been criticized for exaggerating the risk of racial stigmatization presented by affirmative action programs. Preferential policies, it is argued, do not label minorities as incompetent or unable to succeed without special help. Rather, racial stereotypes derive from cultural perceptions deeply rooted in the society's history. A successful program might even defeat stigma, if it followed that white males no longer were perceived as having achieved success against limited competition. Social science data exist for the proposition that hiring preferences actually may be effective in defeating minority stereotypes. The premise is that, as institutions become culturally diversified, uninformed perceptions vanish. Race-conscious remedies also have been described as a response to rather than the cause of stereotypes.

Harm to innocent victims constitutes a reference point that candidly identifies societal aversion to or reserve in assuming the burdens of remediation. Critics of affirmative action maintain that, regardless of how structured, preferential policies cause discernible harm to white males who themselves are blameless.[204] A counterpoint is that individual innocence is illusory because whites as a group have benefited from advantages obtained and accumulated at the expense of minorities.[205] A similar point, expressed less provocatively and without implications of blame, may be that innocence is irrelevant when advantage has compounded from a profound wrong and thus should not be a bar to its undoing.

The Court's emphasis upon the risks of racial polarization has been faulted on grounds it reflects a selective and belated jurisprudential concern. Race was a central factor in the distribution of civil and political rights when the republic was founded and when the Fourteenth Amendment was fashioned.[206] Long after the Reconstruction amendments were adopted, race-dependent policies minimized black influence in the political process.[207] Even now, race is a significant determinant of voting patterns.[208] Tribal politics also characterized the debate over the Civil Rights Act of 1990, which Congress passed and the president vetoed. Opponents of the bill, particularly the chief executive, were criticized for exploiting white resentment of minorities with misleading claims that it would require hiring quotas.[209] Racial antagonism is a crucial factor in modern politics because, as one political consultant noted, it is an "issue [that] moves numbers."[210] Given a well-established history of racial politics, concern that affirmative action will fuel or foster such tribalism attaches unique significance to a common and durable phenomenon. Disapproving references to racial politics, in a society still inclined toward race-specific classifications and governed by competing interest groups, thus elicit criticism for their selective focus.

Factional favoritism is an undeniable feature of a political system that is defined by interest groups and that routinely dispenses special advantages. Congress, for instance, has awarded benefits to workers dislocated from industries adversely affected by government regulation.[211] The Court itself has upheld veterans' benefits programs against challenges of overbreadth and intrinsic unfairness which have ensnared race-conscious remediation.[212] Because legislatively conferred group advantage is the norm, foreclosure of racial preferences may be susceptible to argument that the preclusion is race-dependent itself.

Efforts to reckon with the nation's legacy of discrimination confront daunting impediments attributable to modern standards of review. Discriminatory purpose requirements, as discussed in Chapter 5, confound proof of an equal protection violation. Despite its reality, general societal discrimination has been precluded as a permissible basis for remediation. Accounting for discrimination, absent congressional action pursuant to adequate findings, is limited to rare provable instances of specific discrimination. Even when permitted, therefore, racially focused remediation is bound by the prerequisite of proving discriminatory motive. The net consequence for modern purposes is doctrine that is inapt at discerning subtle or unconscious discrimination against minorities but usually fatal to policies that would reckon with it.

When detached from the context of race and its historical tendency to distort perception, remedial accounting for a particular group or interest is recognizable as a common and generally uncontroversial political phenomenon. When economic opportunity is impaired by systemic dysfunction, for instance, intervention to undo excessive accumulations of power and advantage and open up or maximize opportunity is a regulatory norm. Antitrust laws, for instance, originated from a sense that the

system of production and of exchange is having that tendency which is sure at some not very distant day to crush out all small men, all small capitalists, all small enterprises. This is being done now. We find everywhere over our land the wrecks of small, independent enterprises thrown in our pathway. So now the American Congress and the American people are brought face to face with this sad, this great problem. Is production, is trade, to be taken away from the great mass of the people and concentrated in the hands of a few men who... have been enabled to aggregate to themselves large, enormous fortunes.[213]

Even without constitutional direction akin to the equal protection decree, Congress and the judiciary have directly fashioned redistributive doctrine calculated to optimize the allocation of economic power.[214] The breakup of American Telephone and Telegraph Company disclosed a willingness to restructure the nation's central communications system out of concern with accumulated advantage, dominance, and influence.[215] Refashioning of the industry was characterized by repudiation of rationales often used to defeat race-conscious remediation. Relief was neither foreclosed nor delayed by concerns that special relief or attention would stigmatize or stereotype AT&T's competitors. Enhanced economic opportunity was regarded as a legitimate objective.[216] Nor were consequent restrictions on the dominant company regarded as harm to an innocent victim. Rather, the district court emphasized that it may be necessary to "pry open to competition a market that has been closed" by illegal action.[217] Consequent restrictions were imposed despite a possible argument that AT&T was blameless in having acquired its preeminent position.[218]

Claims that innocent parties were victimized surfaced in a comparable context, when the Federal Communications Commission ordered persons or entities owning a daily newspaper and broadcasting station in the same community to divest one or the other property.[219] Cross-ownership was a function of prior Commission policies encouraging publishers to acquire radio and television properties.[220] Despite such inducement and consequent reliance, "innocent" publishers were obligated to surrender their holdings in the interest of enhanced opportunity and diversity.[221]

Because remediation of dysfunction and redistribution of advantage are policy norms in the economic marketplace, the Court's resistance to preferential policies continues to elicit criticism as being exaggerated and misplaced. Even if the objections are accepted as apt, the case against race-conscious remediation is not without cogent reason. Contrary to the Court's sense that racial preferences are dangerously potent, such programs have been characterized as too feeble insofar as they account mainly for interests of a relatively elite and qualified subgroup.[222] Consequent concern that such policy diverts attention from more profound disadvantage to the interests of persons likely to succeed without special attention is reducible to an inexpensive and relatively low impact form of racial justice, and may foster a self-subverting sense of victimization.[223] Even if societal discrimination were allowed as a permissible reference point for remedial initiative, the argument is that a policy of favoritism would not be substantially related to its declared aim. A counterpoint is that affirmative action need not operate to the exclusion of other methodologies for effecting racial justice.[224] Given a history bereft of policy calculated to account comprehensively for racial disadvantage, however, reality may favor identifying and emphasizing options with maximum potential. In a culture generally hostile to the notion of racial preferences, the case against affirmative action might profit from enhanced attention to whether remediation actually achieves its stated aims.[225]

Such review would demonstrate that the challenge for equal protection, now as in 1868, is to actualize doctrine that accounts effectively for original concern with race-dependent impediments to opportunity. The desegregation mandate was successful only in securing a consensus for the principle that palpable official discrimination is constitutionally unacceptable. The primary value of group-referenced remedial concepts thus may relate less to actual results than as a reminder of and leverage point for attention and progress necessary for effectuating genuine color blindness.

Given the difficulties of proving purposeful discrimination, and thus a constitutional violation, doctrinal resistance to remediation of societal discrimination strikes critics as selective and misplaced.[226] Judicial decisions unrelated to race, but nonetheless implicating profound constitutional concerns, disclose that standards of review are not always unrelenting and may even be accommodating to state interests. The Court has noted, for instance, that "[f]rom the beginning of civilized societies, legislators and judges have acted on various unprovable assumptions . . . [that] underlie much lawful state regulation."[227] Even when protection has been sought for trenchant constitutional interests, the Court has adhered to the principle that "unprovable assumptions about what is good for the people [are] not a sufficient reason to find [a statute] unconstitutional."[228] If viewed as general economic or social policy, remediation would merit a deferential judicial response.[229] Because racial classifications have had such disabling consequences over the course of the nation's history, few would argue for an entirely relaxed review of them. Still, undifferentiated evaluation of racial classifications risks criticism that the Court, like its predecessor a century ago, is more interested in formal imagery than the underlying realities of discrimination.

Typifying such reproval of modern equal protection jurisprudence is the report of a national civil rights organization headed by the former chair of the U.S. Commission of Civil Rights. The study criticized judicial performance during the 1980s as "appearing increasingly hostile toward civil rights advocates."[230] Judicially crafted standards that complicate proof of discrimination, except when remediation is at issue, were characterized as the product of an "overwhelmingly white, conservative, wealthy and male... federal court bench."[231] Such outcomes are attributed to the Reagan administration, which followed the well-established tradition of court packing and, as a result of detailed screening and opportunities to appoint judges, was successful in securing its agenda.[232] By 1991, the Reagan and Bush administrations had appointed 70 percent of the nation's federal judges.[233]

The report essentially complained of a federal judiciary that has reverted toward insensitivity to or fatigue with racial realities. It objects specifically to nascent standards of constitutional color blindness "rest[ing] on the notion that America no longer has a duty to act affirmatively in order to overcome the legacy of slavery and government sanctioned segregation... [but] ignor[ing] the well-documented realities of continuing discrimination and its effects."[234] The study concluded that "a major segment of the nation's minority population continues to suffer the legacy of years of oppression and discrimination."[235] As constitutional theories and standards continue to be debated, such observations afford a reminder of how unfinished the business of 1787, 1868, and 1954 remains.

NOTES

1. Plessy v. Ferguson 163 U.S. 537, 559 (1896) (Harlan, J., dissenting).

2. *Id.*

3. *See* Lawrence, *The Id, the Ego and Equal Protection: Reckoning with Unconscious Racism*, 39 Stan. L. Rev. 317, 339–44 (1987).

4. De Funis v. Odegaard, 416 U.S. 312 (1974).

5. *Id.* at 350 (Brennan, J., dissenting). The principle of mootness operates when the facts and circumstances generating a claim no longer present an actual case or controversy. In *De Funis*, the claimant was nearing the end of his legal education and the law school had indicated it would allow him to graduate. The Court determined that a judgment would not have affected the parties' legal relationship, and thus the controversy was considered academic. *See id.*

6. *Id.*

7. Regents of the University of California v. Bakke, 438 U.S. 265 (1978).

8. *Id.* at 277–78.

9. 18 Cal.3d 34, 132 Cal. Rptr. 680, 553 P.2d 1152 (1976).

10. Regents of the University of California v. Bakke, 438 U.S. at 320 (Powell, J.); *id.* at 421 (Stevens, J., Burger, C.J., Stewart and Rehnquist, J. J., concurring and dissenting).

11. *Id.* at 324–79 (Brennan, White, Marshall, and Blackmun, J.J., concurring and dissenting). Title VI of the Civil Rights Act of 1964, 42 U.S.C. §§ 2000d to 2000d–7, prohibits racially based exclusion from "any program or activity receiving Federal financial assistance." *Id.*, § 2000d.

12. *Id.* at 408–21 (Stevens, J., Burger, C.J., Stewart and Rehnquist, J.J., concurring and dissenting).

13. *Id.* at 272–320 (Powell, J.).

14. *Id.* at 320 (Powell, J.).

15. *See id.* at 325–26 (Brennan, White, Marshall, and Blackmun, J.J., concurring and dissenting).

16. *Id.* at 291 (Powell, J.).

17. Gunther, *Foreword: In Search of Evolving Doctrine on a Changing Court: A Model for a Newer Equal Protection*, 86 Harv. L. Rev. 1, 8 (1972).

18. *See* Regents of the University of California v. Bakke, 438 U.S. at 305 (Powell, J.).

19. *Id.* at 306 (Powell, J.).

20. *Id.* at 307 (Powell, J.).

21. *Id.* at 307–09 (Powell, J.).

22. *Id.* at 309–10 (Powell, J.).

23. *Id.* at 310–11 (Powell, J.).

24. *Id.* at 310 (Powell, J.).

25. *Id.* at 314 (Powell, J.).

26. *Id.* at 311–15 (opinion of Powell, J.); *id.* at 362 (Brennan, White, Marshall, and Blackmun, J.J., concurring and dissenting).

27. *Id.* at 320 (opinion of Powell, J.).

28. *Id.* at 355 (Brennan, White, Marshall, and Blackmun, J.J., concurring and dissenting).

29. *Id.* at 357 (Brennan, White, Marshall, and Blackmun, J.J., concurring and dissenting).

30. *Id.* at 361–62 (Brennan, White, Marshall, and Blackmun, J.J., concurring and dissenting).

31. *Id.* (Brennan, White, Marshall, and Blackmun, J.J., concurring and dissenting).

32. *Id.* at 362 (Brennan, White, Marshall, and Blackmun, J.J., concurring and dissenting).

33. *Id.* at 375 (Brennan, White, Marshall, and Blackmun, J.J., concurring and dissenting).

34. *Id.* at 387–96 (Marshall, J., concurring and dissenting).

35. *Id.* at 402 (Marshall, J., concurring and dissenting).

36. *Id.* at 407 (Blackmun, J., concurring and dissenting).

37. *Id.* at 416–18 (Stevens, J., Burger, C.J., Stewart and Rehnquist, J.J., concurring and dissenting).

38. *Id.* at 418 (Stevens, J., Burger, C.J., Stewart and Rehnquist, J.J., concurring and dissenting).

39. *Id.* at 403 (Blackmun, J., concurring and dissenting).

40. Fullilove v. Klutznick, 448 U.S. 448 (1980).

41. *Id.* at 456–92 (plurality opinion). A plurality opinion is one that receives more votes than any concurrence, but falls short of attracting a majority necessary for precedential significance.

42. *Id.* at 517–22 (Marshall, Brennan, and Blackmun, J.J., concurring).

43. *Id.* at 522–32 (Stewart and Rehnquist, J.J., dissenting).

44. *Id.* at 532–54 (Stevens, J., dissenting).

45. *Id.* at 492 (plurality opinion).

46. *Id.* at 472–80 (plurality opinion).

47. *Id.* at 480 (plurality opinion).

48. *Id.* at 480–81 (plurality opinion).

49. *Id.* at 480 (plurality opinion).

50. *Id.* at 481–82 (plurality opinion).

51. *Id.* at 502 (Powell, J., concurring).

52. *Id.* at 508 (Powell, J., concurring).

53. *Id.* (Powell, J., concurring).

54. *Id.* at 520–21 (Marshall, J., concurring).

55. *Id.* at 523 (Stewart, J., dissenting).

56. Plessy v. Ferguson, 163 U.S. at 560.

57. Fullilove v. Klutznick, 448 U.S. at 537 (Stevens, J., dissenting).

58. *Id.* at 542 (Stevens, J., dissenting).

59. *Id.* at 538–41 (Stevens, J., dissenting).

60. *Id.* at 553 (Stevens, J., dissenting).

61. 476 U.S. 267 (1986).

62. *Id.* at 274 (plurality opinion).

63. *Id.* at 276 (plurality opinion).

64. *Id.* at 274 (plurality opinion).

65. *Id.* at 275–76 (plurality opinion) (citations omitted).

66. *Id.* at 277 (plurality opinion).

67. *Id.* at 277–78 (plurality opinion).

68. *Id.* at 279 (plurality opinion).

69. *Id.* at 279–80 (plurality opinion).

70. *Id.* at 280–81 (plurality opinion).

71. *Id.* at 280–81 (plurality opinion).

72. *Id.* at 282–83 (plurality opinion) (emphasis in original).

73. *Id.* at 284 (plurality opinion).

74. *Id.* at 286 (O'Connor, J., concurring).

75. *Id.* at 290 (O'Connor, J., concurring).

76. *Id.* at 287 (O'Connor, J., concurring).

77. *Id.* at 295 (Marshall, J., dissenting).

78. *Id.* at 296, 307 (Marshall, J., dissenting).

79. *Id.* at 307 (Marshall, J., dissenting).

80. *Id.* at 307–08 (Marshall, J., dissenting).

81. *Id.* at 308 (Marshall, J., dissenting).

82. *Id.* at 310 (Marshall, J., dissenting).

83. *Id.* at 312 (Marshall, J., dissenting).

84. *Id.* at 313 (Stevens, J., dissenting).

85. *Id.* at 315 (Stevens, J., dissenting).

86. *Id.* at 315–16 (Stevens, J., dissenting).
87. *Id.* at 316–17 (Stevens, J., dissenting).
88. *Id.* at 317 (Stevens, J., dissenting).
89. *Id.* at 318 (Stevens, J., dissenting).
90. *Id.* (Stevens, J., dissenting).
91. *Id.* at 318–19 (Stevens, J., dissenting).
92. *Id.* at 319 (Stevens, J., dissenting).
93. *Id.* at 320 (Stevens, J., dissenting).
94. United States v. Paradise, 480 U.S. 149 (1987).
95. *Id.* at 163 (plurality opinion).
96. *Id.* at 185–86 (plurality opinion).
97. *Id.* at 167 (plurality opinion).
98. *Id.* at 171–86 (plurality opinion).
99. *Id.* at 182–83 (plurality opinion) (citations omitted).
100. *Id.* at 186 (Powell, J., concurring).
101. *Id.* at 193 (Stevens, J., concurring).
102. *Id.* at 198–99 (O'Connor, J., dissenting).
103. *Id.* at 200 (O'Connor, J., dissenting).
104. *Id.* at 199 (O'Connor, J., dissenting).
105. 109 S. Ct. 706 (1989).
106. *Id.* at 723–24 (plurality opinion); *id.* at 735 (Scalia, J., concurring).
107. *Id.* at 735 (Scalia, J., concurring).
108. *Id.* at 712–14 (plurality opinion).
109. *Id.* at 714 (plurality opinion).
110. *Id.* at 719 (plurality opinion).
111. *Id.* (plurality opinion).
112. *Id.* (plurality opinion).
113. *Id.* at 721 (plurality opinion).
114. *Id.* (plurality opinion).
115. *Id.* (plurality opinion).
116. *Id.* (plurality opinion).
117. *Id.* at 722 (plurality opinion).
118. *Id.* (plurality opinion).
119. *Id.* at 724 (plurality opinion).
120. *Id.* (plurality opinion).
121. *Id.* (plurality opinion).
122. *Id.* at 728 (plurality opinion).
123. *Id.* (plurality opinion).
124. *Id.* (plurality opinion).
125. *Id.* (plurality opinion).
126. *Id.* at 723–24 (plurality opinion).
127. *Id.* at 729 (plurality opinion).
128. *Id.* (plurality opinion).
129. *Id.* (plurality opinion).
130. *Id.* at 730 (plurality opinion).
131. *Id.* at 727 (plurality opinion).
132. *Id.* at 730 (plurality opinion).
133. *Id.* at 731–32 (Stevens, J., concurring).

134. *Id.* at 735 (Scalia, J., concurring).

135. *Id.* (Scalia, J., concurring).

136. *Id.* (Scalia, J., concurring).

137. *Id.* (*citing* Lee v. Washington, 390 U.S. 333 (1968) (Black, Harlan, and Stewart, J.J., concurring)).

138. *Id.* at 737 (Scalia, J., concurring).

139. *Id.* at 738 (Scalia, J., concurring) (emphasis in original).

140. *Id.* at 739 (Scalia, J., concurring).

141. *Id.* (Scalia, J., concurring) (emphasis in original).

142. *See* Rowan, Thomas hearings split blacks along class lines, Detroit *Free Press*, Sep. 24, 1991, §A, at 13, cols. 1–3.

143. *Id.* at 740 (Marshall, J., dissenting).

144. *Id.* at 739–40 (Marshall, J., dissenting).

145. *Id.* at 740 (Marshall, J., dissenting).

146. *Id.* at 740–43 (Marshall, J., dissenting).

147. *Id.* at 743 (Marshall, J., dissenting).

148. *Id.* at 744 (Marshall, J., dissenting).

149. *Id.* at 746 (Marshall, J., dissenting).

150. *Id.* (Marshall, J., dissenting).

151. *Id.* (Marshall, J., dissenting).

152. *Id.* (Marshall, J., dissenting).

153. *Id.* at 749 (Marshall, J., dissenting).

154. *Id.* at 748 (Marshall, J., dissenting).

155. *Id.* at 750 (Marshall, J., dissenting).

156. *Id.* (Marshall, J., dissenting).

157. *Id.* at 752 (Marshall, J., dissenting).

158. *Id.* (Marshall, J., dissenting) (citations omitted).

159. *Id.* (Marshall, J., dissenting).

160. *Id.* at 753 (Marshall, J., dissenting).

161. *Id.* at 752 (Marshall, J., dissenting).

162. *Id.* (Marshall, J., dissenting).

163. Civil Rights Cases, 109 U.S. 3, 25 (1883). *See generally* City of Richmond v. J. A. Croson Co., 109 S. Ct. at 740 (Marshall, J., dissenting).

164. City of Richmond v. J. A. Croson Co., 109 S. Ct. at 754–57 (Marshall, J., dissenting).

165. *Id.* at 756 (Marshall, J., dissenting) (emphasis in original).

166. *Id.* (Marshall, J., dissenting).

167. *Id.* at 757 (Marshall, J., dissenting).

168. *See* Plessy v. Ferguson, 163 U.S. at 550.

169. City of Richmond v. J. A. Croson Co., 109 S. Ct. at 756–57 (Marshall, J., dissenting).

170. *Id.* at 757 (Blackmun, J., dissenting).

171. *Id.* (Blackmun, J., dissenting).

172. Metro Broadcasting, Inc. v. Federal Communications Commission, 110 S. Ct. 2997 (1990).

173. *See id.* at 3004–05.

174. *Id.* at 3008.

175. *Id.* at 3008–09.

176. *Id.* at 3009.
177. *Id.* at 3010.
178. *Id.*
179. *Id.*
180. *Id.* at 3019.
181. *Id.* at 3016.
182. *Id.* at 3016–17.
183. *Id.* at 3016–27.
184. *Id.* at 3016.
185. *Id.* at 3024.
186. *Id.* at 3025.
187. *Id.* at 3026.
188. *Id.*
189. *Id.* at 3029 (O'Connor, J., dissenting).
190. *Id.* (O'Connor, J., dissenting).
191. *Id.* at 3030 (O'Connor, J., dissenting).
192. *Id.* at 3030–32 (O'Connor, J., dissenting).
193. *Id.* at 3031–3041 (O'Connor, J., dissenting).
194. *Id.* at 3046 (Kennedy, J., dissenting).
195. *Id.* (Kennedy, J., dissenting).
196. *Id.* at 3047 (Kennedy, J., dissenting).
197. *Id.* at 3008 n.12 (majority opinion).
198. *Id.*
199. *See* Metro Broadcasting, Inc. v. Federal Communications Commission, 110 S. Ct. at 3032–43 (O'Connor, J., dissenting); *id.* at 3044–46 (Kennedy, J., dissenting); City of Richmond v. J. A. Croson Co., 109 S. Ct. at 721.
200. When asked "Do you believe that because of past discrimination against black people, qualified blacks should receive preference over equally qualified whites in such matters as getting into college or getting jobs?" 72 percent of whites and 42 percent of blacks answered negatively. *Newsweek Poll of April 23–25, 1991*, Newsweek, May 6, 1991, at 24, col. 3.
201. *See, e.g.*, Ely, *The Constitutionality of Reverse Discrimination*, 41 U. Chi. L. Rev. 723, 735–36 (1974).
202. *See id.*
203. *See supra* notes 61–93 and accompanying text.
204. *See* F. Lynch, Invisible Victims: White Males and the Crisis of Affirmative Action (1989).
205. *See* Ross, *Innocence and Affirmative Action*, 43 Vand. L. Rev. 297, 301 (1990).
206. *See* Chapters 1 and 2.
207. *See* Chapters 3 and 4.
208. *See* Pinderhughes, *Legal Strategies for Voting Rights: Political Science and the Law*, 28 How. L.J. 515, 531 (1985).
209. *Panel Attacks Bush on Civil Rights Work*, Miami Herald, April 18, 1991, at 17A, cols. 1–2.
210. *The New Politics of Race*, Newsweek, May 6, 1991, at 22, col. 1.
211. The Clean Air Act, for instance, provides for compensation for workers displaced by increased regulation. *See* 42 U.S.C. §§ 7621–22 (1977).

212. *See* Personnel Administrator v. Feeney, 442 U.S. 256, 280–81 (1979).

213. 21 Cong. Rec. 2548 (1870) (Sen. George).

214. *See* Northern Pacific R.R. v. United States, 356 U.S. 1, 4 (1956); Sherman Act, 15 U.S.C. §§ 1–2 (1890).

215. *See* United States v. American Telephone & Telegraph Co., 552 F. Supp. 131 (D.D.C. 1982), *aff'd*, 460 U.S. 1001 (1983).

216. *See id.* at 149.

217. *Id.* at 150 (quoting International Salt Co. v. United States, 332 U.S. 392, 401 (1947)).

218. *See* P. Areeda & L. Kaplan, Antitrust Analysis 527 (1988).

219. *See* Federal Communications Commission v. National Citizens Committee for Broadcasting, 436 U.S. 775, 787 (1978).

220. *See id.* at 782–83.

221. *See id.* at 783–84.

222. *See* W. Wilson, The Declining Significance of Race 110 (1978).

223. *See* S. Carter, Reflections of an Affirmative Action Baby (1991); S. Steele, The Content of Our Character (1990); W. Wilson, *supra* note 222.

224. *See, e.g.,* Kennedy, *Persuasion and Distrust: A Comment on the Affirmative Action Debate*, 99 Harv. L. Rev. 1327, 1333–34 (1986).

225. Criticism of the premises of affirmative action are detailed, for instance in T. Sowell, Civil Rights: Rhetoric or Reality? (1984).

226. *See* Kennedy, *supra* note 224, at 1334–36.

227. Paris Adult Theater I v. Slaton, 413 U.S. 49, 61 (1973).

228. *Id.* at 62.

229. *See* City of New Orleans v. Dukes, 427 U.S. 297, 303 (1976).

230. *Panel Attacks Bush on Civil Rights Work, supra* note 209.

231. *Id.*

232. *See* Lively, *The Supreme Court Appointment Process: In Search of Constitutional Roles and Responsibilities*, 59 S. Cal. L. Rev. 551, 564 (1986).

233. *See There Goes the Judge*, Newsweek, April 22, 1991, at 31, cols. 2–3.

234. *Panel Attacks Bush on Civil Rights Work, supra* note 208.

235. *Id.*

Chapter 7

Original Imperatives and Doctrinal Possibility

The legacy of slow, delayed, and incomplete responses to the imperatives of the Fourteenth Amendment has created a constitutional distortion that perverts not only the law but also critical response to it. Failure to account fully for the amendment's central aims results in justifiable frustration, as commitment to civil rights and equality redundantly is articulated, only to be qualified by subsequent limiting principles. Critical review of equal protection jurisprudence reveals a history of doctrinal potential and incomplete actualization. Although analytical failures may be apparent as evidenced by the limited reach, effect and unwinding of the desegregation mandate and by contemporary intent standards which thwart equal protection claims, the possibility of viable alternative premises is confounded by theories that tend to be disputable and thus unserviceable. Much of the Fourteenth Amendment's original business in the meantime remains unfinished and lost between cramped jurisprudence and overly grand or novel response. Given the amendment's existence as an extension of supreme democratic will and the consequent indefeasibility of its core aims, a redirection of attention to original meaning might help ameliorate the abiding tension between doctrinal possibility and actuality.

Even if measured according to the expectations of its framers,[1] the Fourteenth Amendment has been a qualified success at best. The rights to travel without inordinate constraint;[2] to own, possess, and convey property;[3] and to make contracts,[4] for instance, have been secured in varying degree. Even so, jurisprudence continues to struggle with and shrink from those core interests of the Fourteenth Amendment. In recognizing that Congress has secured the right to contract, for instance, the Supreme Court refused to extend the federal interest to post-formation harassment.[5] Such analysis in 1989 disregarded the general principle, enunciated more than a century before, that remedial legislation is to be construed not restrictively but liberally and flexibly to realize its corrective aims.[6] Although the formality of a dual system of criminal justice has been erased, moreover, the Court accepts "[a]pparent discrepancies in sentencing [as] an inevitable part of our criminal justice system,"[7] even when the disparities are pronounced.

Whether evaluated by the minimal demands of original intent contemplating accommodation of "[m]ere discriminations" or by criteria more ambitiously accounting for a discriminatory legacy, the Fourteenth Amendment in general and equal protection in particular have been substantially underachieved. Because standards have been calibrated so that they reach only obvious discrimination, constitutional radar is as defective now as it was more than a century ago when the Court in *Virginia v. Rives* refused to reckon with discrimination that did not overtly disclose its true character.[8] During the 1980s, the Court identified only three instances in which racial minorities were or may have been denied equal protection. In *Batson v. Kentucky*, it determined that a prosecutor may not use peremptory challenges in a racially discriminatory fashion to remove potential jurors and thereby overturned a contrary holding from the past.[9] The Court also found in *Washington v. Seattle School District No. 1* that a ballot initiative, transferring power to order busing from school boards to the state legislature,[10] constituted a breach of equal protection. What was perceived as an impermissible, race-dependent transfer of power in *Washington* did not influence review in *Crawford v. Board of Education*, which upheld voter ratification of a constitutional amendment prohibiting busing absent *de jure* segregation.[11] An equal protection deprivation also was recognized in *Hunter v. Underwood*,[12] when the Court invalidated a state criminal law enacted nearly a century earlier for patently discriminatory reasons.[13] The decisional significance of *Hunter* is minimized by the fact that the law at issue was a relic of official segregation and thus did not present the modern problem of proving wrongful intent. The decision also left open the possibility that the law might be reenacted pursuant to a racially neutral purpose.[14]

Such limited constitutional yield reflects the Court's reticence to probe the implications of egregious racial disparities in settings descending directly from official dualism[15] and contrasts with sharply increased attention and hostility to affirmative action during the same period.[16] Pursuant to modern criteria, the equal protection guarantee affords no meaningful way of confronting and accounting for sophisticated or subtle practices that in modern times deny equal opportunity and connote inferiority as effectively, and perhaps even more insidiously, than did the overt methods of the past. Contemporary analysis as a consequence falls short not only of the potential *Brown* but also of *Strauder*.[17]

Fourteenth Amendment jurisprudence over the course of its existence has disclosed a persistent and as yet unresolved conflict. While acknowledging the interests generally established by the Fourteenth Amendment, the Court seldom and only sporadically has accounted meaningfully for them. Case law in large part consists of statements of principle qualified by limiting or conditioning precepts, which retard doctrinal operation or efficacy. The Court initially held the Fourteenth Amendment captive to narrow state action concepts and perceptions of "mere" and "reasonable" discrimination. Not until 1954 did the Court activate equal protection in a way that made serious demands for societal change. The anti-discrimination phase proved unique in its initial dictate but ultimately became normative as its final contours were narrowed and its demands were reduced. The consequent emergence of motive-based standards and undifferentiating color-blind criteria effectively has resulted in a judiciary that is minimally interventionist when minorities press their claims but more aggressive when the majority complains. Forceful actualization of the federal interest underlying the Fourteenth Amendment, rarely evidenced except for a relatively brief interval from the 1950s to 1970s, ironically did not materialize until state and local governments endeavored to repair rather than maintain a discriminatory heritage.

The formulation of and investment in Fourteenth Amendment doctrine that is inchoate or a step behind the realities of racial injustice has proved more common than exceptional. It is evidenced not only by qualification of the anti-discrimination principle[18] but also by resistance to more remedy-friendly doctrine. Not surprisingly, such performance has resulted in critical attention to theories and principles that might reckon more directly and effectively with the nation's legacy of discrimination. Consistent with the Court's own sense that motive-based inquiry should be avoided when constitutional "stakes are [too] high,"[19] for instance, it has been suggested that review should assess not the intent but the racial significance of a challenged action.[20] Such a focus has been touted for its utility in reaching modern variants of subtle, unconscious, and otherwise constitutionally insignificant racism.[21] Instead of performing a predictably vain search for intent, the Court would assess whether an official action could be perceived as racially stigmatizing.[22]

The notion that equal protection results would vary if standards were simply retooled and made more sensitive to the nature of contemporary racial realities probably represents a false lead. Recognition of societal wrongdoing already is apparent in constitutional renderings that acknowledge "the sorry history of both private and public discrimination in this country."[23] Operative standards, despite such perception, are notable for their capacity to avoid accountability that would significantly contest societal norms or demand substantial revision of the established order. Anticipation of different results pursuant to alternative standards disregards a central lesson provided by two centuries of racial jurisprudence. Despite an understanding of the nation's legacy of discrimination, the Court, except during the desegregation era, has refrained from doctrine that would challenge established practice or custom.

Reality is that even the discriminatory purpose test could establish constitutional offense if facts and circumstances were examined in a more rigorous and sensitive fashion.[24] Continuing adherence to criteria that are largely unresponsive to minority discrimination claims, and disowned in other constitutional circumstances,[25] suggests that they endure because their deficiencies actually are strengths. Jurisprudence that articulates a broad commitment to eliminating all vestiges of discrimination[26] trades in false imagery insofar as the Constitution itself has not been regularly interpreted in such terms. National policy, which has hedged between support of anti-discrimination principles and inadequate enforcement or remedial efforts, offers a more accurate reflection of a societal determination qualified by competing priorities. Even if doctrine was redirected to account for racially significant events or policy, the standard still would be susceptible to qualifying standards that would limit or negate its utility. History thus suggests the improbability that substantially different equal protection results would eventuate from a simple recasting of analytical criteria.

Evidence that equal production unproductivity is not simply a function of technical standards comes from a variety of constitutional contexts where cultural significance is a pertinent consideration. In *City of Memphis v. Greene*, for example, a traffic barrier between black and white neighborhoods was challenged as a "badge of slavery" at odds with the Thirteenth Amendment.[27] The Court's failure to recognize the barrier's manifest racial significance showed that review was no more discerning than if performed pursuant to Fourteenth Amendment standards.

Modern establishment clause review further demonstrates that the Court may not necessarily discern or acknowledge the cultural significance of a challenged state action. Like Thirteenth Amendment analysis, which considers whether government action has racial significance, establishment clause review inquires into religious significance.[28] Findings that nativity scenes,[29] references to God on coinage,[30] and legislative prayer[31] do not have such meaning suggest that the results are less the function of operative standards than of an unresponsiveness to minority perceptions or a disinclination to probe imagery or practices that reflect cultural norms.

In the freedom of speech and press contexts, where sensitivity to diversity is indispensable, the Court has been criticized for an "acute ethnocentric myopia . . . and depressing inability to appreciate that in our land of cultural pluralism, there are many who think, act and talk differently from the Members of this Court, . . . and who do not share their [fragile] sensibilities."[32] In finding that commonly used profanities were unfit for general public consumption via the airwaves,[33] the Court disregarded or discounted the significance of expression with culturally specific meaning at odds with its own perceptions.[34] As Justice Brennan noted, "The words . . . [found] so unpalatable may be the stuff of everyday conversations in some, if not many, of the innumerable subcultures that compose this Nation."[35] He thus alluded to academic evidence that "[w]ords generally considered obscene . . . are considered neither obscene nor derogatory in the [black] vernacular except in particular contextual situations and when used with certain intonations."[36] Judicial insensitivity to that reality has manifested itself in a ruling that, instead of examining rap music in its cultural context, found certain lyrics obscene pursuant to general community standards.[37] Such analysis reinforces a sense that results would not change if racial significance rather than discriminatory purpose was the touchstone. Development of new theories to animate equal protection may generate intellectual attention and even acclaim, but the exercise is purely academic if the societal norms and priorities defining equal protection do not accommodate their implications.

A final reckoning with equal protection requires appreciation of the disparity between formal appearance and real achievement. The *Brown* decision is commonly regarded as a monument to racial equality. The desegregation mandate and consequent anti-discrimination principle present powerful rhetorical imagery, but, pursuant to subsequent limiting principles, actual performance has not lived up to its billing. Qualification of the desegregation requirement, as noted in Chapter 5, effectively exchanged "separate but equal" for "separate and unequal." The original decision in *Brown* delayed relief in hopes of securing popular acceptance. As desegregation demands narrowed and weakened, deferral in large part translated into denial.

A fundamental tenet of *Brown* was that desegregation was essential for equal educational opportunity and thus was a means rather than a mere end in itself. The Court thus characterized education as "the most important function of state and local governments. . . . the very foundation of good citizenship. . . . succe[ss] in life. . . . [and] a right which must be made available to all on equal terms."[38] Post-*Brown* jurisprudence largely has foreclosed the possibility of equal educational opportunity as a function of constitutional imperative. By concluding that education is not a fundamental right,[39] wealth classifications are not suspect[40] and racially disproportionate impact by itself is insufficient to establish constitutional responsibility,[41] the Court has more than repudiated *Brown*'s potential. It also has recalibrated standards to the point that constitutional capability may be even less than under the separate but equal principle. Implicit in the delay of immediate relief was the prospect of more profound long-term constitutional results. The narrowing of standards and accommodation of functional racial separation and distinction, however, have diminished if not defeated that possibility. The desegregation thesis, suggesting enhanced Fourteenth Amendment performance, thus has proved subject to antithesis in a dialectic that arguably has yielded doctrinal regression.

The jurisprudence of race over two centuries has consistently frustrated initiatives and theories that might animate the Constitution in a way that would significantly account for minority interests. Rejection of color-blind criteria a century ago when segregation was challenged, and subscription to such standards as race-conscious remediation has become a prominent issue, illustrate the adaptability of rationales in forging constitutional results consonant with dominant impulses. The influence of cultural norms and priorities upon equal protection's coursing has been well-understood by those who have sought to redirect it. In *Brown* itself, the constitutional challenge stressed how segregation harmed not only minorities but the entire society. Argument thus was offered that desegregation would enhance the image of the United States as it vied for international favor during the early phases of the Cold War.[42] Considerations of international image, when the North was courting international favor during the Civil War, influenced emancipation. Modern arguments for remediation have referred to a general interest in maximizing human resources to enhance global competitiveness. Equal protection's adaptability in constitutionalizing concerns unrelated to race[43] denotes further a guarantee not fixed by a transcendent limiting principle but animated selectively by priority.

With or without judicial inspiration, equal protection over the course of its existence has not amounted to much more than cultural norms will allow. Under any circumstances when minority concerns are being pressed and doctrine propounded without clear charter sanction, judicial renderings are susceptible to allegations of usurping legislative power. Crucial to an effective equal protection guarantee therefore is a clear sense of what is truly vulnerable to charges of anti-democratic functioning. Ideological output concerning the proper limits of judicial review is extensive. Theories of restraint account for concepts of literalism,[44] originalism,[45] and neutrality,[46] which collectively vie with non-interpretive notions that the Constitution realistically cannot be vitalized without reference to external values.[47] Debate over the general role of the judiciary is compounded in the equal protection context, where intervention on behalf of minorities clearly confronts majoritarian rule, by premises competing to minimize and to enhance the guarantee's vitality.

A survey of pertinent literature discloses no shortage of alternatives to modern equal protection theory. Paul Brest argues that courts should construe the equal protection clause as an anti-discrimination principle directed toward race-dependent practices.[48] Owen Fiss maintains that courts should focus on group disadvantage because proving discrimination is problematic and strains judicial resources.[49] Charles Lawrence suggests analysis that considers the cultural significance of government action to determine if it is racially stigmatizing or implies inferiority.[50] Bruce Ackerman proposes an equal protection jurisprudence that moves beyond process defect theory and formulates "a legally cogent set of higher-law principles."[51] Such theories contrast with the minimalist views that would narrowly delineate equal protection's operation. Chief Justice Rehnquist, for instance, has favored an equal protection guarantee responsive only to racial discrimination and would limit close scrutiny to instances in which wrongful intent is established.[52]

No matter how artfully framed and persuasively justified, equal protection doctrine is unlikely to be widely accepted if it evokes charges that it is anti-democratic. Without clear and well-accepted constitutional grounding, courts that confront the political process and threaten to retool legislative output more favorably toward minority interests invite resistance prompted or at least referenced to anti-democratic perceptions. History reveals, despite some prominent exceptions, that jurisprudence generally has avoided disruptive consequences even at the expense of constitutional imperative.

Maximizing not just the potential but also the actual efficacy of equal protection doctrine requires understanding and accepting institutional resistance to unsettling consequences. It also is essential to realize that theory not clearly tied to manifest constitutional concern can be attacked by competing perspectives and perverted as a result of altered circumstance. Doctrine premised on political science, as discussed later, has been victimized by its own creativity and uncertain linkage to constitutional design. Although a reference point for racial jurisprudence of the past half century,[53] the concept of process dysfunction as a basis for equal protection animation is largely anachronistic. The right to vote is largely secured, and actual representation is defined by the extent of electoral participation.[54] If contemporary exclusion from the legislative process is a function of self-determination rather than official discrimination, concern with systemic distortion exaggerates the significance of an increasingly irrelevant factor, while inviting unnecessary resistance to modern political output. Attention to process defects resulted in strict scrutiny of racial classification. Judicial review itself has become distorted and the original theory perverted, however, to the extent exacting review now is reserved primarily for remedial policies enacted by democratically elected agents. Rigorous review detached from its original justification thus has evolved as accounting methodology for persons who never have been excluded from the political process or part of a historically disadvantaged group.

Doctrine that feeds anti-democratic perceptions risks defiance and evasion if jurisprudential demands are substantial and underwrites constitutional torpor or incongruity if the Court lacks the resolve to make meaningful demands. Modern equal protection doctrine is especially unsatisfactory to the extent it offers unacceptable options and ultimately confounds constitutional reckoning. A choice between high conflict/high risk doctrine and avoidance/abdication is especially remiss when basic and indisputable aims of the Fourteenth Amendment remain unsatisfied.

Jurisprudence may challenge or displace legislative enactment and popular sentiment, but, to the extent clearly referenced to original intent or consensual understanding, it is safe from allegations of anti-democratic tendencies. Failure to mine fully the possibilities of originalism may be due to an awareness of the overtly racist sentiment and limited aims that inspired the Fourteenth Amendment. A consequent motivation for more exotic doctrine may be a sense that work influenced by such attitudes and aspirations itself is infected or spoiled. For all the sophisticated theories competing to animate doctrine more aggressively and expansively, they are pragmatically doomed to the extent they would unsettle cultural norms and be objected to as fundamentally anti-democratic.

Equal protection for practical purposes is reducible to the art of the possible within a framework now, as always, limited but not without significant opportunity for achievement. Society and its governing agents are bound by constitutional baselines that reflect the paramount explications of democratic consent. As noted in Chapter 2, the central and consensual aims of the Fourteenth Amendment were to ensure basic economic opportunity for material self-development and to provide for strict parity within the legal system, regardless of race. The implications of these core interests and the existence of less certain concerns might be debated—and avoided to the extent that clear reference points did not exist. Because the essential agenda is so indisputable, equal protection vitality would be enhanced by identifying and effectuating the logical radiations of original design, which remain pertinent to a legacy of discrimination more than a century after the Fourteenth Amendment's introduction. Consequent doctrine closely tied to facilitating elemental opportunity and equality of legal status would begin with the significant advantage of immunity to anti-democratic perceptions and debate that respectively cripple and enervate other alternatives.

Movement toward theory and consequent standards that are rooted

in original soil but more productive in their yield necessitates a reexamination of some old shibboleths. Modern notions of suspect classifications and strict scrutiny evolved from the sense that discrete and insular
minorities traditionally were excluded from or underrepresented in the
legislative process and thus merited special judicial attention.[55] Review
of racial classifications evolved to the point that it was characterized as
"strict in theory and fatal in fact."[56] Such scrutiny may have been pro-
democratic rather than anti-democratic insofar as it accounted for defects in the representative process. It was especially apt when enactments
that implied inferiority, perpetuated privilege, or denied opportunity
were at issue. As traditionally disadvantaged minorities have enhanced
their political identity and influence, in a system predicating success on
effective coalition building and brokering among interest groups, special
jurisprudential attention is more difficult to justify on the grounds of
process defect. Evidence suggests that blacks in recent years have increased their influence in the political system. The Civil Rights Act of
1991,[57] passed by Congress in response to restrictive Supreme Court
readings of civil rights laws, illustrates how a group that was once entirely
excluded from the legislative process now participates in alliances that
yield political accomplishments.[58] Congress, in the previous year, failed
to override a presidential veto of a similar enactment.[59] The experience
suggests at least on the federal level that a previously outcast group no
longer is entirely disabled by prejudice and, like other non-dominant
groups, may prevail in some proportion to its actual numerical strength.

Jurisprudence that justified special constitutional attention when the
political system was grossly distorted actually may imperil the representative process when it has become more responsive to all citizens. As
localities with a long and pervasive history of discrimination have attempted to reckon with their past, the Court has confounded their efforts. Constitutional impedance is a function of strict scrutiny, deriving
from now misplaced assumptions of exclusion from or unrepresentation
in the political process. The consequent anomaly is that the harshest
standard of review, for practical purposes, has been reserved primarily
for constitutional claims by the dominant racial group. It is ironic that
the Court, which vitalized the equal protection guarantee with notions
of suspect classification and strict scrutiny when the political process was
perceived as dysfunctional is cramping the system as it approaches the
ideal that the Court identified. Analytical standards introduced to repair
process defect thus may be responsible for its aggravation.

Even with its limited aspirations, the Fourteenth Amendment was
supported by a significant sense of obligation to account for racial disadvantage. The notion that race never can be a factor in official action
may represent a desirable ideal and may afford neat symmetry to the
extent it touts general color blindness, but it denies the methodology for

a constitutionally sanctioned reckoning. By making race unmentionable, even though its presence and implications are pervasive and selectively unattended to, jurisprudence seriously confounds even the limited aims of the Fourteenth Amendment. The Court actually may impede progress toward real color blindness insofar as premature insistence on neutrality may deter morally inspired initiatives intended to remedy the consequences of past policy and practice. Categorical prohibition of racially referenced policy, to the extent premised upon legal criteria of color blindness, establishes a constitutional standard incongruent with the reality of persisting color-consciousness. It thus leaves the Court vulnerable to criticism that it has fast-tracked legal standards beyond society's actual moral development. Even worse, such legal principles project imagery of societal development that may engender complacency and actually deter individual or collective attention to moral reality.

Equal protection's potential has been constrained by a sense of the judiciary in competition with the representative process and thus the consent of the governed. The indisputable albeit limited aims of the Fourteenth Amendment, however, are a supreme extension of rather than a challenge to popular will. No higher expression of democratic consent exists than what the Constitution itself ordains. Doctrine neither should be cast in terms of creative theory, therefore, nor should it negate credible initiatives aimed at transforming ideals into reality. Rather, equal protection theory and principle should maximize the possibilities of linkage to cognizable and incontrovertible interests and present themselves with the certainty that constitutional aims and democratic imperatives are coextensive and essentially the same. Original design may not support the most expansive or exotic notions of equality, but it affords the opportunity for confident enunciation of assertive and meaningful standards for interests that still await a full accounting.

Pragmatic vitalization of the Fourteenth Amendment favors divesting anachronistic and uncertain theories and attending instead to the amendment's credible emanations. Such review essentially would be a function of how closely related a claimed interest is to original or consensual goals of the Fourteenth Amendment. As the relationship between modern policy and original or consensual agenda becomes less fathomable, scrutiny of a challenged circumstance or action should intensify. Correlatively, as the nexus becomes more discernible, scrutiny should be less rigorous. Review would be in inverse proportion to the close or distant association with the original agenda and consensual glosses on it. As amended by subsequent experience, constitutional concern would extend to any form of official racial discrimination or stigmatization manifestly inimical to equal protection criteria established in 1954.

Fourteenth Amendment analysis thus should focus upon (1) whether a challenged policy or action implicates a clear original or consensual concern and (2) whether the policy or action credibly conforms with or contravenes amplified original interest. Race-conscious policies advancing basic elements of the amendment's historical agenda should be subject to less than strict scrutiny. Conversely, when the relationship between central aims and a challenged action is attenuated or uncertain, review should be more rigorous. Such a sliding scale would calibrate judicial concern not to secondary or peripheral matters—including motive, process defect, cultural significance, and even disputable implications of a classification—but rather to more justifiable constitutional concerns.

The efficacy of the equal protection guarantee consequently would be enhanced but not to the point it would be an uncontrollable peril to all legislation that classifies or has disparate effects. The parade of horribles, referred to by the Court in justifying motive-based inquiry,[60] would never materialize. General tax legislation that routinely classifies, for instance, would not implicate original or consensual concern and thus not be subject to serious equal protection challenges.[61] Similarly a reduction in public benefits that disproportionately affects the poor may not be proximately related to cognizable Fourteenth Amendment concerns, even if it affects one racial group more than another.[62] Disparate impact would have constitutional significance to the extent it related to venues and circumstances close to acknowledged Fourteenth Amendment concerns with basic opportunity and a fair system of justice. Although probity would diminish as ties to the original agenda became more distant, it would not be categorically discounted.

A fortified jurisprudence of original design should closely examine disproportionality not only in employment and business venues but also in areas that are critical to economic opportunity, such as education. Instead of limiting principles that gloss the funding differentials among racially identifiable schools that are not officially segregated, a constitutional duty would exist to provide quality education. To the extent a traffic barrier between black and white neighborhoods does not impede basic opportunity, it would survive equal protection review. Attention to original aims, however, might engender more sensitive Thirteenth Amendment analysis that recognized how such official acts may be consistent with reducing a particular group to the status of a subject race. Disparities in the criminal justice system's operation would be closely scrutinized pursuant to original concern with equal status before the law.

Initiatives to facilitate equal economic opportunity for racial minorities should be constitutionally permissible if they effectuate core Fourteenth Amendment aims and if their adoption is not procedurally irregular.[63] Standards of review should be receptive to voluntary efforts to integrate the educational system or the workplace as policies legitimately tied to Fourteenth Amendment aims. Presumptively valid would be a diversification scheme, such as the plan defeated in *Wygant v. Jackson Board of*

Education, designed to facilitate basic opportunity and subscribed to without procedural aberration.[64] Attention to the link between policy and original aim, unlike an entirely deferential mode of review, would enable the Court to identify and invalidate schemes that were inadequately rooted in original design. The possibility that a locally powerful minority might enact policy to secure unfair advantage, which worried the Court in *City of Richmond v. J. A. Croson Co.*,[65] still could be discerned pursuant to a credibility standard. Even if such a program fit within a clear concern of the original agenda, it would fail if not accounting for a legitimate interest under the circumstances and if proper procedures were not followed. The inquiry should remain fixed, however, on whether the plan credibly reckoned with a persisting discriminatory legacy of recognizably constitutional significance.

Even if affirmative action presents some of the negatives and risks that the Court has catalogued,[66] judicial intervention is unjustified when the representative process is not dysfunctional but rather is effectively accounting for original imperatives. Holding society and its legislative agents to an as yet unrealized standard, in the form of color blindness, detaches law from morality without compelling justification. It also represents social engineering and micromanagement, which proponents of restraint supposedly condemn, and defines and limits policies that may compete for moral subscription.

Jurisprudence that speaks in idealistic flourishes and then manipulates doctrine so that the results comport with actual moral circumstance is the preface for an Orwellian legacy. Society has not evolved to the point that racial distinctions are no longer pertinent or prominent. Race-dependent attitudes and judgments always have been and remain rooted in the nation's traditions and conscience as defining societal characteristics. Review that suggests a deep and broad spectrum commitment to erasing discrimination, even as it effectively avoids the task, not only transcends original vision. It also is delusionary and obstructive to society's own confrontation with and even consciousness of racial reality. A culture indulged by constitutional imagery, suggesting a higher state of moral development than actually exists, is the victim of an especially insidious form of judicial activism insofar as its incentive for real moral growth is diminished.

The jurisprudence of race now, as over the course of two centuries, is reducible to a doctrine of affordability. Slavery was accommodated at the republic's inception after factoring in the toll otherwise to a viable political and economic union. The separate but equal doctrine calculated the cost of insisting that society abandon its established traditions and attitudes. Curtailment of the anti-discrimination principle generally, and the desegregation mandate particularly, likewise reflects a sense that jurisprudence cannot impose demands that are too unsettling or in conflict with higher priorities. Standards as they have evolved so far denote the reality of a society not disposed toward absorbing fully the cost of accounting for racial discrimination. What remains affordable and serviceable, but largely neglected, is doctrine that would achieve the central and consensual aims of the Fourteenth Amendment. The interests of constitutional productivity point not to doctrinal creativity that will be disputed and defeated but to maximization of an original agenda that affords an irrefutable constitutional baseline for policy and review. The alternative is constitutional law presuming a society that is mythical rather than real and a source of disputable theories instead of real accomplishments.

NOTES

1. *See* Chapter 2.
2. Civil Rights Act of 1964, 42 U.S.C. § 2000a to 2000b (1964), precludes discrimination in public accommodations and facilities that otherwise limited eating and shelter options appurtenant to travel. *See, e.g.,* Katzenbach v. McClung, 379 U.S. 294, 304 (1964); Heart of Atlanta Motel v. United States, 379 U.S. 241, 258 (1964).
3. For instance, the Court has held that racially restrictive covenants violate both the Thirteenth and Fourteenth Amendments. *See* Shelley v. Kraemer, 334 U.S. 1, 20–21 (1948).
4. *See, e.g.,* Patterson v. McLean Credit Union, 109 S. Ct. 2363, 2370 (1989) (42 U.S.C. § 1981 precludes racial discrimination with respect to making and enforcing contracts).
5. The Court held that Section 1981 does not reach racial harassment that occurs after formation of an employment contract. *See* Patterson v. McLean Credit Union, 109 S. Ct. at 2373–74. The dissent argued that the majority failed to recognize that racial harassment during employment "denie[s] the right to make an employment contract on [an equal] basis." *Id.* at 2393 (Brennan, J., dissenting).
6. In striking down a state law excluding blacks from juries, the Court emphasized that the Fourteenth Amendment was to be interpreted in a way that implemented its remedial purpose. Strauder v. West Virginia, 100 U.S. (10 Otto) 303, 307 (1880). Such interpretive philosophy characterizes the review of modern federal regulation in general. The federal securities laws, for instance, are to "be construed 'not technically and restrictively, but flexibly to effectuate [their] remedial purposes.' " Herman & McLean, Inc. v. Huddleston, 459 U.S. 375, 386–87 (1983) (quoting Securities and Exchange Commission v. Capital Gains Research Bureau, Inc., 375 U.S. 180, 195 (1963)).
7. McCleskey v. Kemp, 481 U.S. 279, 312 (1987).
8. Virginia v. Rives, 100 U.S. (10 Otto) 313 (1879).
9. Batson v. Kentucky, 476 U.S. 79 (1986).
10. Washington v. Seattle School District No. 1, 458 U.S. 457 (1982).
11. Crawford v. Board of Education, 458 U.S. 527 (1982).
12. 471 U.S. 222 (1985).

13. *Id.* at 233.

14. *Id.*

15. *See* McCleskey v. Kemp, 481 U.S. at 279, 329–33, 343–44 (Brennan, J., dissenting).

16. *See* Martin v. Wilks, 109 S. Ct. 2180 (1989); City of Richmond v. J. A. Croson Co., 488 U.S. 469 (1989); United States v. Paradise, 480 U.S. 149 (1986); Local 28, Sheet Metal Workers International Association v. EEOC, 478 U.S. 421 (1986); Local No. 93, International Association of Firefighters v. Cleveland, 478 U.S. 501 (1986); Wygant v. Jackson Board of Education, 476 U.S. 267 (1986); Firefighters Local Union No. 1784 v. Stotts, 467 U.S. 561 (1984); Minnick v. California Department of Corrections, 452 U.S. 105 (1981); Fullilove v. Klutznick, 448 U.S. 448 (1980).

17. The *Strauder* Court, as noted in Chapter 3, intimated that the Fourteenth Amendment was concerned with discrimination "implying inferiority." Strauder v. West Virginia, 100 U.S. (10 Otto) at 308.

18. See Chapter 5.

19. United States v. O'Brien, 391 U.S. 367, 384 (1968).

20. *See* Lawrence, *The Id, the Ego and Equal Protection: Reckoning with Unconscious Racism*, 39 Stan. L. Rev. 317, 355–62 (1987).

21. *See id.* at 349–50.

22. *See id.* at 354–55.

23. City of Richmond v. J. A. Croson Co., 109 S. Ct. at 706, 724.

24. Cases involving grossly disparate applications of the death penalty and state-facilitated segregation of city and suburban schools appear on their face to be constitutionally violative, even under a rigorous discriminatory intent test. Yet, the Court explained away duality in the death penalty context as a mere "discrepancy that appears to correlate with race...[and] an inevitable part of our criminal justice system." McCleskey v. Kemp, 481 U.S. at 312. The Court set aside a trial court's findings of fact in a school segregation case in order to avoid ordering intermunicipal desegregation. *See* Milliken v. Bradley, 418 U.S. 717, 745–47 (1974).

25. *See, e.g.,* United States v. O'Brien, 391 U.S. at 383–84.

26. *E.g.,* Columbus Board of Education v. Penick, 443 U.S. 449, 459 (1979).

27. City of Memphis v. Greene, 451 U.S. 100, 124 (1981). The city had a long and pervasive history of official segregation, as well as traditions connoting racial inferiority. *See id.* at 137 (Marshall, J., dissenting). The city erected the barrier at the request of residents in the white neighborhood. *See id.* at 135 (Marshall, J., dissenting).

28. *See* Lawrence, *supra* note 20, at 319.

29. *See* Lynch v. Donnelly, 465 U.S. 668, 685 (1984).

30. *See id.* at 676.

31. *See* Marsh v. Chambers, 463 U.S. 783, 795 (1983).

32. Federal Communications Commission v. Pacifica Foundation, 438 U.S. 726, 775 (1978) (Brennan, J., dissenting).

33. The specific language contained in a broadcast satire of social usage and response to certain words is reproduced in the appendix to the court's opinion. *See id.* at 751–55.

34. *See id.* at 750 (characterizing broadcast of language at issue as equivalent to "a pig [in the] parlor").

35. *Id.* at 776 (Brennan, J., dissenting).

36. *Id.* (quoting Bins, *Toward an Ethnography of Contemporary African American Oral Poetry*, in Language and Linguistics Working Papers No. 5, at 82 (1972)).

37. *See* Skywalker Records, Inc. v. Navarro, 739 F. Supp. 578 (S.D. Fla. 1990).

38. Brown v. Board of Education, 347 U.S. 483, 493 (1954). In mandating desegregation of federal schools in the District of Columbia, despite the absence of an explicit equal protection provision in the Fifth Amendment, the Court reinforced the notion that education was a fundamental right. *See* Bolling v. Sharpe, 347 U.S. 497, 499–500 (1954).

39. *See* San Antonio Independent School District v. Rodriguez, 411 U.S. 1, 36 (1973).

40. *See id.* at 28–29.

41. *See id.*

42. *See, e.g.*, Amicus Curiae Brief for American Civil Liberties Union at 28–31, Brown v. Board of Education, 347 U.S. 483 (1954); Amicus Curiae Brief for American Federation of Teachers at 25–26, Brown v. Board of Education, 347 U.S. 483 (1954).

43. Modern equal protection addresses classifications based on gender, alienage, and illegitimacy and also covers discriminatory acts impacting on fundamental rights. It thus would be a source of surprise to early observers who "doubt[ed]...very much whether any action of a State not directed...against the negroes...will ever be held to come within the purview of this provision." Slaughter-House Cases, 83 U.S. (16 Wall.) 36, 81 (1872).

44. Strict constructionism is predicated on the notion that "the Court has no power to add or subtract from the procedures set forth by the Founders." In re Winship, 397 U.S. 358, 377 (1970) (Black, J., dissenting). The doctrine directs courts to construe the Constitution "in a straightforward manner...paying close attention to its words and avoid twisting or stretching their meanings [so] there will be few occasions for controversies that can be manipulated." L. Tribe, God Save This Honorable Court 41 (1985). Given the inadequacy of a purely textual approach to construing the many critical open-ended terms of the Constitution, it is not surprising that strict constructionists constitute "a very unpopulated subgroup." G. Gunther, Constitutional Law 518 n.11 (1991).

45. Originalism requires that courts confronted with vague or indeterminate constitutional provisions construe those provisions with reference to the subjective intent of the framers of the Constitution. *See* D. Lively, Judicial Review and the Consent of the Governed: Activist Ways and Popular Ends 56–59 (1990). The theory is susceptible to the same criticisms leveled against the Court's motive-based Fourteenth Amendment inquiry.

46. Neutrality calls on courts to employ objective interpretive principles that favor no particular group, even when the interpretation proves subjectively unsatisfying. *See* Bork, *Neutral Principles and Some First Amendment Problems*, 47 Ind. L.J. 1, 6–7 (1971); Tushnet, *Following the Rules Laid Down: A Critique of Interpretivism and Neutral Principles*, 96 Harv. L. Rev. 781, 805–06 (1983); Wechsler, *Toward Neutral Principles of Constitutional Law*, 73 Harv. L. Rev. 1, 11–12, 15 (1959). The neutral principles model suffers from a misplaced assumption that

a singular principle links serial decisions and that factors invariably can be advanced, as in the case of affirmative action, to distinguish circumstances from the general rule.

47. *See, e.g.*, Grey, *Do We Have an Unwritten Constitution?*, 27 Stan. L. Rev. 703, 706 (1975); Tushnet, *supra* note 46.

48. *See* Brest, *Foreword: In Defense of the Antidiscrimination Principle*, 90 Harv. L. Rev. 1, 6 (1976).

49. *See* Fiss, *Groups and the Equal Protection Clause*, 5 Phil. & Pub. Aff. 107, 153–54 (1976).

50. *See* Lawrence, *supra* note 20, at 355–62.

51. Ackerman, *Beyond Carolene Products*, 98 Harv. L. Rev. 713, 744 (1985).

52. Sugarman v. Dougall, 413 U.S. 634, 649–57 (1973) (Rehnquist, J., dissenting).

53. The Court's strict scrutiny of racial classifications is rooted in the premise that prejudice against discrete and insular minorities may distort the political process otherwise relied upon for protection. *See* United States v. Carolene Products Co., 304 U.S. 144, 152 n.4 (1938).

54. The Voting Rights Act of 1965, 42 U.S.C. § 1973 (1988), continues to secure voting rights and political participation in states that historically denied or impaired the franchise on racial grounds. In the 1988 presidential election, 50.2 percent of the voting age population actually cast ballots. Statistical Abstract of the United States 258 (table 433) (1989). During the 1986 congressional election, 46 percent of the eligible population voted. Statistical Abstract of the United States 249 (table 418) (1988).

55. *See* United States v. Carolene Products Co., 304 U.S. at 152 n.4. The concepts of suspect classification and rigid scrutiny made their literal debut in Korematsu v. United States, 323 U.S. 214, 216 (1944).

56. Gunther, *Foreword: In Search of Evolving Doctrine on a Changing Court: A Model for a Newer Equal Protection*, 86 Harv. L. Rev. 1, 8 (1972).

57. *See* S. 1745, 102nd Cong., 1st Sess. (Nov. 1991) (Lexis, Genfed Library, Bills File). The law, among other things, curtails belated challenges to consent decrees incorporating affirmative action plans, places upon employers the burden of showing that practices having a racially disparate impact are justified by business necessity, and extends protection against racial discrimination in employment contracts to post-formation harassment. The enactment thus displaces case law discussed *supra* at notes 4–6 and accompanying text, and in Chapter 5, notes 182–86 and accompanying text.

58. Unlike other interest group efforts, organized initiatives toward securing racial justice are qualified by standards prohibiting a remedial focus that is race-conscious. *See* City of Richmond v. J.A. Croson Co., 109 S. Ct. 721.

59. *See* 136 Cong. Rec. S 16,562, S 16,589 (Oct. 24, 1990).

60. The Court has reasoned that without a discriminatory intent standard for the Fourteenth Amendment, "a whole range of tax, welfare, public service, regulatory, and licensing statutes" would be endangered. Washington v. Davis, 426 U.S. 229, 248 (1976).

61. A tax that without adequate justification singled out an interest protected by the equal protection guarantee, however, would be susceptible to constitutional challenge. *Cf.* Minneapolis Star & Tribune Co. v. Minnesota Commissioner

of Revenue, 460 U.S. 575, 585 (1983). Although not directly referring to the equal protection guarantee, the Court cited to authority for the proposition that such regulation, even if unrelated to suppression of expression, would be "pres-umptively unconstitutional." *Id.* (citing Police Department of Chicago v. Mosley, 408 U.S. 92, 95 (1972)).

62. Denial of government funds for abortions thus would not be likely to present an equal protection claim under the proposed standards. *See, e.g.,* Harris v. McRae, 448 U.S. 297, 326 (1980); Maher v. Roe, 432 U.S. 464, 469–70 (1977).

63. Judicial scrutiny to determine whether laws were enacted in conformance with procedural norms would be intended to ensure that any preferential scheme emerged from a fair process. *See* Wygant v. Jackson Board of Education, 476 U.S. 267, 317 (1986) (Stevens, J., dissenting).

64. *See id.*

65. *See* City of Richmond v. J. A. Croson Co., 109 S. Ct. at 722.

66. *See id.* at 721. The Court's objections to affirmative action are examined in Chapter 6.

Bibliography

BOOKS

Abraham, H., Justices and Presidents (1974).

Allen, R., The Life and Experience and Gospel Labors of the Rt. Rev. Richard Allen (1960).

Areeda, P., & Kaplan, L., Antitrust Analysis (1988).

Baer, J., Equality under the Constitution: Reclaiming the Fourteenth Amendment (1983).

Bell, D., And We Are Not Saved (1987).

Bell, D., Race, Racism and American Law (1973).

Berger, R., Government by Judiciary (1977).

Bickel, A., The Supreme Court and the Idea of Progress (1970).

Black, C., Jr., Structure and Relationship in Constitutional Law (1969).

Bork, R., The Tempting of America (1990).

Carter, S., Reflections of an Affirmative Action Baby (1991).

Cover, R., Justice Accused (1975).

Du Bois, W.E.B., The Suppression of the African Slave-Trade to the United States of America, 1638–1870 (1896).

Dunham, A., & Kurland, P., eds., Mr. Justice (1964).

Elliot, J., ed., The Debates in the Several State Conventions of the Adoption of the Federal Constitution (1901).

Fairman, C., History of the Supreme Court of the United States, Reconstruction and Reunion (1971) (1987).

Farrand, M., ed., The Records of the Federal Convention of 1787 (1937).

Fehrenbacher, D., The Dred Scott Case (1978).

Finkelman, P., An Imperfect Union (1981).

Goldwin, R., & Kaufman, A., eds., The Constitution, Equality and Race (1988).
Graham, H., Everyman's Constitution (1968).
Gunther, G., Constitutional Law (1991).
Hall, K., ed., The Law of American Slavery (1987).
Higginbotham, A., Jr., In the Matter of Color (1978).
Hyman, H., A More Perfect Union (1973).
Hyman, H., & Wiecek, W., Equal Justice under the Law (1982).
Jacobs, P., Prelude to Riot: A View of Urban America from the Bottom (1967).
Jordan, W., White over Black: American Attitudes Toward the Negro (1968).
Kaczorowski, R., The Politics of Judicial Interpretation: The Federal Courts, Department of Justice and Civil Rights, 1866–1876 (1985).
Karst, K., Belonging to America (1989).
Karst, K., ed., Civil Rights and Equality (1989).
Kettner, J., The Development of American Citizenship, 1608–1870 (1978).
Kluger, R., Simple Justice (1975).
Kurland, P., Politics, the Constitution, and the Warren Court (1970).
Lewis, A., Portrait of a Decade: The Second American Revolution (1964).
Lively, D., Judicial Review and the Consent of the Governed: Activist Ways and Popular Ends (1990).
Lynch, F., Invisible Victims: White Males and the Crisis of Affirmative Action (1989).
Lynd, S., Class Conflict, Slavery and the United States Constitution (1967).
Mason, A. The Supreme Court from Taft to Warren (1958).
Mason, A. William Howard Taft—Chief Justice (1964).
Myrdal, G., An American Dilemma (1944).
Nelson, W., The Fourteenth Amendment: From Political Principle to Judicial Doctrine (1988).
Phillips, U., American Negro Slavery (1918).
Ripple, K., Constitutional Litigation (1984).
Sowell, T., Civil Rights: Rhetoric or Reality? (1984).
Steele, S., The Content of Our Character (1990).
Story, J., Commentaries on the Constitution (1905).
ten Broek, J., Antislavery Origins of the Fourteenth Amendment (1951).
Tribe, L., American Constitutional Law (1988).
Tribe, L., God Save This Honorable Court (1985).
Tushnet, M., The American Law of Slavery (1981).
Wiecek, W., The Sources of Antislavery Constitutionalism in America, 1760–1848 (1977).
Wilson, W., The Declining Significance of Race (1978).
Woodward, C., The Burden of Southern History (1960).

ESSAYS

Ackerman, *Beyond Carolene Products*, 98 Harv. L. Rev. 713 (1985).
Bins, *Toward an Ethnography of Contemporary African American Oral Poetry*, in Language and Linguistics Working Papers No. 5 (1972).
Bork, *Neutral Principles and Some First Amendment Problems*, 47 Ind. L.J., 1 (1971).

Brest, *Foreword: In Defense of the Antidiscrimination Principle*, 90 Harv. L. Rev. 1 (1976).

Ely, *The Constitutionality of Reverse Discrimination*, 41 U. Chi. L. Rev. 723 (1974).

Fehrenbacher, *Slavery, the Framers, and the Living Constitution*, in Slavery and Its Consequences: The Constitution, Equality and Race (R. Goldwin & A. Kaufman eds. 1988).

Finkelman, *Prigg v. Pennsylvania and Northern State Courts*, in The Law of American Slavery (R. Hall ed. 1987).

Fiss, *Groups and the Equal Protection Clause*, 5 Phil. & Pub. Aff. 107 (1976).

Goodman, *De Facto School Segregation: A Constitutional and Empirical Analysis*, 60 Calif. L. Rev. 275 (1972).

Graham, The Early Antislavery Backgrounds of the Fourteenth Amendment, 1950 Wis. L. Rev. 610 (1950).

Grey, *Do We Have an Unwritten Constitution?*, 27 Stan. L. Rev. 703 (1975).

Gunther, *Foreword: In Search of Evolving Doctrine on a Changing Court: A Model for a Newer Equal Protection*, 86 Harv. L. Rev. 1 (1972).

Kennedy, *Persuasion and Distrust: A Comment on the Affirmative Action Debate*, 99 Harv. L. Rev. 1327 (1986).

Lawrence, *The Id, the Ego and Equal Protection: Reckoning with Unconscious Racism*, 39 Stan. L. Rev. 317 (1987).

Levy, *Plessy v. Ferguson*, in Civil Rights and Equality (K. Karst ed. 1989).

Lively, *The Supreme Court Appointment Process: In Search of Constitutional Roles and Responsibilities*, 59 S. Cal. L. Rev. 551 (1986).

Lively & Plass, *Equal Protection: The Jurisprudence of Denial and Evasion*, 40 Am. U.L. Rev. 1307 (1991).

Marek, *Education by Decree*, New Perspectives, Summer 1985, at 36.

Marshall, *An Evaluation of Recent Efforts to Achieve Racial Integration in Education through Resort to the Courts*, 21 J. Negro Education 316 (1952).

Meese, *The Law of the Constitution*, 61 Tul. L. Rev. 979 (1987).

Pinderhughes, *Legal Strategies for Voting Rights: Political Science and the Law*, 28 How. L.J. 515 (1985).

Ross, *Innocence and Affirmative Action*, 43 Vand. L. Rev. 297 (1990).

Sandalow, Constitutional Interpretation, 79 Mich. L. Rev. 1033 (1981).

Sullivan, *Sins of Discrimination: Last Term's Affirmative Action Cases*, 100 Harv. L. Rev. 78 (1986).

Tushnet, *Following the Rules Laid Down: A Critique of Interpretivism and Neutral Principles*, 96 Harv. L. Rev. 781 (1983).

Wechsler, *Toward Neutral Principles of Constitutional Law*, 73 Harv. L. Rev. 1 (1959).

Index

Ableman v. Booth, 32, 37n.
Abolitionism, 13–14, 22, 34–35nn.
Ackerman, Bruce, 175
Affirmative action. *See* Race-conscious policies
Allen, Richard, 2
Allgeyer v. Louisiana, 95, 105n.
American Insurance Co. v. Canter, 14, 35–36nn.
Anti-miscegenation laws, 28, 103–4
Antitrust policy, 159–60
Articles of Confederation, 3, 11, 68

Barron v. Mayor and City Council of Baltimore, 30, 57n.
Batson v. Kentucky, 87n., 170, 182n.
Berea College v. Kentucky, 94–95, 105n.
Berger, Raoul, 49–50, 52
Bill of Rights, 7, 44–45, 49, 73
Black Codes, 42–43, 47, 51, 72, 77, 89
Blackmun, Harry, 140, 152, 155
Board of Education of Oklahoma City Public Schools v. Dowell, 127, 135n.
Bolling v. Sharpe, 112, 125, 131n., 134n., 183n.

Bradley, Joseph, 67, 73–74, 79
Brennan, William, Jr., 140, 147, 152, 155–56
Brest, Paul, 175
Briggs v. Elliott, 109–10, 130n.
Brown v. Board of Education: criticism, 129–30; generally, 3, 6, 9n., 17, 35n., 65, 77, 87n., 106–7nn., 109–20, 125–30, 130–35nn., 171, 173–74, 183n.; limiting principles, 7, 120–28, 130, 173–74, 180–81; litigation history, 109–10; reaction, 6–7, 114–19; relief, 6–7, 112–14
Buchanan v. Warley, 94–95, 105n.
Burger, Warren, 119, 141
Bush, George, 162
Busing. *See* Desegregation

Capital punishment, 128, 170
Citizenship: early concepts, 17–18; effect of Civil War, 42; effect of Fourteenth Amendment, 48–56, 67–74; interpretation in *Scott v. Sandford*, 27–29
Civil rights, 6, 40–56
Civil Rights Act of: 1866, 6, 45–51,

54, 61–62, 68–69, 73, 129; 1871,
75; 1875, 55, 62, 78–84; 1964, 55,
62, 65, 129, 138; 1990, 159; 1991,
177
Civil Rights Cases, 6, 9n., 55, 59n., 62,
78–84, 84nn., 87–88nn., 89, 104n.,
125, 166n.
Civil War, 39–44, 83, 174
Cleveland, Grover, 96
Colfax Massacre, 66, 75
Color-blind standards, 5–6, 66, 84,
92–93, 137, 142, 148–51, 156–59,
174, 177–78, 180
Commonwealth v. Aves, 19–20, 35n.
Compromise of 1850, 23
Contract rights, 6, 62–63, 69, 74, 95–
97, 129, 170
Constitutional Convention: accommo-
dation of slavery, 1–6, 180–81;
general purpose, 1–7
Cooley, Thomas, 52
Cooper v. Aaron, 114–15, 131n.
Corfield v. Coryell, 46–47, 68, 74, 86n.
Crawford v. Board of Education, 116–
17, 132n., 170, 182n.
Criminal justice, 128, 170, 179
Cumming v. Board of Education, 93–94,
105n.

Dawes, Thomas, 4
Declaration of Independence, 28, 41,
44–45, 49, 73
DeFunis v. Odegaard, 138, 162n.
Democratic Party, 24–26, 31–32, 49
Desegregation: busing, 116–18, 170;
District of Columbia, 112; generally, 98–102, 109–30; graduate and
professional schools, 98–102; implementation, 112–19; interdistrict
remedies, 122–24; limiting principles, 120–28, 130, 173–74, 180–81;
resegregation, 124–28; resistance
to, 114–19
Discriminatory effect, 77–78, 120–30,
137, 179, 184n.
Discriminatory intent, 63, 77–78,
120–30, 137, 159, 170–72, 179,
184n.

Diversification policies, 139–40, 145–
46, 155–58, 179–80
Douglas, Stephen A., 26
Dred Scott case. *See Scott v. Sandford*
Due process clause: Fifth Amend-
ment, 14, 30, 44, 71; Fourteenth
Amendment, 51–52, 71, 77, 94–97,
112

Economic rights. *See* Contract rights;
Fourteenth Amendment; Property
rights
Education, 6, 47, 89, 91, 93–95, 97–
102, 109–30, 179
Eisenhower, Dwight, 114
Emancipation Proclamation, 40
Enforcement Act of 1870, 54
Equal protection: early interpretation, 71, 75–78, 90–91, 98; modern
application, 101–4, 109–30, 137–
62, 169–74; original purpose, 51;
theories of review, 7, 129–30, 174

Field, Stephen, 52, 72–74
Fifteenth Amendment: congressional
enforcement power, 54, 56, 65,
97–98; early court decisions, 61,
97–98; framing and ratification, 6,
33, 51, 54, 63–64; modern application, 65–66; purpose, 6, 33, 51, 54,
61; southern resistance, 64
Fisher v. Hurst, 100, 106n.
Fiss, Owen, 175
Force Acts, 64
Fourteenth Amendment: citizenship
(*see* Citizenship); congressional enforcement power, 49, 52–56, 62,
65, 72, 79–84, 141–42, 177; debate
over its meaning, 7, 49, 52; early
interpretation, 6, 61, 66–84, 171;
economic rights doctrine, 51–52,
67, 72–74, 94–97; framing and ratification, 6, 33, 45–53, 56, 68, 111;
fundamental rights, 7, 51–52, 55,
61, 68, 74, 94–97; incorporation, 7,
44, 49; Lochnerism (*see* Lochnerism); non-race dependent interests,
51–52, 55, 61, 67, 72–74, 94–97;

purpose, 6, 33–34, 45–53, 56, 61,
  68, 75–84, 176–81; redistribution
  of federal and state powers, 48,
  52–53, 56, 61, 66, 70–72, 75, 79–
  84, 127–28; separate but equal (*see*
  Segregation, separate but equal
  doctrine); voting rights, 65
Free soil, 24–25, 31–32
Freedmen's Bureau, 43–44
Fugitive Slave Act of: 1793, 15–16,
  21–23, 25, 83; 1850, 23, 32, 40
Fugitive slave clause, 1–2, 11, 15–16,
  21–23, 30–31
Fugitive slave controversy, 6, 14–16,
  19–25, 29–32, 83
Fullilove v. Klutznick, 141–42, 164n.,
  182n.

Garrison, William, 14, 22
*General Building Contractors Association,
  Inc. v. Pennsylvania*, 63, 85n.
Giles v. Harris, 9n., 64, 85n., 97–98,
  106n.
Gong Lum v. Rice, 98, 106n.
*Green v. County School Board of New
  Kent County, Virginia*, 115–17, 123,
  132n., 134n.
Griffin v. Breckenridge, 62, 85n.
*Griffin v. County School Board of Prince
  Edward County*, 115, 117
Guinn v. United States, 64, 85n.

Hamilton, Alexander, 52
Harlan, John, Sr., 82–84, 92–94, 137,
  142
Harrison, Benjamin, 96
Holmes, Oliver, Jr., 6, 64, 98
Hunter v. Underwood, 170, 182n.

Integration maintenance, 126–28
Iredell, James, 8n.

Jefferson, Thomas, 12
Jim Crow laws, 89–90, 121
Johnson, Andrew, 43, 48, 53
Jones v. Alfred H. Mayer Co., 59n., 62,
  84n.
Jordan, Winthrop, 4

Josefa Segunda, The, 19, 35n.
Jury selection, 75–78, 170

Kansas-Nebraska controversy, 24–26
Kennedy, Anthony, 156–57
Keyes v. School District No. 1, 120–24,
  133nn.
Ku Klux Klan Act, 54
Korematsu v. United States, 103, 107n.,
  157, 184n.

Lawrence, Charles, 175
Lincoln, Abraham: reaction to *Scott v.
  Sandford*, 32; reconstruction, 41;
  Thirteenth Amendment views, 41–
  42; views on race, 32–33
Literalism, 30, 174, 183n.
Lochner v. New York, 86n., 95–96, 102,
  104, 105n.
Lochnerism, 95–97
Loving v. Virginia, 104, 107n.

Madison, James, 3, 5, 8n., 12
Marbury v. Madison, 3, 8n., 131n.
Marshall, John. 3
Marshall, Thurgood: as Justice, 109,
  122, 124–25, 140–42, 144–45, 152–
  55; with NAACP, 98–102, 109,
  154–55
Mason, George, 4
*McCabe v. Atchison, Topeka & Santa Fe
  Railway Co.*, 94, 105n.
McCleskey v. Kemp, 128, 135n., 182n.
*McLaurin v. Oklahoma State Regents for
  Higher Education*, 100–102, 106–
  7nn.
Memphis, City of, v. Greene, 63, 85n.,
  172, 182n.
*Metro Broadcasting, Inc. v. Federal
  Communications Commission*, 9n.,
  155–57, 166–67nn.
Miller, Samuel, 67, 71, 74
Milliken v. Bradley, 9n., 122–24, 133–
  34nn., 182n.
Missouri ex rel. Gaines v. Canada, 98–
  100, 106n.
Missouri Compromise, 12, 24–25, 31,
  33

Moore v. Illinois, 25, 36n.
Motive-based inquiry, 63, 77–78, 120–30, 137, 148, 159, 170–72
Munn v. Illinois, 74, 87n.

National Association for the Advancement of Colored People, 98–104, 114
Natural law, 7, 34–35nn., 44
Necessary and proper clause, 3, 30, 65, 79
Neutrality, 174, 183–84nn.
Nixon, Richard, 118
North Carolina State Board of Education v. Swann, 116, 132n.
Northwest Ordinance and Territory, 2, 11–12, 29

O'Connor, Sandra Day, 144, 147, 148–50, 151, 152, 156–57
Originalism, 174, 183n.

Pace v. Alabama, 103, 107n.
Parker, John, 110
Pasadena City Board of Education v. Spangler, 124–25
Patterson v. McLean Credit Union, 57n., 63, 85n., 129, 135n., 181n.
Plessy v. Ferguson, 5, 9n., 16, 34, 90–99, 104–7nn., 111–12, 125, 127, 131n., 134n., 137, 157, 162–63nn., 166n.
Political rights, 6, 47, 50–54, 56, 64–66, 130, 175–76, 184n.
Popular sovereignty, 24–26
Powell, Lewis, 119, 121–22, 125–26, 138–40, 142–44, 146–47
Prigg v. Pennsylvania, 20–25, 35–36nn.
Privileges and immunities: Art.IV, §2, 14, 17, 28, 68; Fourteenth Amendment, 48–50, 67–74
Process defect, 175–77, 180
Property rights, 6, 13, 29–31, 62, 69, 94–95
Public accommodations, 78–83

Quotas, 117–18, 139, 146–47

Race-conscious policies: congressional enactments, 141–42, 148, 155–57; desegregation (*see* Desegregation); generally, 5–7, 137–62, 177–80; rationales against, 6, 139–40, 142–44, 147–52, 156–61; rationales for, 139–42, 144–47, 152–61
Racial disparity or disproportionality. *See* Discriminatory effect
Racial preferences, 137–62
Reagan, Ronald, 162
Reconstruction: aims and policies, 6, 40–56, 61–62; disagreement between executive and legislative branches, 41, 44–48, 53; southern response, 42–45, 48–51, 54
Regents of the University of California v. Bakke, 9n., 138–43, 146, 162–63nn.
Rehnquist, William, 126, 141–42, 147, 156, 175
Republican party, 31–33, 39–40, 45, 49–53, 130
Richmond, City of, v. J. A. Croson Co., 5–6, 148–55, 165–67nn., 179, 182n., 184–85nn.
Roberts v. City of Boston, 16–17, 35n., 104n.
Roosevelt, Franklin, 52
Runyon v. McCrary, 62–63, 85n.

San Antonio Independent School District v. Rodriguez, 125, 134n., 183n.
Scalia, Antonin, 147, 151–52, 156
Scott v. Sandford, 2–3, 6, 8n., 13, 16–17, 19–20, 24, 26–34, 36–37nn., 39–41, 45, 71, 89, 92
Segregation: affirmance of, 5, 90–104; challenge to, 98–104; de facto, 120–26, 130; de jure, 120–26, 128, 130; District of Columbia, 47, 91, 110–12; funding of schools, 93–94, 97, 101; intangibles, 101; northern, 2, 16–18, 33, 89–91, 110, 118–27; separate but equal doctrine, 5, 34, 64, 66, 90–104, 157, 181
Sipuel v. Board of Regents, 99–100, 106n.

Slaughter-House Cases, 66–74, 76, 79, 83, 85–86nn., 95, 183n.
Slavery: abolition, 33, 39; badges and incidents, 62, 172; District of Columbia, 13, 16, 40; fugitive slaves (*see* Fugitive Slave Act; Fugitive slave clause; Fugitive slave controversy; generally, 1–6, 11–34, 48, 51, 53, 83, 180–81; original accommodation, 1–6, 11, 16, 34, 180–81; property rights, 13, 28–31; slave trade, 1, 5, 7, 18–19, 30–31; Texas, 13–14
Souter, David, 157
South Carolina v. Katzenbach, 59n., 65, 85n.
Southwest Territory, 12
Standards of review: intermediate scrutiny, 139–40, 153–56; rational basis, 139, 143; strict scrutiny, 138–40, 142–44, 147–49, 151–53, 156–57, 184n.
State action principles, 77, 79–83
Statistical disparity. *See* Discriminatory effect
Stevens, John, 141–42, 145–47
Stewart, Potter, 141–42
Story, Joseph, 21–22, 34n.
Strader v. Graham 24, 26–27, 36n.
Strauder v. West Virginia, 75–79, 82, 87n., 89–90, 104–5nn., 129, 177, 181–82nn.
Strict constructionism. *See* Literalism
Strong, William, 75–76
Swann v. Charlotte-Mecklenburg Board of Education, 117–19, 132n., 134n.
Sweatt v. Painter, 100–102, 106n.

Taft, William, 96
Taney, Roger: in *Ableman v. Booth*, 32; as attorney general, 17–18; in *Barron v. Mayor and City Council of Baltimore*, 30; liberates own slaves, 12; in *Prigg v. Pennsylvania*, 21–23; in *Scott v. Sandford*, 2–3, 16, 27–33, 39, 71, 89

Territorial expansion and controversy, 6, 11–14, 23–25, 29, 32–33
Territory clause, 14, 29
Thirteenth Amendment: congressional enforcement power, 41, 56, 62, 79–84, 141–42; early court decisions, 61–62, 75–84, 90; framing and ratification, 6, 33, 41–42, 51; modern application, 62–63; purpose, 6, 33–34, 39, 41–42, 44–45, 56, 61, 63, 78–84; Southern response, 43–44, 48
Thomas, Clarence, 157
Travel, right to, 169

United States v. Carolene Products Co., 102–3, 107n., 184n.
United States v. Cruikshank, 74–75, 87n.
United States v. Harris, 75, 87n.
United States v. Paradise, 147, 164–65nn.

Vinson, Fred, 101
Virginia, Ex parte, 77, 87n.
Virginia v. Rives, 77, 87n., 170
Voting rights, 6, 47, 50–54, 56, 64–66, 130, 175–76, 184n.
Voting Rights Act of 1965, 65, 184n.

Wallace, George, 118
Wards Cove Packing Co. v. Atonio, 129, 135n.
Warren, Earl, 101–2, 119
Washington, Bushrod, 46, 69
Washington v. Seattle School District No. 1, 116–17, 132n., 170, 182n.
West Coast Hotel v. Parrish, 102, 107n.
White, Byron, 122, 140
White primaries, 64–65
Wiecek, William, 4–5
Wright v. City Council of Emporia, 116, 132n.
Wygant v. Jackson Board of Education, 143–46, 150, 164n., 179, 185n.

About the Author

DONALD E. LIVELY is Professor of Law at the University of Toledo College of Law. He is the author of *Modern Communications Law* (Praeger, 1991) and *Essential Principles of Communications Law* (Praeger, 1991).